British Studies Series
General Editor JEREMY BLACK

Published

John Charmley **A History of Conservative Politics, 1900–1996**
David Childs **Britain since 1939**
David Eastwood **Government and Community in the English Provinces, 1700–1870**
Brian Hill **The Early Parties and Politics in Britain, 1688–1832**
Kevin Jefferys **Retreat from New Jerusalem: British Politics, 1951–1964**
T. A. Jenkins **The Liberal Ascendancy, 1830–1886**
David Loades **Power in Tudor England**
Alexander Murdoch **British History, 1660–1832: National Identity and Local Culture**
Anthony Musson and W. M. Ormrod **The Evolution of English Justice: Law, Politics and Society in the Fourteenth Century**
Murray G. H. Pittock **Inventing and Resisting Britain: Cultural Identities in Britain and Ireland, 1685–1789**
Andrew Thorpe **A History of the British Labour Party**

Forthcoming

D. G. Boyce **Britain and Decolonisation**
Glenn Burgess **British Political Thought from Reformation to Revolution**
J. B. Christoph **The Twentieth-Century British State**
Gary De Krey **Restoration and Revolution in Britain**
W. H. Fraser **The Rise and Fall of British Trade Unionism**
Jeremy Gregory **The Long Reformation: Religion and Society in England *c.* 1530–1870**
Katrina Honeyman **Women and Industrialization**
Jon Lawrence **Britain and the First World War**

(List continued overleaf)

F. J. Levy **Politics and Culture in Tudor England**
Allan Macinnes **The British Revolution**
G. I. T. Machin **The Rise of British Democracy**
Thomas Mayer **Britain, 1450–1603**
Michael Mendle **The English Civil War and Political Thought**
W. Rubinstein **History of Britain in the Twentieth Century**
Howard Temperley **Britain and America**

British Studies Series
Series Standing Order
ISBN 0–333–71691–4 hardcover
ISBN 0–333–69332–9 paperback
(*outside North America only*)

You can receive future titles in this series as they are published by placing a standing order. Please contact your bookseller or, in case of difficulty, write to us at the address below with your name and address, the title of the series and the ISBN quoted above.

Customer Services Department, Macmillan Distribution Ltd
Houndmills, Basingstoke, Hampshire RG21 6XS, England

THE EVOLUTION OF ENGLISH JUSTICE

LAW, POLITICS AND SOCIETY IN THE FOURTEENTH CENTURY

Anthony Musson
Barrister, the Middle Temple, and Associate of the Centre for Medieval Studies, University of York

and

W. M. Ormrod
Professor of History, University of York

First published in Great Britain 1999 by
MACMILLAN PRESS LTD
Houndmills, Basingstoke, Hampshire RG21 6XS and London
Companies and representatives throughout the world

A catalogue record for this book is available from the British Library.

ISBN 0–333–67670–X hardcover
ISBN 0–333–67671–8 paperback

 First published in the United States of America 1999 by
ST. MARTIN'S PRESS, INC.,
Scholarly and Reference Division,
175 Fifth Avenue, New York, N.Y. 10010

ISBN 0–312–21748–X

Library of Congress Cataloging-in-Publication Data
Musson, Anthony, 1966–
The evolution of English justice : law, politics, and society in
the fourteenth century / Anthony Musson and W.M. Ormrod.
p. cm. — (British studies series)
Includes bibliographical references and index.
ISBN 0–312–21748–X (cloth)
1. Law—England—History. 2. Courts—England—History.
3. Justice, Administration of—England—History. 4. Great Britain–
–Politics and government—1066–1485. I. Ormrod, W. M., 1957–
II. Title. III. Series.
KD610.M87 1998
349.42—dc21   98–22634
                                                                            CIP

© Anthony Musson and W. M. Ormrod 1999

All rights reserved. No reproduction, copy or transmission of this publication may be made without written permission.

No paragraph of this publication may be reproduced, copied or transmitted save with written permission or in accordance with the provisions of the Copyright, Designs and Patents Act 1988, or under the terms of any licence permitting limited copying issued by the Copyright Licensing Agency, 90 Tottenham Court Road, London W1P 9HE.

Any person who does any unauthorised act in relation to this publication may be liable to criminal prosecution and civil claims for damages.

The authors have asserted their rights to be identified as the authors of this work in accordance with the Copyright, Designs and Patents Act 1988.

This book is printed on paper suitable for recycling and made from fully managed and sustained forest sources.

10 9 8 7 6 5 4 3 2 1
08 07 06 05 04 03 02 01 00 99

Printed in Hong Kong

Contents

Preface viii
List of Abbreviations ix

1 Introduction: The Evolution of English Justice 1
  A Century of Revolution? 1
  A Century of Evolution 4
  A Palimpsest of Jurisdictions 8
  Attitudes to Justice 10

2 Royal Justice at the Centre 12
  Structures 12
    The *curia regis* and its offshoots 12
    The court of common pleas 14
    The court of king's bench 17
    The council and its offshoots 20
    The chancery 23
    Parliament 25
  Personnel 28
    Education 29
    Recruitment and promotion 32
    Public and private service 36
  Conclusion 40

3 Royal Justice in the Provinces 42
  Structures 43
    The general eyre 43
    Assizes and gaol delivery 45
    Commissions of oyer and terminer 48

Keepers and justices of the peace	50
Personnel	54
Judges and serjeants of the central courts	58
Men of law	62
Landed society: gentry and magnates	68
Conclusion	73

4 External Influences on the Evolution of Justice — 75
War — 77
   War and disorder — 78
   The royal response — 80
   The politics of war — 85
Economic Crises and Popular Disturbances — 89
   The great famine and its aftermath — 90
   The plague and its aftermath — 93
   The Peasants' Revolt and its aftermath — 96
Constitutional Conflict — 101
   The tyranny of Edward II and the minority of Edward III — 102
   The personal rule and tyranny of Richard II — 106
Conclusion — 111

5 Internal Influences on the Evolution of Justice — 115
'Consumer Demand' — 116
   Special commissions of oyer and terminer — 119
   The assize of novel disseisin — 122
   Other manifestations of 'consumer demand' — 125
   The inclusivity of royal justice: justice for all? — 127
   New methods for prosecuting crime — 134
The Judicial Profession — 139
   Legal service — 140
   The fashioning of an intellectual domain — 144
Legislation — 146
   Making and presenting parliamentary petitions — 147
   The translation of petitions into statutes — 151
Conclusion — 157

6 Conclusion: Attitudes to Justice — 161
Discourses on Justice — 161
   Didactic discourses — 162
   Remedial discourses — 163

Satirical discourses	166
Polemical discourses	171
Responses to Complaint	175
The accessibility of the judicial system	177
The responsibilities of justices, lawyers and jurors	181
Conclusion	189
Appendix: The Sessions and Itineraries of the Court of King's Bench and Parliament, 1290–1399	194
Notes	206
Select Bibliography	239
Index	242

Preface

This book is intended both as an introduction to the history of English justice in the fourteenth century and as a new interpretation of the changes effected in the judicial system during that period. It arose from our concern to provide an accessible description of the structure of the royal courts in the later Middle Ages and our conviction that the political and social context of law in the fourteenth century had yet to be fully explored and satisfactorily explained. In the latter respect, we were partly motivated by the significant research of Dr A. J. Verduyn, who was originally to have joined us in co-authoring this book. While his own commitments prevented this, his unpublished thesis and recent articles have informed our own approach, and we are very grateful for the positive encouragement he gave the project at the outset. We should stress, however, that he is not responsible for the opinions expressed here: the book would undoubtedly have been different had he been involved in the writing of it, just as it would have been if only one of the remaining two had undertaken to produce it.

The debts that we owe to other scholars in the field will, we hope, be apparent from our notes and bibliography, even if we have sometimes – and, we trust, courteously – departed from their interpretations. We are also grateful to the undergraduate and postgraduate students at the University of York on whom so many of our ideas have been tested, and to all those who have coped with the complications of our respective domestic and professional lives during the writing of this book.

York　　　　　　　　　　　　　　　　　　　　　　　　ANTHONY MUSSON
　　　　　　　　　　　　　　　　　　　　　　　　　　　　MARK ORMROD

List of Abbreviations

BIHR	*Bulletin of the Institute of Historical Research*
CCR	*Calendar of Close Rolls*
CFR	*Calendar of Fine Rolls*
CPR	*Calendar of Patent Rolls*
EGW	J. F. Willard, W. A. Morris, J. R. Strayer and W. H. Dunham (eds), *The English Government at Work, 1327–1336* (Cambridge, MA: Medieval Academy of America, 1940–50)
EHD, vol. 3	H. Rothwell (ed.), *English Historical Documents, 1189–1327* (London: Eyre & Spottiswoode, 1975)
EHD, vol. 4	A. R. Myers (ed.), *English Historical Documents, 1327–1485* (London: Eyre & Spottiswoode, 1969)
EHR	*English Historical Review*
HMSO	Her Majesty's Stationery Office
JBS	*Journal of British Studies*
LQR	*Law Quarterly Review*
Musson, *Public Order*	A. Musson, *Public Order and Law Enforcement: The Local Administration of Criminal Justice 1294–1350* (Woodbridge: Boydell Press, 1996)
Palmer, *English Law*	R. C. Palmer, *English Law in the Age of the Black Death, 1348–1381: A Transformation of Governance and Law* (Chapel Hill, NC: University of North Carolina Press, 1993)
P&P	*Past and Present*

Powell, 'Administration'	E. Powell, 'The Administration of Criminal Justice in Late-Medieval England: Peace Sessions and Assizes', in R. Eales and D. Sullivan (eds), *The Political Context of Law* (London: Hambledon Press, 1987), pp. 48–59
Powell, *Criminal Justice*	E. Powell, *Kingship, Law, and Society: Criminal Justice in the Reign of Henry V* (Oxford: Clarendon Press, 1989)
Putnam, *Enforcement*	B. H. Putnam, *The Enforcement of the Statute of Labourers*, Columbia University Studies in History, Economics and Public Law 32 (New York, 1908)
Putnam, *Shareshull*	B. H. Putnam, *The Place in Legal History of Sir William Shareshull* (Cambridge: Cambridge University Press, 1950)
Putnam, 'Transformation'	B. H. Putnam, 'The Transformation of the Keepers of the Peace into the Justices of the Peace, 1327–1380', *Transactions of the Royal Historical Society*, 4th series, 12 (1929), pp. 19–48
Putnam (ed.), *Proceedings*	B. H. Putnam (ed.), *Proceedings before the Justices of the Peace in the Fourteenth and Fifteenth Centuries* (London: Ames Foundation, 1938)
RP	*Rotuli parliamentorum* (London: House of Lords, 1783)
RS	Rolls Series
SR	*Statutes of the Realm* (London: Record Commission, 1810–28)
SCCKB	G. O. Sayles (ed.), *Select Cases in the Court of King's Bench*, Selden Society 55, 57, 58, 74, 76, 82, 88 (London, 1936–71)
SS	Selden Society
TRHS	*Transactions of the Royal Historical Society*
Verduyn, 'Attitude'	A. J. Verduyn, 'The Attitude of the Parliamentary Commons to Law and Order under Edward III', University of Oxford DPhil thesis (1991)

Unless otherwise stated, all unpublished documents are in the Public Record Office.

1
Introduction: The Evolution of English Justice

A Century of Revolution?

The century between the 1290s and the 1390s witnessed some of the most far-reaching changes ever effected in English justice. Three particular developments form the subject matter of this book. First, the fourteenth century saw a major expansion in the scope of the common law, that body of legal processes and remedies that had developed since the twelfth century to make available and apply the judicial customs of the king's court in a standard (or 'common') form throughout the realm. Secondly, the same period marked a fundamental reform of the structure of the courts which enforced that law, as an earlier system heavily dependent on the use of centralised agencies and itinerant commissions gave way to a more elaborate hierarchy radiating out from the Westminster courts of king's bench and common pleas through the circuit commissions of assize and goal delivery to the regular quarter sessions held by the justices of the peace in the shires. Thirdly, the period witnessed the emergence of a distinctive English judiciary comprising two groups: the formally qualified, full-time lawyers employed in the higher courts; and the part-time commissioners (many of them also having legal training and experience), drawn from provincial political society, who performed so many essential judicial (and, later, administrative) tasks on the county benches. These three developments proved remarkably enduring, helping to create a judicial system that survived in essence until the nineteenth century and was only formally dissolved in a bout of modern rationalisation during the 1970s.

They have also had a profound effect on the way that historians write about the development of law in medieval England. Their influence may be discerned, again, in three ways. The first is the widespread belief that royal justice developed not in a linear manner but in a series of steps: short phases of dramatic change interspersed with longer periods of comparative stability. One such cluster of changes came in the mid-twelfth century with the creation of the common law and the beginnings of the transcendent judicial authority of the state; another occurred in the mid- to late thirteenth century as a result of a major extension in the range of civil and criminal actions dealt with by the king's courts; a third is represented by the establishment of the commissions of the peace and a further notable extension of common law processes in the years around 1350; and yet another occurred in the mid- to late fifteenth century with the institutionalisation of royal prerogative justice and the application of new processes that fell outside the scope of the common law. The assumption behind such an approach is that the long lulls between periods of intense activity provided a kind of breathing space during which society, and the judicial system itself, could assimilate such change.

Secondly, this notion of the pace of change has greatly influenced the language we use to characterise the development of the law. Doris Mary Stenton's description of the emergence of the common law in the twelfth century as a great 'leap forward' has become rooted in the historiography of the Angevin state.[1] More particularly for present purposes, Bertha Haven Putnam and Robert C. Palmer both used the word 'transformation' in the titles of seminal works on the fourteenth century, Putnam in relation to the emergence of the justices of the peace, and Palmer with reference to the expansion of common law processes in the third quarter of that century.[2] Although legal historians generally eschew the more violent connotations of the word 'revolution', their choice of vocabulary deliberately evokes images of the 'breakthrough', a sudden upward movement that liberates the legal system from earlier restrictions and allows it to respond to new demands and challenges. The language of transformation is particularly relevant in the present context, since the period *c.* 1290–1360 has long been recognised as witnessing major changes not just in the law, but also in other functions of government. Indeed, at least two of these other changes have recently been characterised as 'revolutions' in their own right: the 'military revolution' and 'fiscal revolution' brought about through the new and unprecedented pressures of war.[3] Given that historians tend, in such contexts, to use the word 'revolution' as synonymous with 'transformation', it is obviously tempting to fit the processes at work in English justice during the same period – particularly the changes in the structure of the judiciary – into a still wider thesis that identifies the period c. 1290–1360 as a crucial phase in the development of the English state.[4]

The third feature of the historiography of fourteenth-century justice that needs to be identified is the search for explanations. If the law, and the judicial system that served it, tended to grow by fits and starts, then it is reasonable to suppose that it changed only when some new variable was introduced and forced it to respond. Historians have long argued that there were two overriding influences at work upon English justice in the fourteenth century: war and plague. They have also generally argued that these phenomena had contrasting effects. The wars with Scotland and France are assumed to have had a largely disruptive influence, by distracting the energies of the state away from its obligation to maintain justice: indeed, the era between the abandonment of the general eyre (see Chapter 3) in 1294 and the statutory confirmation of the commissions of the peace in 1361, far from being identified as one of formative development (as in the 'state-building' model outlined above), is more usually characterised as a kind of limbo during which the crown manifestly failed to devise any coherent programme of law-keeping. Richard W. Kaeuper's terminology nicely encapsulates this argument: as the thirteenth-century 'law state' gave way to the fourteenth-century 'war state', the crown repeatedly compromised its judicial functions for the sake of its military enterprises.[5]

In striking contrast, the Black Death has come to be seen as a great catalyst for change. Putnam believed that the justices of the peace, although emerging from a series of judicial experiments of the first half of the fourteenth century, only became an established part of the system in the aftermath of the plague, when the crown faced the challenge of enforcing the Ordinance (1349) and Statute (1351) of Labourers, the new legislation brought in to deal with the economic emergency precipitated by the death of over a third of the population.[6] More recently, Palmer has argued vigorously that the new common law processes emerging in the second half of the fourteenth century may be directly explained as a response to the perceived breakdown of social obligations after the plague and a means by which those obligations might be legally enforced.[7] The result of this continuing emphasis on two great forces, the one disruptive and the other dynamic, is simply to confirm the first premise outlined above, that developments in the law tend to occur in short bursts of intense activity – in this case, a flurry of reforms in the generation or so after the Black Death.

A Century of Evolution

This book proposes that the changes evident in English justice between the 1290s and the 1390s may be more meaningfully represented as a process of *evolution*. The difference between 'revolution' and 'evolution' is often blurred in historical discourse, where the distinction is usually assumed to be one of relative speed: revolution denotes a series of dramatic events or marked changes occurring within a short and self-contained block of time, whereas evolution implies a process of gradual, often imperceptible, development over an extended period. However, a deeper exploration of modern evolution theory not only helps to refine this definition but also provides a conceptual framework that may be applied particularly fruitfully to the subject matter of this book.

Modern evolution theory encompasses a wide range of approaches and opinions.[8] Evolution as understood by Darwinians is, as in the general usage outlined above, a long-term, gradual process of change. Thereafter, however, the theory diverges from the popular understanding in several key respects. First, to some neo-Darwinians, the process of change is not a linear one: because life forms have a tendency to stasis, they only adapt and develop when forced to do so by environmental changes. Stephen Jay Gould has described this process as one of 'punctuated equilibrium':

> Lineages change little during most of their history, but events of rapid speciation [the branching off of new species from a persisting parental stock] occasionally punctuate this tranquillity. Evolution is the differential survival and deployment of these punctuations.[9]

The terminology may be off-putting, but the theory obviously applies itself neatly to the development of English justice in the fourteenth century. At first sight, it appears to validate the conventional argument outlined above that the sudden arrival of the plague, and the 'environmental' changes thus brought about in society and the economy, provoked a great re-organisation of the judicial system. On the other hand, Gould's explanation begs the question as to why the other primary force conventionally identified as acting upon the judicial system in the fourteenth century – the pressure of war – did not also precipitate positive, as well as merely negative, changes. To adopt the model of 'punctuated equilibrium' is therefore also to call for a more systematic analysis of the whole range of 'environmental' factors – economic, political and cultural – that may have influenced the development of the law in the course of the fourteenth century. This book attempts to provide that analysis.

There is a second, and still more important, way in which modern theory differs from popular understanding: it treats evolution not as progress but merely as change. Neo-Darwinians have repudiated the notion that evolution represents a process of advancement in favour of a neutral stance which judges change by its success or failure in adapting to new environmental conditions: 'if an amoeba is as well adapted to its environment as we are to ours, who is to say that we are higher creatures?'[10] This moral neutrality has particular advantages for the study of later medieval English law, since fourteenth-century political rhetoric was often preoccupied with a perceived deterioration of public order and the apparent reduction in the will, or the capacity, of the crown to deliver justice to its subjects. This has generally been attributed to the process of 'devolution', whereby the primary responsibility for law-enforcement came increasingly to be delegated to the localities through the commissions of the peace; the result, supposedly, was that royal justice was effectively privatised and was run as a mafia-style operation serving the interests only of the wealthy and powerful.[11] It has been accepted for some time, however, that increasing public criticism is no real measure of the supposed failure of the late medieval judicial system: indeed, as K. B. McFarlane pointed out, it can actually imply the exact opposite, by signifying that society had higher expectations of that system and was more conditioned to working with, rather than against, it.[12] Evolution theory here allows us to avoid assumptions about whether the judicial system became either 'better' or 'worse' in the course of the fourteenth century, and instead calls for a more objective assessment of the extent to which the law and its agencies, as social institutions, adapted successfully to the environmental changes going on around them.[13]

Thus far, then, modern evolution theory appears to provide a valuable conceptual framework in which to carry out a re-evaluation of the 'transformations' that occurred in royal justice during the fourteenth century. To allow that analysis to proceed, however, it is important to refine our notion of the influences that act upon a given system to induce change. Because evolution theory has developed specifically in reference to the natural sciences, it tends to view forces for change as being chiefly 'exogenous': that is, independent, external triggers which tend to arise in a sudden and unpredicted manner and are often dramatic in their impact (pandemics, ice ages, and so on). On the other hand, natural scientists recognise that change can also occur 'endogenously' – from *within* – and may be a result of autonomous development rather than a reaction to external challenges. The distinction between exogenously and endogenously induced change is particularly important in relation to the social sciences, since it recognises that human organisations and societal norms are not simply conditioned by external pressures but may also be affected by new cultural influences developing from within.[14]

Historians may also usefully deploy this distinction, not merely because it facilitates a rational categorisation of 'factors' in any given debate, but, more importantly, because it allows us to differentiate between the mere *speed* and *extent* of change on the one hand, and the actual *direction* and deeper *implications* of change on the other. This methodology has been much developed in recent years by historians of population, and it is from their work that the present approach chiefly derives.[15] It has particular relevance to the subject of this book, dominated as it is by a discourse which tends to see one particular exogenous shock – the Black Death – as both the catalyst and the determinant of change in the legal system of fourteenth-century England. For some years now, demographic historians have pointed to the fact that, while the appalling loss of lives as a result of plague may have determined the *speed* of change encountered, for example, in the conditions of work and in patterns of nuptiality, it did not necessarily alter the *direction* of development of such fundamental social structures as the family, the household and the community. As P. J. P. Goldberg has put it, 'The nature of the response was culturally determined, the level of mortality shaping only the extent of the response.'[16] This example therefore provides a timely reminder, first that monocausal explanations are almost always inadequate, and secondly that, simply because things happen after a given event, they are not necessarily 'caused' by it.

This new and more sensitive approach to causality and change has special relevance for the history of justice, since it explicitly recognises an important distinction between the internal dynamics of the law and the external influences that so often determined the personnel and structures of the judicial system. Legal historians have long recognised that the law has an existence of its own which is constantly re-shaped by the practical needs of those who seek its remedies and the intellectual processes of those who practise it. In this sense, law can change, develop and grow from within, as legislators, judges and pleaders respond to influences from the society of which they are part. Political historians, on the other hand, tend to think of the law chiefly in terms of the judicial system that serves it, and therefore assume that law is somehow changed when the method of enforcement is altered. Furthermore, the latter approach often explains those changes not in terms of a general striving for the common good but in specifically political – even conspiratorial – terms, whereby the state is induced to apply the law in ways that are to the advantage of particular interest groups.

This distinction between the 'legal' and the 'political' interpretation of justice should not be over-drawn, but it has obvious applications to the subject matter of this book. For Palmer, taking a socio-legal approach, the 'transformation' of the law that occurred in the third quarter of the fourteenth century may have been precipitated by exogenous (that is, plague-induced) change, but it was actually effected endogenously as a result of the ability of lawyers to devise and implement new common law processes from within the system.[17] Putnam's thesis, on the other hand, taking a primarily political approach, explains the emergence of the justices of the peace in terms of a debate between the crown and parliament in which the exogenous forces of war and plague provided the commons with the political leverage they required to create their own preferred, and devolved, system of justice: the commissions of the peace, in other words, represented a defeat for the centralising state and a triumph for provincial political society.[18] By recognising that the development of the legal system could be affected *both* by endogenous influences within the law *and* by exogenous influences acting upon the judicial system, the present study attempts to provide a fuller, and a more balanced, explanation of why that system developed in the particular way that it did.

A Palimpsest of Jurisdictions

Before we proceed to that analysis, it is necessary to provide a brief outline of the fuller range of judicial structures that existed in fourteenth-century England.[19] A number of distinct legal systems operated in the Middle Ages, and it is important to establish that this book deals with only one of them: namely, the king's law, dispensed through the common law and prerogative courts. The two other most important systems were provided by the church and by the customary courts.

The ecclesiastical courts are fairly easily distinguished from royal tribunals and may be treated succinctly: they operated under a different legal tradition (canon law); they dealt with a specific range of business relating to a particular group (the clergy); and they took cognisance of a limited range of cases involving the laity (such as matrimonial or testamentary disputes and sexual offences).

The customary courts are rather less easy to understand at first, since they overlapped more obviously with the common law courts of the king; they therefore require fuller treatment. They consisted of two main types: the communal courts of the county, the hundred, the borough and the vill; and the feudal (private, or seigneurial) courts of the honor and the manor. Between them, these courts dispensed law derived from 'custom': that is, they interpreted law according to local convention. One of the things that distinguished the customary courts from the common law courts, then, was that the former were not standardised, whereas the conventions and judgments of the latter held good throughout the realm.

Another difference was the degree of royal control. Although the county courts were convened by the king's representative, the sheriff, many hundred and borough courts were alienated to, or appropriated by, noblemen, ecclesiastical institutions and urban corporations in the course of the twelfth and thirteenth centuries, with the result that their proceedings – and their profits – fell outside the king's reach. Under Henry III and Edward I, the crown attempted to regulate this process of alienation by launching *quo warranto* inquiries to investigate the 'warrant' or authority under which such 'franchises' were held.[20] These inquiries were abandoned in the 1290s (another frequently cited example of the apparent shift from 'law state' to 'war state'), and the crown thereafter largely accepted the untidy patchwork of jurisdictions thus preserved – even if it often squabbled with the franchise-holders over the harbouring of criminals or the sharing out of judicial profits.[21]

It is important to realise, however, that the areas in which such franchises were exercised – known as liberties – were still subject to royal justice: even the greatest of the liberties, the palatinates of Chester, Durham and (after 1351) Lancaster, remained bound by common and statute law.

The fact that two systems – royal and customary – could operate within the same locality may seem curious to the modern mind. To medieval society, however, the distinction was readily explicable in terms of the business undertaken in different courts. The common law, as it had emerged in the twelfth and thirteenth centuries, had been chiefly concerned with litigation between the proprietary classes over land and rights, and with the trial and punishment of capital offences, especially homicide (cases such as this, reserved for trial before the king's justices at common law, were known as 'pleas of the crown'). Although, as we shall see, the king's courts greatly extended the range of their business in the course of the later thirteenth and fourteenth centuries, the crown lacked the vision, the incentive and the resources to become the *sole* source of dispute settlement in the realm. Indeed, the king's courts actively discouraged minor litigation in order not to be overwhelmed with petty business, and after 1278 officially excluded all cases involving claims of under £2.[22] A great mass of petty litigation continued, therefore, to be heard in the customary courts. Moreover, because the king's courts were open only to *free* men (and free women, if they were unmarried or widowed), those who held land in customary or servile tenure, and were designated as villeins or unfree, were simply not recognised by the common law. It was in the manor court that the relationship between the lord and his villeins, and disputes between tenants of servile status, continued to be regulated.[23]

It can thus be seen that there were certain geo-political areas and certain sections of society which, through their privileged or servile status, remained to a greater or lesser extent outside the normal scope of the king's courts. That said, it should also be understood that the later Middle Ages witnessed a gradual but remarkable erosion of the jurisdiction particularly of the customary courts and a concomitant increase in the competence of the royal judicial system. This process can be traced in a number of ways. The sheriffs, as presidents of the customary courts of county and hundred, had already been deprived of their right to judge pleas of the crown under the terms of Magna Carta in 1215.[24] By the beginning of the fourteenth century their function of receiving indictments in the customary courts was already being superseded by the newly emerging keepers of the peace, who operated under common law conventions; the transfer of authority from sheriffs to justices of the peace was finally completed in 1461.[25] More especially, as we shall see in the ensuing chapters, the late thirteenth and fourteenth centuries witnessed a great expansion in the quantity of business, and the range of social classes, accommodated within the royal courts. The process by which the state overrode customary law – and particularly seigneurial rights – to create a truly unitary system of law was inevitably very protracted: although the Tudor regime was to make much headway in this respect, some vestiges of the older traditions continued into the early twentieth century.[26] Nevertheless, the developments are sufficiently impressive to suggest that the later Middle Ages witnessed not just a relative standardisation, but a veritable 'nationalisation' of English justice:[27] a process – and a terminology – which provides an important counterbalance to the better known notions of devolution and privatisation discussed earlier in this chapter.

Attitudes to Justice

It is this very process of nationalisation, however, that also creates such problems for the historian attempting some general evaluation of fourteenth-century attitudes to the law. Precisely because the later Middle Ages witnessed an increase in the range of civil and criminal actions available in the common law courts and in the range of people taking advantage of those actions, so it becomes increasingly difficult to determine the degree to which the law was respected, flouted, revered or despised by the society subject to it. The standard response to this issue, much strengthened by Palmer's recent work, is to assume that there were discernible and contrasting 'class' attitudes to the law in late medieval England, with landed society using (and, when necessary, abusing) the law to maintain its rights, and the peasantry becoming increasingly alienated from a system so obviously weighted against the interests of the lower orders. The law thus takes centre stage in explanations of the social tensions that emerged in the generation after the Black Death and sparked the Peasants' Revolt of 1381. To push these arguments further and argue that the whole system of royal justice became a ritualised form of class conflict is, however, to give less than due credit to the ambitious scope of the judicial structure that had developed by the fourteenth century. The perennial complaints about justice in the later Middle Ages – that it was prohibitively expensive, that it was open to manipulation, that it was unduly protracted and inefficient – have therefore to be set alongside evidence that demonstrates the active engagement of a remarkably wide cross-section of society in the processes of the common law.[28]

One way of reconciling the apparent discrepancy between high levels of litigation on the one hand and disillusionment with the legal system on the other is to return to the distinction made above between the law itself and the judicial structure that enforced it. The major challenge facing the state during the fourteenth century was not to convince its subjects of the general desirability of a national system of law, but to provide a structure capable of responding to public expectations and delivering both the quantity and the quality of the justice demanded. In taking the morally neutral stance advocated by evolution theory, this book does not seek to avoid the methodologically awkward question of evaluating contemporary perceptions. Instead, it takes those perceptions not as its starting point, but as its culmination. The discussion of the structure of royal justice in Chapters 2 and 3, and the analysis of exogenous and endogenous influences for change in Chapters 4 and 5, aim to assess the evolution of justice in an objective manner, free from the moral hyperbole of medieval – and of some modern – commentators. In Chapter 6, however, we shall return to the contemporary debates and attempt to determine whether the changes wrought in the law and the judicial system during the fourteenth century really did respond appropriately to the needs of fourteenth-century society. To the extent that it attempts a critical re-assessment of political mentality, this book therefore represents a contribution to the cultural, as well as the legal, history of later medieval England.

2
Royal Justice at the Centre

This chapter aims to do two things: to outline the structures of the central courts in the fourteenth century; and to examine the personnel of those courts in order to understand something of the social and political context in which they operated. It must be appreciated that up to 1300, and for some way beyond, the 'centre' denoted not so much a fixed geographical point as the place within the realm where the king's government happened to be functioning. Not least of the interesting features of royal justice in the fourteenth century, however, is the contribution made by the senior courts to the development of Westminster and London as the administrative capital of England.[1]

Structures

The Curia Regis *and its Offshoots*

Most of the powers exercised by the central courts in the fourteenth century stemmed originally from the authority of the *curia regis*, the omnicompetent royal court operated by the Normans and early Angevins.[2] As the work of government expanded, so did the amount of business entertained by the *curia regis*, and throughout the twelfth and thirteenth centuries new tribunals emerged to deal with discrete areas of this court's jurisdiction.

The earliest of these tribunals was the exchequer, whose 'barons', or judges, are known to have been functioning by 1110. In its origins, the exchequer was a court only in so far as it was concerned with financial administration, and it did not begin to develop a recognisably public judicial role until somewhat later in the twelfth century. By the thirteenth century, private individuals were taking advantage of its expertise as a revenue court to bring debt litigation before the barons. The exchequer enjoyed particular autonomy in this respect, since it had its own duplicate copy of the king's great seal and could therefore issue writs (the instructions necessary to instigate common law actions) without reference to the only other source of such documents, the chancery. In 1280, however, it was agreed that such private litigation was impeding the prosecution of the king's business, and the exchequer's jurisdiction was thereafter severely curtailed.

By that stage, another common law court had already emerged to take on such business and provide the normal tribunal for debt cases, as indeed for a whole range of civil litigation. In Henry II's reign, the records allow us to identify a court called 'the bench' which was distinct from the *curia regis* on the one hand and from the general eyre on the other. This new court had particular responsibility for 'common pleas': that is, for private litigation under the common law. Under King John there emerged yet another offshoot of the *curia regis* in the form of the court *coram rege* ('before the king'), a peripatetic tribunal which initially had particular responsibility for safeguarding the king's interests but then took over the jurisdiction of the bench – whose own proceedings were accordingly suspended in 1209. Clause 17 of Magna Carta (1215) declared that 'common pleas shall not follow our court but shall be held in some fixed place', thereby restoring a notional division of responsibilities, with common pleas being entertained in the bench, and criminal prosecutions, together with civil actions in which the crown had an interest, being restored to the court *coram rege*.[3] Although pleas *coram rege* were in turn suspended during the minority of Henry III, the two courts became clearly established as a result of the emergence of separate series of records – the *coram rege* rolls and the *de banco* rolls – after 1234 (the exchequer also began to preserve its own plea rolls from 1236). While they continued for a long time to be referred to as the 'the bench' and the court *coram rege*, it is less ambiguous and more convenient to refer to these tribunals respectively by their later titles of common pleas and king's bench.

The Court of Common Pleas

By declaring that common pleas ought to be held 'in some fixed place', Magna Carta did not originally imply that the bench should be resident only in a *single* place, or indeed that this had to be Westminster. Rather, its concern was to ensure that private litigants seeking access to the common law should not be impeded by the king's peripatetic lifestyle. The intention appears to have been that common pleas ought only to be heard in *established* centres of royal government – which included the county towns and other bases commonly visited by the justices in eyre as well as the royal palace of Westminster. By the end of the thirteenth century, however, Magna Carta was already being glossed to signify that common pleas ought normally to be heard at Westminster.[4]

The only recognised exception to this was when the exchequer moved from its Westminster base and located closer to the royal household in order to provide the king with convenient financial services during his wars in Wales or Scotland. On these occasions, the close association between the bench and the exchequer became manifest, and common pleas moved out of its accustomed headquarters in the great hall of Westminster Palace to take up residence, first in Shrewsbury during Edward I's campaign against the Welsh (1277), and then on several occasions at York during successive campaigns launched by the first three Edwards against the Scots (1298–1304, 1319–20, 1322–3, 1327 and 1333–8).[5] For half a century after 1338, however, common pleas remained at Westminster. The only disruptions to its routine during this period occurred when natural disasters and political crises necessitated temporary closure: this happened during the plague in 1349, 1361 and 1368, upon the death of Edward III in 1377, and at the time of the Peasants' Revolt in 1381.[6] Common pleas (and the exchequer) sat on only one further occasion at York, in 1392–3, when Richard II quarrelled with the authorities in London and attempted to punish the city by temporarily removing the offices of state from the capital. Interestingly, however, Richard's own rebuilding of the great hall of Westminster Palace in the 1390s provided symbolic confirmation that Westminster had indeed become the recognised headquarters of English royal justice.[7]

The establishment of the court of common pleas 'in some fixed place' did much to enhance its accessibility and thus to increase its business. All procedure in common pleas was instigated by an 'original writ', so called because it originated, or instigated, an action. Original writs were available from the chancery as a matter of course (they were thus classified as writs *de cursu*). They were not necessarily free: the standard payment for such a document was 6d., and the chancery clerks were often accused of charging more – though there is also good evidence that fees were often dropped in cases of need.[8] The writ consisted of an instruction (in Latin) to the sheriff of the county in which the defendant resided; it had to be returned to the relevant court at a specified date, along with the sheriff's response, in order to prove that the instruction had been fulfilled and to allow the case to proceed. The subsequent stages through which the case passed were known as 'mesne process' and were also directed by a series of 'judicial' writs issued not by the chancery but by the justices: in 1344 both common pleas and king's bench were provided with their own copies of the great seal in order to validate these orders and, in the process, to make more money for the crown (a judicial writ now cost a standard 7d.).[9] If the case represented a breach of the king's peace (or, after 1351, was a plea of debt), and the defendant refused to appear in court, the sheriff was empowered to arrest him by a writ of *capias*; if two such writs were issued without success, the defendant was subject to 'exigent', the process leading to outlawry. In the event that the defendant did appear in the king's court, trial was normally by a jury drawn (at least in theory) from the 'visne', the neighbourhood in which the alleged offence had taken place.[10] Mesne process was often protracted, not least because common pleas (like the courts of king's bench and exchequer) was in session only during the four legal terms of Michaelmas, Hilary, Easter and Trinity. Depending on the dates of moveable religious feasts, this meant a total of about four months' work a year, interspersed with three short vacations and a much longer break between early July and early October.[11]

The viability of the actions available in common pleas would have been jeopardised had all the parties been required to attend in person. In fact, two conventions emerged during the thirteenth century to ease the logistical challenges created by the transfer of cases from far-flung corners of the realm to the great hall at Westminster Palace. First, both plaintiffs and (in many civil actions) defendants were permitted to attend by proxies or 'attorneys', the forebears of modern solicitors (see Chapter 5). Secondly, there was the practice, formalised in 1285, of allowing cases to be transferred out of the central courts and to be heard (though not brought to judgment) locally, before the justices of assize. This process was known as *nisi prius*, from a clause inserted in common law writs requiring the action to proceed in the central courts 'unless before then' the king's justices should have come into the relevant county. *Nisi prius* obviously offered particular attractions to the jurors summoned in a given case. It was possible not least because the judges of the central courts were usually members of the assize commissions, and visited the shires in this capacity during the vacations between the law terms at Westminster. It therefore provides a good example of the integration between central and local justice that is discussed more fully in Chapter 3.

The three most important categories of original writ were the *praecipe*, the petty assizes (which are discussed in Chapters 3 and 5) and the *ostensurus quare*.[12] The first of these, which developed in the generations after the Norman Conquest, instructed the sheriff to order (*praecipe*) the defendant to remedy the grievances of the plaintiff; only if the defendant refused to do so and chose to plead his case was he required to appear before the king's justices. The *ostensurus quare*, by contrast, which developed in the course of the thirteenth century, omitted the first stage of the *praecipe*, instead requiring the sheriff to instruct the defendant to appear before the king's justices and 'show why' he had committed the alleged wrong. Although the first stage of action upon the writ *praecipe* seems rapidly to have become a mere matter of form, the *ostensurus quare* obviously offered the plaintiff a speedier form of redress, and the great expansion in the number of common law writs available from the chancery during the thirteenth century is largely explained by the increasing number of remedies provided under the latter form of action.

By far the most important sub-classes of the *ostensurus quare* were the writ of trespass *vi et armis* and the writ of trespass on the case. Trespass *vi et armis* (by force and arms) developed in the thirteenth century to cover a wide range of civil injuries – to land, to chattels and to the person – not recognised on the criminal side of royal justice: the Latin phrase *vi et armis*, rendered in law French as *tort et force*, provides the basis for 'tort' in modern common law. The notion that an alleged trespass was only admissible in court if it was accompanied by violence rapidly became a fiction, and by the mid-fourteenth century the chancery was admitting a wide range of cases under this category. More importantly, the courts also began to develop a whole new range of trespass actions 'on the case', in which the detailing of the alleged wrong allowed a case of trespass to be made where no general writ had previously been available. Of particular importance in this respect was the new writ of assumpsit, which allowed those dissatisfied with the services of a whole range of professionals and craftspeople to use trespass litigation as a means of suing for damages in the king's courts (see Chapter 5).

The Court of King's Bench

Whereas the political community had attempted to restrict the movements of the court of common pleas since 1215, it openly acknowledged that the court *coram rege* had an intimate relationship with the ruler: indeed, in 1300 it was specified that the king's bench should follow the person of the king.[13] In a literal sense, this had already ceased to happen: it was another tribunal, the court of the verge, that more usually represented the king's right to dispense personal justice in the fourteenth century by exercising special jurisdiction within a twelve-mile radius of the itinerant household.[14] In a deeper sense, however, the king's bench retained a particular association with the sovereign by safeguarding the king's rights and upholding his particular responsibilities at law. In this respect, its work can be distinguished from that of common pleas in three particular ways.

First, the king's bench was charged to hear appeals from lesser common law courts, including common pleas (though not, after the mid-fourteenth century, the exchequer). This obviously gave it a certain superiority and dignity in the judicial hierarchy.

Secondly, and more substantially, in the fourteenth century the king's bench came to have special jurisdiction over criminal cases of treason and felony. The *coram rege* rolls differ from the *de banco* rolls in that they contain a separate section annotated *rex*, to denote criminal proceedings in which actions of felony were brought formally in the name of the king against persons accused of breaking his peace (in trespass cases, by contrast, the plaintiff made his or her own case, even though it might subsequently be taken up by the crown).[15] There were six crimes designated as felonies: homicide, rape, robbery, larceny, arson, and breach of prison while under arrest for felony.[16] Prosecution for felony was initiated by appeal (oral complaint either by the victim or by accomplices who turned king's evidence), or by indictment (written accusation made by individuals or by a jury of presentment in the county where the alleged crime took place, and sometimes endorsed by a grand jury). The defendant had to be arrested and kept in custody pending trial, so the king's bench maintained its own prison known as the marshalsea. Whereas trespass was almost always punishable by a money fine, felony was (at least formally) punishable by death and the confiscation of estates for a year and a day.

Until the early fourteenth century, the king's bench had only a subsidiary role to play in the pursuit of felony: criminal justice was dispensed in the localities where the offences occurred, through the eyre and the justices of gaol delivery (see Chapter 3), and the central court was only usually involved in appeals against judgments given in lower courts or in difficult and doubtful cases.[17] Occasionally before 1323, however, and as established practice thereafter, the king's bench assumed responsibility over all pleas of the crown in the shire where it sat and undertook to deliver the local gaols of all prisoners pending trial. As a result, the regional visitations of the king's bench took on the function previously fulfilled by the justices in eyre and the commissions of trailbaston (see Chapter 3). Furthermore, it became much more common as the fourteenth century progressed for cases of felony brought by appeal or indictment before local justices of oyer and terminer or justices of the peace (and, indeed, for many trespass cases instigated in those courts) to be transferred into the king's bench for trial and judgment.[18] This practice illustrates the close coordination that existed between central and local justice, as well as demonstrating the establishment of the king's bench as a superior criminal court.

The third particular function of the king's bench which distinguished it from common pleas was its right to instigate actions of trespass not on the basis of original writs supplied by the chancery, but by bill. The bill was a written petition, made in the name of the plaintiff, requesting the court to initiate action to redress a wrong.[19] It had its origins in the oral *querelae* and plaints that were lodged in chancery as a means of suing out the appropriate original writs. Prior to the fourteenth century, however, the itinerant justices in eyre had taken cognisance of bills delivered by residents in the shires where they sat, on the grounds that, since the sheriff was present at the session, it was unnecessary to issue him with an original writ to initiate proceedings. The king's bench assumed the right to hear cases brought by bill when it sat in the provinces, and during its long sojourn at York in 1318–20 it began properly to systematise this area of its business.[20] From 1323 it was authorised to deal with all bills presented by suitors for the king's justice, and thus to act as a court of first instance for all indictments. The acceptance of procedure by bill helped to distinguish the work of the king's bench from other judicial agencies operating in the localities, and gave it a particularly powerful role in the early fourteenth-century campaign against lawlessness.

The geographical orbit of that campaign can be ascertained from the Appendix, which summarises the known details of the itinerary of the king's bench for the century after 1290. It shows how, after moving around in conjunction with Edward I's military campaigns during the 1290s, the court settled virtually continuously at Westminster for the period 1305–18. From that date, however, and more particularly from 1322, it was frequently out of the capital, and continued to make visitations of the shires on a reasonably regular basis until the 1360s. The choice of York, which hosted more sessions than any other provincial centre, is obviously explained by the use of this city as a northern capital during the Scottish wars.[21] Other venues, however, may have been chosen specifically because their hinterlands were believed to be particularly crime-ridden and in general need of a direct assertion of royal judicial authority: the north, and the counties bordering the Welsh marches, were particularly obvious targets for government attention in this respect (see Chapter 4).

It is now fashionable to emphasise the limitations of this policy of using the king's bench as what has been called a 'superior eyre'.[22] The movements of the court were arguably too random, too swift, and too unevenly distributed to make a real and lasting impact on the operation of criminal justice in the shires. There is some evidence, as we shall see in Chapter 5, that the business of the king's bench when on provincial circuit was more extensive than its plea rolls allow; this goes some way to answering the charges of inadequacy. However, a major practical problem remained: the court could only be in one place at a time, and lacked the resources to maintain a nationwide policy on law and order. The more sedentary tendencies of the court during the second half of the century, evident from the Appendix, must therefore be taken as something of an admission of defeat. For thirty years between 1362 and 1392 the king's bench remained at Westminster; and after a flurry of regional sessions in the reign of Henry V, it settled in the capital more or less permanently.[23]

This in turn meant a major change in the nature and balance of its work. The criminal side of king's bench business remained relatively stable during the second half of the fourteenth century because, as indicated above, it had become common practice for cases of felony instigated by indictments before the justices of the peace in the localities to be transferred into this superior court: in this respect, indeed, the real geographical range of the court remained wide, and the judicial system as a whole remained remarkably integrated.[24] On the civil side, however, the court's business dwindled rapidly as a result of the fact that it was now able only to receive bills of trespass from the county of Middlesex. Although the 'bill of Middlesex' was in turn to open the way for a series of legal fictions that greatly enlarged the competence of this court in the later fifteenth century, the king's bench must be said to have played an increasingly subsidiary role to the court of common pleas in the processing of private litigation during the latter part of the period covered by this book.[25]

The Council and its Offshoots

Beyond the courts of king's bench, common pleas and exchequer, there was a whole array of other tribunals within the structure of central government that enjoyed judicial authority, but which did not usually act within the sphere of the common law. Most of these courts may be said to have derived their jurisdiction from the authority retained by the *curia regis* after the emergence of common pleas and king's bench in the thirteenth century. The title *curia regis* begins to look rather antiquated in the fourteenth century, and historians refer to this body simply as the 'council'. Just as the *curia regis* had delegated responsibility for the common law to separate tribunals in the thirteenth century, so in the fourteenth did the council begin to develop, and devolve, forms of justice that remained outside the common law. In that their activities represented the king's right to provide 'prerogative' justice, it is easy to assume that there was something vaguely sinister about the motives and procedures of the new conciliar courts. On the other hand, it must be acknowledged that their emergence had as much to do with pressure from litigants as it did with the ambitions of a thrusting monarchy: it is sufficient for the present to see their evolution as complementing, rather than deliberately competing with, the jurisdiction of the common law courts.

The king's council had many manifestations: the one that immediately concerns us here is the inner circle of ministers and judges who determined the routine work of government, implemented policy decisions in their respective departments, and sat in judgment in most of the judicial cases reserved for the attention of the council.[26] This body met wherever was convenient for its members and (to a lesser extent) for the king; but the increasing tendency for the major offices of state to adopt fixed headquarters clearly impacted upon the council itself: in *c.* 1343 it was provided with its own 'new chamber' (later the Star Chamber) within the royal palace of Westminster. Because the council was not a court of record, it kept no organised archive. Enough evidence survives, however, to suggest something of the distinctive part that it played in the maintenance of justice.

Most of this judicial work was undertaken by the principal officers of state: the chancellor and treasurer, the chief justices and justices of king's bench and common pleas, and the barons of the exchequer. The influence of the common lawyers upon the workings of the conciliar courts was therefore strong. Process before the council was initiated by a petition. This was very similar to the bill of trespass as entertained in the eyre and the king's bench, except that the plaintiff addressed the request for remedy specifically to the king and council. Issues that were obviously provided for by standard criminal procedure and by actions at common law were regularly sent on to the relevant courts: the council saw no benefit in being flooded with routine business. The onus was on the petitioner to indicate why the case deserved special treatment – either because it was unresolvable at common law or because it involved issues in which the king might have a particular interest. The business of the council therefore tended to fall into certain categories: cases of serious violence (which were often, in turn, delegated to special commissions of oyer and terminer, discussed in Chapter 3); litigation on fraud (forged charters, false claims, counterfeit money, malicious indictments, and so on); accusations of heresy, sorcery and witchcraft; maritime and mercantile disputes; and litigation arising from 'uses' (trusts).

So far as the absolute and relative scale of such work is concerned, the extant records provide only a very rough guide. In the course of the fourteenth century, however, various aspects of the council's jurisdiction began to be delegated to specialised tribunals, and this process provides at least some glimpse of the likely growth areas in conciliar judicial business. It used to be thought that the court of chivalry, which had special powers over cases arising from acts of war, disputes over armorial bearings and appeals of treason, grew from just such a process in the second half of the fourteenth century.[27] Although the origins of this court are now argued to have developed earlier, under Edward I, and to have emerged out of the special responsibilities undertaken by the constable and marshal in organising the king's household for war,[28] it is still possible that the council actively encouraged its development in the period of military activity against Scotland and France. This certainly seems to have been the case with the court of admiralty, which emerged when the council began to send mercantile disputes for settlement before the admirals in the 1340s: the increase in such business as a result of the Anglo-French wars provided an obvious incentive for the establishment of a specialised court.[29] Finally, in the mid-fourteenth century the council superseded the king's bench in hearing appeals on cases brought in the exchequer: this right was asserted for the chancellor, treasurer, and two justices in 1348, and in 1357 was formalised in another specialised branch of the council known as the court of exchequer chamber.[30] Again, it seems likely that the new tribunal was a response to the increasing burden of such business.

The conciliar courts later had a reputation for giving swift, if somewhat brutal, justice, and important advances were made during the fourteenth century in establishing the characteristic processes that created this reputation. The very informality of its business could, in certain respects, cause problems. Although the council (unlike the common law courts) was technically always open for business, its sessions had sometimes to be adjourned because members were absent.[31] Without its own properly regulated prison, it also experienced its fair share of difficulties in finding safe places of detention for those pending trial.[32] Above all, the early fourteenth-century council lacked effective means to ensure the attendance of defendants at its sessions. Around the middle of the century, however, it found a solution at least to the latter problem in the form of the personal summons: that is, a writ addressed directly to the defendant (rather than, as in common law practice, being addressed to, and then served by, the sheriff).[33] Such writs had hitherto only been issued to persons of some rank, or to royal office-holders, and had generally specified the reasons for which they should appear before the council. From 1346, however, personal summonses began at once to be issued to a wider range of defendants and to omit the reason for which attendance was required. In the early 1350s such summonses also began to include a penalty clause (*sub pena...*) threatening a fine in case of default. Thus emerged the famous *sub pena* writ, the most potent of all the instruments of late medieval prerogative justice. By *c.* 1390 *sub pena* writs summoning persons before the council were being issued under the privy seal, whose clerks had, since the middle of the century, been providing the basis of a new conciliar secretariat. The fact that the privy seal was denied any role in the processes of the common law serves to highlight the difference between the established and highly formalised actions available in the courts of king's bench and common pleas, and the more immediate and summary forms of justice increasingly available before the council and its offshoots.

The Chancery

At the beginning of the fourteenth century the chancery was an administrative office, responsible for writing the charters, letters patent and letters close (writs) issued under the great seal. By the end of the century, it had emerged as a 'court of conscience': that is, as a tribunal which exercised the king's right of discretion by allowing a plaintiff to set out the full details of his case and request that due consideration be given to special circumstances inadmissible at common law.[34] As in the council, process was begun by a petition from the plaintiff; if the chancery accepted the case, the defendant was usually summoned to appear by a writ of *sub pena* under the great seal. As in the council too, justice was summary: there was no jury, and the chancellor, as president of the court, simply declared a judgment when sufficient evidence had been collected. By the end of the fourteenth century, then, the chancery had begun to take on the role that would, by the sixteenth century, result in its emergence as a court of equity.

How and why did this change in the chancery's jurisdiction come about? Scholars are divided as to whether the chancery's judicial function stemmed from its own administrative responsibilities or by delegation from the council: it may be, to exercise the historian's prerogative of compromise, that it derived from both. Not least of the factors that facilitated the development of the court of chancery was the gradual removal of the office of the great seal from the king's entourage and its establishment, by the late 1330s, in the great hall of Westminster Palace, in close proximity to both the common law and the conciliar courts.[35] To understand how the traditions of those courts informed the development of chancery jurisdiction, it is necessary to appreciate that the chancery developed two sides to its judicial business: the 'Latin' side, which was a natural extension of its administrative responsibilities; and the 'English' or equity side, so called because, by the fifteenth century, the petitions and pleadings were normally in English (in the late fourteenth century they were, in fact, more usually in Anglo-Norman French). From the 1340s there were important developments on both sides which indicate that the office was taking a more active role in the provision of royal justice.

On the Latin side, the chancery had a dual responsibility. There were matters *de cursu* over which the office had immediate jurisdiction: these included the authority to issue original writs and to carry out certain routine judicial processes. But the chancery also dealt with matters *de gratia* (of grace) which involved the exercise of royal discretion and normally required a warrant from the king to validate the appropriate document issued under the great seal. It was from the latter responsibility that the chancellor derived his role as keeper of the king's grace and used it to intervene in common law process to safeguard the king's prerogative rights. In the 1340s, for example, successive chancellors made aggressive use of the writ *scire facias* ('make known...') to have suits pending before both king's bench and common pleas adjourned into the chancery on the grounds that such cases involved the dispensation of patronage, the disposal of estates held in chief of the king, or the misuse of documents issued under the great seal.[36] Thus far, then, chancery was apparently content to undertake specific responsibilities for maintaining the king's rights, rather than intervening more generally and assertively in the processes of the common law.

On the English side, however, the fourteenth-century developments in chancery jurisdiction were much more far-reaching. The most significant change occurred when suitors began formally to recognise the emerging judicial role of the chancery by addressing their petitions for relief not to the king and council, but directly to the chancellor: this practice may again be dated from the mid-1340s.[37] Between that date and the late 1380s, when the earliest surviving records of chancery proceedings begin, we know little of the extent to which the chancellor exercised his emergent authority. It is generally accepted, however, that the chancery's particular role as a court of conscience developed in large part from its involvement in 'uses', the trusts that became popular among the landed classes in the fourteenth century as a means of establishing stability of succession and the rights of the family. The use gave formal legal title to a group of trustees ('feoffees to use') who held the land for the benefit of another (*cestui qui use*). While legal title allowed the trustees rights enforceable in the common law courts, the beneficiary was not recognised there; the latter, who had a superior right in conscience, looked instead to the prerogative courts to uphold his interests.[38] At what precise point such cases became a notable responsibility of the chancery still awaits further clarification: the date has been successively pushed back from the late 1380s, through the early 1380s, to the early 1370s.[39] Whatever the case, it is evident that the chancellor had begun, in the course of the second half of the fourteenth century, to exercise a discernible role in the dispensation of royal grace and to fill an important gap in the provision of the 'equal and right justice and discretion' that lay at the heart of medieval concepts of royal governance.[40]

Parliament

Parliament was still a relatively new institution at the beginning of the fourteenth century. It had grown out of plenary sessions of the king's council in the reign of Henry III, and it clearly retained its conciliar – and therefore also its judicial – character well into the reigns of Edward I and II. In the late thirteenth century, however, and more particularly under Edward III, the composition and business of the assembly altered dramatically: parliament became a predominantly fiscal and political institution where the representative element, the commons, used its control over taxation as an opportunity to extract concessions from the crown in the form of statutory legislation (see Chapters 4 and 5).[41] Partly because of this shift in business, and partly because of the advent of some of the new judicial tribunals outlined above, parliament's particular identity as a court waned as the fourteenth century progressed. Nevertheless, it continued to fulfil a number of important functions with regard to the law which gave it an acknowledged and, in some respects at least, an exceptionally powerful position in the hierarchy of the courts. In the present context, the most important of these functions was parliament's role as a high court.[42]

Parliament was an extraordinary assembly: although it was common for two or three meetings to be held every year under Edward I, there was a marked decline in frequency during the second half of the fourteenth century, when it was not unknown for two or three years to pass without parliaments. Such assemblies were summoned at the king's will, and met wherever was convenient for him (see Appendix): although most sessions were held at Westminster, which became the established location between 1338 and 1378, earlier parliaments had been held at Berwick, York and Carlisle during Edward I's northern campaigns, and at York and Lincoln periodically until the 1330s; and it is interesting that Richard II revived his predecessors' freedom of action in this respect by calling parliaments at a number of provincial venues including Gloucester, Northampton and Shrewsbury. The extraordinary nature of parliament emphasises its distinction from the common law courts: like the council, it could sometimes undertake actions at common law, but it was not an organised court of record and primarily dispensed prerogative justice.

In acting as a high court, parliament had three responsibilities: as a court of appeal; as a tribunal for the resolution of difficult cases; and as a venue for state trials. All three functions were closely related with the work of what would later be called the house of lords, the group of archbishops, bishops, abbots, dukes, earls, barons and officers of state who received personal summonses to attend the assembly: a full session of the lords was often called a 'great council'. In fact, the first two functions outlined above seem generally to have been undertaken not in full session, but in smaller committees staffed mainly by the official element, the ministers and judges who also, as we have seen, dominated the judicial work of the council. Thus, appeals were occasionally made in parliament on errors in any other court, including both the king's bench and the council. Difficult cases (those where the common law failed to provide a clear means of resolution or where there was some disagreement over procedure) were also referred into parliament either at the instigation of one of the parties or by the court where the business originated.[43] This was an important area of parliamentary business in the early fourteenth century, as the anonymous legal treatise *Fleta* (*c*. 1290) clearly acknowledged: 'The king has his court in his council in his parliaments...[where] are terminated doubts concerning judgments, and new remedies are devised for new wrongs which have arisen, and justice is done to each one according to his deserts.'[44] It was in order to guarantee a forum for the same business that the Ordinances of 1311 demanded that there should be at least one parliament held every year, 'and that in a convenient place'.[45] In 1340, however, the crown agreed to set up a permanent commission of magnates and ministers to deal with problems outside sessions of parliament. Although this body never developed in a formal sense, its role seems to have been assumed by the administrative council; consequently, by the 1370s difficult cases were no longer seen as the special responsibility of the great council in parliament.[46]

By contrast, parliament's role as the venue for state trials seems to have become more important as our period progressed.[47] The crown itself encouraged this development: when taking proceedings against discredited ministers such as Adam Stratton in 1279 and Walter Langton in 1307, or when conducting purges of central and local government in 1289 and 1340, Edward I and Edward III publicly invited all those who had grievances against royal officials to submit bills in parliament which could then be used to supplement the charges brought against such ministers before the lords in great council.[48] This did not at first restrict such proceedings to sessions of parliament – or, indeed, guarantee the defendant a fair trial. However, in 1341, when Edward III attempted to take his revenge on the former chancellor and president of the council, John Stratford, for the failure of the diplomatic and financial policies employed in the opening stages of the French war, the lords in parliament extracted a statute guaranteeing that 'no peer of the land, either officer or other, shall ... be arrested, imprisoned, outlawed or exiled ... or be judged ... except by award of the ... peers in parliament'.[49] The Statute of Treasons of 1352 effectively put an end to arbitrary judgments 'on the king's record', and thereafter it was tacitly agreed that all state trials involving allegations of high treason had to take place before a full session of the lords in parliament. Although the process of trial once more became somewhat summary under Richard II, there was no real dispute over the appropriate venue: even at the height of his 'tyrannical' regime in 1397–8, Richard was persuaded that the only proper place in which to bring charges of treason against peers of the realm was before the great council in parliament.

Nor was it only the crown and the lords that could bring such charges in parliament. In the last quarter of the fourteenth century the parliamentary commons also took on responsibility for initiating state trials by adopting the process known as impeachment. Impeachment signified an accusation made not by an individual or by a sworn jury, but by a group of people acting collectively to initiate trial on the basis of the notoriety of the defendant.[50] In the Good Parliament of 1376, the commons claimed that the misdeeds of a group of Edward III's courtiers and financiers were notorious, and thus forced the crown to allow judicial proceedings to take place before the lords. The results were spectacular: the public disgrace of the chamberlain, Lord Latimer, the steward, Lord Neville, the king's mistress, Alice Perrers, and the London merchant, Richard Lyons, was hailed as a major political victory.[51] It is not surprising, then, that the process of impeachment was to be used again on a number of occasions under Richard II, most notably in the parliamentary attack on the king's friend and chancellor, Michael de la Pole, earl of Suffolk, in the Wonderful Parliament of 1386.[52] The commons had thus found a very striking method of initiating state trials in parliament when neither the king nor the lords, for various reasons, were prepared to prosecute.

The significance of impeachment should not be overrated. The commons usually charged offenders merely with 'misprision', or abuse of office. Impeachment of treason, by contrast, was rarely used, and when it was – as in 1388 and 1397 – it was closely associated with, and reinforced by, appeals of treason entered by members of the lords.[53] Furthermore, because impeachment was a highly politicised process, it was almost inevitably resisted by the crown. John of Gaunt, acting on behalf of Edward III, systematically reversed the acts of the Good Parliament during the winter of 1376–7; and Richard II pre-empted the formal judgment against de la Pole in 1386 by allowing the latter to escape to the continent. It is not surprising, then, that impeachment was little used in the fifteenth century, and fell into disuse between 1450 and the early seventeenth century. Its brief flourishing at the end of the fourteenth century does, however, remind us both of the effective monopoly that parliament had now developed over state trials and, more generally, of the special and lasting place that was thus accorded to parliament in the judicial structures of the realm.

Personnel

Just as the fourteenth century witnessed important developments in the judicial structure, so did it mark the emergence of a more clearly defined system of training, recruitment and preferment for those who staffed the central judicial agencies. To understand the particular identity, status and attitudes of this group, it is helpful to examine their individual and collective experiences in three respects: their training; their recruitment and promotion in royal service; and the public and private interests they sought to advance through such preferment.

First, however, it is necessary to itemise the posts that form the focus of this discussion. In the later Middle Ages, the king's bench and common pleas each had a chief justice, who acted as president of the court, and a fluctuating number of 'puisne' (junior) justices. King's bench had between two and four puisne justices until the mid-fourteenth century, but only one between 1349 and 1391, after which the number rose again. Common pleas had a rather larger bench of between three and six puisne justices for most of the century. The court of the exchequer was similarly staffed by a panel of judges comprising the chief baron and three (sometimes four) barons. Cases brought at common law in these courts were pleaded by 'serjeants at law', the antecessors of modern barristers. The king employed an attorney (a legal representative) in both king's bench and common pleas, and from the early fourteenth century regularly retained three or four serjeants at law to act as *narratores* (pleaders) for the crown: the members of this latter group took a special oath to serve the interests of the king, and are known as the king's serjeants.[54]

The president of the court of chancery was the chancellor, or, in his absence, the keeper of the rolls (that is, the clerk responsible for the archives of the office). The latter was one of the twelve senior clerks who also exercised considerable discretion in the Latin and, subsequently, the English sides of chancery business; by the time of Richard II's chancery ordinances (*c*. 1389), these clerks were already being referred to as the 'masters' in chancery, the title by which they were known in the more developed court of conscience of the fifteenth century.[55] The council, as we have seen, derived its personnel from the common law courts and the offices of state; its president was the king's senior minister, the chancellor. The chancellor and treasurer, along with the judges, the king's serjeants, and the barons of the exchequer, all received personal summonses to parliament and provided the body of legal expertise required there both to deal with judicial problems and to draft statutory legislation (see Chapter 5). The senior personnel of the various central courts therefore comprised a remarkably close-knit group with well-defined but overlapping functions, and it is reasonable to suppose that they had a highly developed sense of their own identity and importance.

Education

That sense of identity was very much reinforced in the fourteenth century by the creation of distinct traditions of training and recruitment in the central courts. It was during the reigns of the three Edwards that there emerged, for the first time, a discernible pattern in the qualifications and experience of those appointed to senior positions in the judiciary. After 1290 churchmen ceased to hold a majority of the senior posts in the common law courts, and from the beginning of Edward III's reign the justices of the king's bench and common pleas were, almost without exception, members of the laity. A similar shift may be observed in the post of chief baron of the exchequer, which from the 1310s was held predominantly by laymen. By contrast, until the early fifteenth century the senior chancery clerks and (with a few notable departures from the norm) the chancellors and keepers of the privy seal were all members of the clergy.[56] This difference in status denoted different traditions of education in two entirely separate traditions of law, and does much in turn to explain the increasing divergence evident in the later fourteenth century between the common law courts on the one hand and the prerogative courts on the other.

The common lawyers of late-thirteenth- and fourteenth-century England rarely had any university education, though some of them – William Bereford, William Inge, Henry Scrope and others – can certainly be shown to have had some knowledge of the academic tradition of Roman law.[57] Essentially, however, the future serjeants at law and king's justices learned their business by attending and observing the procedures of the central courts: at the conclusion of a case in 1302, Ralph Hengham, the chief justice of common pleas, specifically addressed the 'apprentices', as this group was called, in order to clarify a point of law. It is now evident that, at least from the late thirteenth century, there was also some formal education available in the technicalities of the common law both in London and Westminster and, indeed, in Oxford (though outside the context of the university, in the schools that offered training in a range of business skills). It remains uncertain as to whether any such instruction was offered in the inns of court, the hostels that sprang up on the western fringes of the city of London during the fourteenth century to provide accommodation for the apprentices at law: although we know that the Inner Temple, the New Temple and Gray's Inn were already functioning in a *domestic* capacity by 1388, and were joined by Lincoln's Inn before 1422, it is not until the mid-fifteenth century that the inns can be shown to have developed a properly organised *educational* role. Whatever the exact nature and location of the training, however, the collegiate ethos promoted both by communal residence and by the acquisition of a common body of arcane and privileged knowledge clearly did much to breed a strong sense of professional solidarity among the future serjeants and justices of the king's courts.

In the early fourteenth century the staff of the royal chancery seem to have received their training in administrative and legal technicalities within the place of employment: partly by recruiting from well-established clerical families, and partly by promoting from within, the senior clerks successfully perpetuated the high standards of accuracy and accountability on which the good reputation of their office depended.[58] This was reinforced by the requirement that chancery clerks should be celibate and live together in the manner of a religious community. While the 'household' of chancery provided only meals and robes for its staff, the majority of clerks therefore gathered in communal domestic units or 'inns' such as the House of Converts, the home of the keeper of the rolls. Although many clerks were only in minor orders, and therefore technically free to marry, very few did so before the end of the fourteenth century – for the very practical reason that they were then forced to set up expensive domestic establishments of their own. Towards the end of the same century, moreover, the senior clerks of chancery realised that their specialist knowledge was a marketable commodity, and began to offer instruction in chancery practice in the 'inns of chancery' that grew up around the House of Converts in Chancery Lane.[59] The fact that the inns of court developed in precisely the same location is, of course, a striking reminder of the overlap between the Latin side of chancery business and the procedures of the common law courts.

At the same time, however, the chancery – and, indeed, the privy seal office – began to demonstrate important signs of an alternative, outside, influence as a result of the recruitment into their ranks of men with formal university qualifications in civil and canon law. The origins of this process lay in the great explosion of diplomatic activity associated with the Scottish and French wars. Although common lawyers such as John Benstead, William Inge, John Stonor and Geoffrey Scrope were intimately involved in diplomatic negotiations down to the 1330s,[60] it became more and more important, as the scale and complexity of that business grew, to involve experts in the academic traditions of civil and canon law which, in turn, provided the medieval equivalent of international law. Both Edward II and Edward III patronised the Universities of Oxford and Cambridge specifically to encourage the development of such skills and prepare men for royal service.[61] During the 1340s, indeed, it became more or less an established convention that chancellors and keepers of the privy seal should be drawn from this background: John Thoresby, Simon Islip and Michael Northburgh at the privy seal, and John Offord and John Thoresby (again) at the chancery, had all begun their careers at Oxford and had served as royal envoys during the opening stages of the French wars.[62] The association of this academic elite with the work of the royal secretariat may also have had important repercussions for the development both of the English side of chancery and of the procedures of the prerogative courts. For example, the training in civil and canon law received by Thoresby, who was chancellor between 1349 and 1356, and by his nephew John Waltham, successively keeper of the rolls and keeper of the privy seal in the 1380s, may well explain the affinity between certain procedures observed in the ecclesiastical courts and the new processes associated with the *sub pena* writ.[63] The presence of an increasing number of civil lawyers in the ranks of the royal administration may also explain the ease with which the emergent courts of admiralty and chivalry adopted Roman law principles in their procedures and judgments.[64] The academic tradition may never have established as strong a hold on royal justice as did the common law, but it is evident that the university connection was becoming a recognised influence within the structure of the central courts.

Recruitment and Promotion

To be recruited into royal service was an important mark of distinction, and the route and speed of preferment was an important measure of royal favour. The first thing that needs to be noted about the men who filled the senior ranks of the judiciary in the fourteenth century is the degree to which theirs was a career open to talent: most of the common lawyers and administrators, and a majority of the graduates, came from relatively obscure backgrounds and were reliant on their personal ability (as well, of course, as the timely intervention of influential patrons) to win them places in royal government. That said, it is also evident that a fairly clear distinction emerged in the fourteenth century between the recruitment systems observed by the common law courts on the one hand and the prerogative courts on the other.

The laicisation of the king's bench and common pleas, which is such a marked feature of the early fourteenth century, was rapidly accompanied by the development of a tradition of promotion from within the legal system: after 1320 it was standard practice to fill vacancies in the judiciary by promoting the king's serjeants to be justices of the two senior courts.[65] In other words, a close and enduring link was established between the bar (the serjeants who pleaded cases in the courts) and the bench (the judges who presided there). This, in turn, meant a relatively internalised and self-regulating judicial system, where promotion depended on experience and the pattern of office-holding was characterised by stability. Of the four king's serjeants appointed in 1315, for example, William Herle became justice (1320–7) and chief justice (1327–9, 1331–5) of common pleas, while Geoffrey Scrope was appointed justice of common pleas (1323) and chief justice of king's bench (1324–9, 1331–2, 1332–8). Later in the century, John Knyvet, king's serjeant from 1356 to 1361, became a justice of common pleas (1361–5) and chief justice of king's bench (1365–72), while his colleague Thomas Ingleby, king's serjeant in 1359–61, went on to be a justice of king's bench from 1361 to 1378.[66] It was not at all uncommon, then, for outgoing chief justices to look back over careers at the bar and the bench that had given them thirty years or more of uninterrupted service in the king's courts.

The principal officials of the prerogative courts – the chancellor, the treasurer, and the keeper of the privy seal – were, by contrast, drawn from more diverse backgrounds and their appointments were subject to a whole range of political as well as purely professional considerations. There was certainly a strong tradition of appointment from within. The close interaction between the secretarial offices, for example, meant that the keepers of the rolls of chancery were not infrequently promoted to the keepership of the privy seal, as in the cases of Richard Airmyn (keeper of the privy seal 1327–8), John Thoresby (1345–7), John Waltham (1386–9), and Nicholas Bubwith (1405–6); and the route from the keepership of the privy seal to the chancellorship, established under Edward II, was perpetuated by Robert Baldock (chancellor 1323–6), Richard Bury (1334–5), John Offord (1345–9), John Thoresby (1349–56) and William Wykeham (1367–71, 1389–91). On the other hand, the selection of such ministers depended less on their command of bureaucratic detail and rather more on their leadership qualities. This explains why so many chancellors continued to be recruited from, or appointed into, the episcopate during the fourteenth century: not only did ecclesiastical office provide handsome incomes for the king's ministers, it also trained and tested the skills of those found worthy to act as members of the royal council.[67]

All that said, it is also evident that, as the fourteenth century progressed, both the range of candidates for such offices and the considerations that underpinned their selection became more varied. Two interconnected trends are of particular relevance here: namely, the laicisation and the politicisation of the major offices of state. In 1340 Edward III suddenly broke with tradition and appointed laymen to the posts of chancellor and treasurer. This decision arose from the political rift between the king and the domestic administration led by Archbishop Stratford: by appointing laymen, who would be liable to investigation in royal courts, Edward intended to override the attempts made by the archbishop and his brother, Robert Stratford, the dismissed chancellor, to claim clerical privilege and immunise themselves from prosecution and punishment. The change was short-lived, and clergy returned to the senior posts in the exchequer and the chancery in 1341 and 1345 respectively. However, in 1371 parliament revived the king's earlier strategy by demanding the replacement of the chancellor, treasurer and keeper of the privy seal with laymen, and for the following six years the crown abided by this request. This politically motivated shift in the pattern of recruitment proved to have more enduring influence, and although the clergy long continued to dominate the three offices of state, there were a number of subsequent appointments under Richard II and Henry IV which signified that the posts of chancellor and (to a greater extent) treasurer had indeed became accessible to the laity.[68]

Who precisely were these new lay ministers of the crown? The first lay chancellors and treasurers were, interestingly, recruited from among the common lawyers: Robert Parving (treasurer, 1341; chancellor, 1341–3) had previously been a king's serjeant (1333–9), and briefly justice of common pleas (1340) and chief justice of king's bench (1340–1); while Robert Sadington (chancellor, 1343–5) had been an advocate in the royal courts before becoming chief baron of the exchequer in 1334. It is significant that these lawyer-chancellors, particularly Parving, made something of an impact in the year books, the lawyers' own records of pleadings in the king's courts, by intervening in the business of king's bench and common pleas to claim special jurisdiction over cases in which the crown had an interest: their influence on the development of the Latin side of chancery jurisdiction may, indeed, have been rather greater than their brief tenure in that office may suggest.[69] In the 1370s, the pattern was repeated. Robert Thorpe moved from being chief justice of common pleas (1356–71) to the chancellorship (1371–2) where, on his death, he was replaced by the chief justice of king's bench, John Knyvet, who served as chancellor until 1377. The influence of these common lawyers may again have been decisive in the development of the chancery's specialised jurisdiction over litigation on uses in the 1370s.[70]

Thereafter, however, it was more common for lay chancellors to be chosen from the secular baronage: Richard Scrope, who was the first lay treasurer (1371–5) since Parving, and who went on to be chancellor in 1378–80 and 1381–2, certainly had powerful connections in the courts (his father, Geoffrey, and his uncle, Henry, had been senior figures in king's bench and common pleas in the first half of the century), but he made his own career and won his place in the peerage through military and political service to the regimes of Edward III and Richard II.[71] The appointment of Richard II's close personal associate, Michael de la Pole, as chancellor in 1383, the latter's elevation to the earldom of Suffolk in 1385, and his subsequent impeachment in the Wonderful Parliament of 1386, are all powerful signs of the way in which the opening up of ministerial positions to laymen had increased both the political profile and the political hazards of royal office-holding.

So far, then, a contrast has been drawn between an internalised and politically neutral judiciary on the one hand and a more diversified and politicised class of ministers on the other. To an extent, this distinction accurately reflects the late medieval convention that, whereas the common law courts should be allowed to undertake their business without undue influence from the crown, the council and its offshoots existed primarily to fulfil the king's will and uphold the royal interest. Certainly, that convention is, in turn, illustrated by relative longevity of tenure. Between 1290 and 1399 the office of chancellor changed hands forty-one times and was held by thirty-three different men. That of chief justice of king's bench, by contrast, changed only nineteen times and was held by seventeen individuals; and that of chief justice of common pleas changed only fifteen times and was held by a total of just thirteen men.[72] To assume from these statistics that the dignity and independence of the common law somehow immunised the staff of the king's bench and common pleas from the vagaries of politics is, however, both to distort the meaning of service as it was understood in the later Middle Ages and, indeed, to forget that the judges often provided some of the principal players – and victims – in major political crises of the fourteenth century. A rather more subtle distinction therefore needs to be drawn between the degree of political influence that acted upon the recruitment and promotion of the king's judges on the one hand and his ministers on the other. That influence can best be discerned through a discussion of the various interests served by the judicial agents of central government in the fourteenth century.

Public and Private Service

The laicisation and professionalisation of the common law courts had a major impact on the manner in which the king's judicial representatives derived their income. Those ministers who continued to be recruited from the clergy were rewarded handsomely for their service to the crown through ecclesiastical preferment: clerical chancellors and treasurers, who could expect incomes of £1500–£3000 a year from bishoprics such as Ely, Winchester and Durham, found themselves on the same economic footing as many of the titled nobility.[73] The lay judges, by contrast, must have considered themselves somewhat shabbily treated. Common lawyers were usually knighted on their promotion to the judiciary and received annuities of £40 a year to sustain this dignity. From at least the 1270s until 1346, the two chief justices also received fees of £40 a year, and the puisne justices 40 marks (£26 13s. 4d.); a few were also retained as feed members of the king's household.[74] In 1346 the crown approved a series of supplementary fees worked out on an incremental basis according to status; these were successively increased over the following decades, and by 1389 stood at 180 marks (£120) for the chief justice of king's bench, 140 marks (£93 6s. 8d.) for the chief justice of common pleas, and 110 marks (£73 6s. 8d.) for the puisne justices.[75] There was also a fixed rate of £20 a year for those central court judges who sat on assize commissions in the localities, and a similar scale of payments for serving on oyer and terminer and other local commissions; judges also received an allowance out of court fees. Even by the early fifteenth century, however, a newly appointed puisne justice could only expect to earn about £250 a year from the crown – a figure which set him significantly lower in the economic hierarchy than the clerical ministers, among the lesser barons and greater knights of the kingdom.[76]

The real anomaly, however, lay in the discrepancy between the incomes of the serjeants at law and the judges. To be promoted from the bar to the bench could actually mean a drop in income, since the lawyer could no longer officially represent his large network of private clients by acting for them in court.[77] In some cases, sound investment of the profits earlier earned from private practice was perhaps sufficient to act as a cushion against (relative) poverty: Sir Geoffrey Scrope, for example, had already begun to build up a large landed estate for himself in Yorkshire before being retained as a king's serjeant and royal justice.[78] On the whole, however, those appointed to the judiciary found it appropriate to supplement their official salaries by continuing to sell their expertise as legal advisors. Although the judges could not, of course, act as counsel in their own courts, their experience and insider knowledge were marketable assets, especially to those powerful individuals and institutions that found themselves regularly involved in legal transactions and litigation. Consequently, a significant number of noble families, urban corporations and ecclesiastical institutions began, from the late thirteenth century, to retain members of the judiciary on a permanent basis. The annuities and fees paid out under this arrangement, often accompanied by liveries (robes, hoods, hats and badges bearing the lord's colours and coat of arms), thus became an established source of additional income to the fourteenth-century judiciary.[79]

While there was nothing necessarily sinister about royal judges providing legal advice, it is easy to see why this practice came to be perceived as corrupt: if a party to a suit before the royal courts had one or more of the king's justices in his pay, how could the system be trusted to deliver impartial judgments? Certainly, while the practice of retaining judges was not necessarily created with the deliberate intention of subverting the law, it is clear that those who employed royal justices in a private capacity were quite prepared to use their contacts to personal advantage. During the early years of Edward III's reign, for example, John Cambridge, a king's serjeant and (from 1331) justice of common pleas, was appointed to a series of judicial commissions investigating the quarrel between the abbot and townspeople of Abingdon; since Cambridge was also retained as the abbot's steward, the results were virtually a foregone conclusion, and in 1332 the claims of the townspeople were decisively quashed.[80] The retaining of royal justices thus became part of an elaborate network of influences acting upon the legal system which, in its more covert and sinister forms, severely hindered the ability and reputation of the common law courts to do right justice to all. These abuses often went by the generic title of 'maintenance', which was understood to include the harbouring of criminals and the packing and intimidation of juries as well as the bribing of lawyers and judges (see Chapter 6).

The crown's response to repeated allegations of corruption in the central courts was reactive and sporadic. In 1289–90 and 1340–1, for example, Edward I and Edward III carried out major purges of the king's bench and common pleas. The circumstances were strikingly similar: both kings had been absent from the realm for lengthy periods, and were persuaded that they should launch inquiries into the iniquitous practices that had supposedly flourished unchecked among their officials in central and local government. The short-term impact on the judiciary was startling. Edward I forced the chief justice of common pleas, Thomas Wayland, into exile and dismissed four of the five justices of common pleas and all three justices of king's bench. These, along with six of the justices in eyre, were forced to pay heavy fines, amounting eventually to some £20 000, to obtain their release and restoration to favour.[81] Edward III similarly dismissed the chief justice of common pleas, John Stonor, and six of the eight justices of that court, subjecting them to trial before a special commission.[82] On the eve of his departure on campaign in 1346, in an apparent attempt to preempt similar scandals, Edward III issued the Ordinance of Justices, which offered a radical solution to the problem of maintenance by requiring all royal justices (those working in the shires as well as those in the central courts) to declare, on oath, that they would take no fees or robes except from the king: it was to recompense them for the resulting drop in income that the same legislation increased the allowances made to the judges out of the royal exchequer.[83] While it is clear that the ordinance did not put a stop to the retaining of senior justices, it did become a form of sanction against corruption in the central courts: Edward III subsequently dismissed William Thorpe on charges of maintenance in 1350, and removed both Henry Green, another chief justice of king's bench, and William Skipwith, chief baron of the exchequer, from his service in 1365.

In most of these cases, it has to be said that the longer-term significance of such scandals was considerably blunted, both by the ability of the lawyers to defend themselves from such charges and by the crown's subsequent willingness to reinstate them. In none of the trials following the dismissals of 1289, 1340 and 1350 did the government manage to come up with any really substantial evidence to support its general charges, and a number of the principal defendants in such trials found their way back into royal service within a remarkably short period. Ralph Hengham, justice of king's bench, who was induced to offer the remarkable fine of 8000 marks (£5333 6s.8d.) for pardon of his alleged trespasses in 1290,[84] was later appointed chief justice of common pleas in 1301; Richard Willoughby, accused in 1341 of perverting the course of justice and selling the laws 'as if they had been oxen or cattle',[85] returned to a long career as justice of common pleas from 1343 to 1357; and William Thorpe, pardoned his offences in 1351, was quickly back in office as second baron of the exchequer in 1352. In certain respects, indeed, these *causes célèbres* did more to vindicate than to discredit the lawyers: both Hengham and Willoughby were cited in the year books for their vigorous denials of malpractice, and thus assumed a certain heroic status in the folklore of the legal profession.[86]

Nevertheless, those who continued to criticise and accuse the lawyers were not entirely thwarted. The allegations against Thorpe were still remembered in 1386 when the commons in parliament cited them as a precedent for one of their accusations against Michael de la Pole.[87] This provides an important link between the intermittent royal campaigns against judicial corruption in the first three-quarters of the fourteenth century and what might be described as the 'direct action' undertaken by the crown's subjects in the reign of Richard II, when first the rebels during the Peasants' Revolt and later the Lords Appellant carried out their own purges of the royal courts and actually executed two chief justices – William Cavendish in 1381 and Robert Tresilian in 1388. These pre-emptive strikes by the king's opponents signified the extent to which the judges, and the courts over which they presided, were perceived to have become contaminated by the social and political influences at work upon them.

Not surprisingly, perhaps, the violent purges of the senior judiciary during the 1380s seem to have had a more radical and enduring impact on the legal profession than did the royal initiatives of the early fourteenth century. In particular, the new men promoted as justices of king's bench and common pleas after 1388 appear to have stopped taking regular fees and robes from private patrons (though they long continued to receive more casual and occasional payments in return for private service and legal advice). This retreat from the formalities of retaining may not have been entirely their own choice: in part, it reflected the better rates of reward offered by the crown after 1389; and it may also have had something to do with the programme of retrenchment forced on ecclesiastical institutions and great noblemen by the economic recession of the late fourteenth century.[88] Certainly, it is difficult to tell whether the change had any impact on public perceptions of judicial integrity: the proverbial evidence suggests that the king's justices, and their fifteenth-century successors, were still thought to be highly susceptible to ad hoc bribes and other sweeteners.[89] On the other hand, the shift away from involvement in aristocratic affinities at a time when the latter were becoming more and more important as a form of political organisation and identity among the gentry (and, therefore, arguably, among the king's justices in the localities) does suggest that a certain cultural shift had taken place, and that a higher premium was now set by all parties – the crown, the judges and the political community – on the independence and impartiality of the central judiciary. We shall return in Chapter 6 to consider whether the higher standards of conduct set for the judges in the king's bench and common pleas adequately served the correspondingly inflated expectations of those who sought satisfaction in those courts.[90]

Conclusion

This chapter has explored the structures and personnel of the central agencies of royal justices in the fourteenth century and described the changes that emerged in the period between the 1290s and the 1390s. The century in question witnessed the emergence of new forms of action in private litigation passing through the court of common pleas and gave the king's bench an important role as the superior criminal court in the land. It also saw the emergence of a whole series of prerogative courts which responded to the limitations of the common law by dispensing the royal grace in a technically arbitrary, but also speedy, manner. The range of remedies available in the central courts therefore increased as the century wore on, and the take-up rate, at least in civil actions, seems to have grown accordingly (see Chapter 5). At the same time, the personnel of the system altered significantly, as the upper levels of the legal profession took on discernible patterns of training and recruitment and began, in response to political pressure, to develop a keener sense of its obligations to uphold and conform to public morality. The degree to which different levels of society in different parts of England were able to engage with the processes of the central courts is clearly an important issue to which we shall have to return. This chapter, however, has already hinted at the close connections between centre and localities, and before we attempt to explain the changes that took place in English justice during the fourteenth century, it is important to describe the structural changes that also came about in the provinces and to examine the personnel that served in the various agencies of royal justice scattered across the shires of medieval England.

3

ROYAL JUSTICE IN THE PROVINCES

Chapter 2 discussed the organisation and staffing of the central courts of justice, institutions lying at the heart of royal government. This chapter complements the previous one by examining the administration of justice as it affected the provinces. A necessary feature of government, both for judicial and for administrative reasons, was the capacity to reach out into the shires and thus enable the king's will to penetrate the consciousness of the individual subject. As early as the twelfth century it was realised that this task could be accomplished through teams of justices travelling around the counties. Establishing such a link with the regions had the added advantage of creating reciprocity: people could bring their complaints and disputes to the king's attention via his itinerant judges. The essential change that occurred during the fourteenth century was the gradual replacement of these periodic provincial visitations with permanent judicial tribunals in the shires, and the resulting creation of a body of king's justices who lived and worked in the localities they served.

It is important to keep in the forefront of one's mind the long-term direction of judicial evolution during the fourteenth century. Largely as a result of the rapid expansion of royal government, the setting up of an effective mechanism to bring justice to the shires was a lengthy and at times seemingly confused or disjointed process. The latter part of the thirteenth and the first half of the fourteenth centuries, in particular, were characterised by improvisation and experimentation. Moreover, much of the government's policy towards justice in the regions was reactive and irregular: judicial commissions were often sent out for specific reasons and were thus intermittent and sporadic in nature. To some extent, this remained a feature of the English judicial system, although over the course of the fourteenth century there was a gradual move towards permanence, represented most obviously by the regular sessions of the justices of assize and the justices of the peace.

The subject of regional justice is therefore best approached through an examination of a wide range of judicial agencies over an extended period of time. This enables us to take account of the rate of change in general terms, and of the process of definition, re-definition and fine-tuning that occurred as the fourteenth century progressed. As in Chapter 2, the basic structure of regional justice will be treated separately from its personnel in order to provide a clearer picture of judicial developments and their wider administrative significance.

Structures

The General Eyre

The general eyre was the principal agency of royal justice in the provinces during the thirteenth century. It comprised a series of powerful commissions headed by a team of itinerant justices who operated on defined county circuits. It began as a means of enforcing the Assize of Clarendon (1166), which regularised forms of action made available upon a chancery writ and established procedures for the presentment of felonies. Empowered to hear all civil pleas (mainly land litigation) as well as pleas of the crown, the justices in eyre were therefore responsible for the administration of both civil and criminal justice.[1] The eyre's jurisdiction over crown pleas was embodied in the 'articles of the eyre' (*capitula itineris*), a list of questions to which juries from the various administrative units and jurisdictions within the county (hundreds, boroughs and liberties) were required to respond.[2] Until the mid-thirteenth century, however, the articles of the eyre betrayed an overriding concern for the king's own rights, with a special emphasis upon the financial gains to be made from the feudal and proprietary rights of the crown and from fines for infringements of royal prerogatives and regulations.[3] At this stage, the criminal side of the articles was subsidiary: the eyre was only really interested in felony, and particularly with hearing appeals and receiving presentments of homicide.

The addition of new articles (*nova capitula*) in 1254 and 1278 greatly extended the competence of the eyre, particularly in the criminal field. The justices were now empowered to investigate two areas of considerable concern to the crown: the usurpation of royal rights (via the *quo warranto* inquiries) and the conduct of royal and seigneurial officials.[4] More generally, the elaboration of the articles of the eyre brought an influx of new business – 'the beginning of a second stream in English law'[5] – in the form of trespass litigation. As the royal courts entertained oral complaints (*querelae*) against the abuses of officials, so a whole range of minor offences against persons and property, previously matters for local courts, came to be accepted and remedied before the king's justices.[6] The recognition of trespass as a crown plea considerably enlarged the scope of royal criminal jurisdiction. Ironically, however, the sheer volume of new business imposed burdens on the workings of the eyre and contributed to its eventual decline. The mammoth task imposed by the *quo warranto* campaigns, which theoretically tested every claim to a franchise or liberty, similarly added to the eyre's unwieldiness – even though it is apparent that such proceedings were rarely as comprehensive as the king envisaged.[7] The expansion of law and government stemming from the additional articles therefore served to highlight the limitations of the eyre as an omnicompetent, non-specialised judicial agency.

In 1294 a new offensive in Gascony led to the suspension of the general eyre and effectively halted the *quo warranto* enquiries, which were considered too unpopular for the political climate.[8] There was no immediate hiatus in judicial terms, however, as no visitation of the eyre in the thirteenth century had ever been carried out exactly as planned. Indeed, following the suspension of the eyre for the second Welsh war (1282–4), and with the king's absence abroad towards the end of that decade, eyres had already become occasional rather than continuous.[9] Contemporaries regarded the withdrawal of the eyre in 1294 merely as a temporary state of affairs and expected it to resume its work in due course.[10] Only gradually over the following quarter-century, therefore, did it cease to be viewed as an integral part of the administration of civil and criminal justice in the shires. Indeed, eyres continued to be employed after 1294, though more for political and fiscal than for judicial reasons. Individual eyres, for instance, were held in certain counties, usually coinciding with a vacancy in the relevant bishopric, and were used by the king to emphasise his transcendent seigneurial authority at moments when his political will was otherwise being challenged.[11]

The general eyre was essentially a product of, and response to, English government and society in the late twelfth century. Unspecialised and omnicompetent, its operation was largely determined by the needs, processes and institutions of that society. Although the eyre was revived briefly during the regime of Isabella and Mortimer, the sheer range of its work made it an unwieldy weapon in the judicial armoury, and it was aborted after only two years, in the winter of 1330–1, with just four counties covered (see Chapter 4).[12] By Edward III's reign, the eyre was of symbolic rather than real significance, and was used simply – and cynically – to the crown's financial advantage: eyres proclaimed in Kent and Durham in 1333, for instance, were bought off by the communities of those counties with fines of 1000 marks (£666 13s. 4d.) each.[13] Changes in society, and in the needs that first gave it birth, had in turn made the eyre redundant. The judges masterminding its revival in 1329 imagined a golden age of peace under the eyres,[14] an inflated opinion entertained still by some historians.[15] Its disappearance, however, certainly left a major gap in the judicial administration which took half a century and more to be adequately filled.

Assizes and Gaol Delivery

Some of the functions of the eyre had already been supplemented and/or devolved upon other agencies prior to its demise. In an attempt to reduce the weight of business in the eyre, the more limited tasks of hearing assizes and delivering gaols were entrusted to itinerant commissioners.[16] In the half-century or so following the suspension of the eyre, a distinct network of assize circuits emerged, incorporating a substantial number of assize venues. A similar arrangement for the delivery of prisoners held in county gaols was developed and became linked to the system for assizes, initially in 1299 and more permanently after 1330. It was intended that the justices should visit the shires during the central courts' vacations, providing brief sessions in one particular area before moving on to the next venue. By this mechanism, it was hoped, the backlog of business that had been so troublesome to the eyre would not be allowed to build up, and regular access to the king's justices could be guaranteed.

Assizes, held under the authority of special and general commissions, embodied the essence of the Angevin administrative 'leap forward': a writ available to all free subjects that was returnable into the king's courts for the hearing of a plea at a specific time and place.[17] The actions available under this writ, known as the possessory or petty assizes, were novel disseisin (remedy for a tenant improperly ejected from his freehold), darrein presentment (determining who exercised the right of patronage to an ecclesiastical benefice) and mort d'ancestor (the transmission of seisin of a dead man to the true heir).[18] Special assize commissions, which were common before the general ones came into use at the end of Henry III's reign, involved only a single action or assize, while general commissions assigned the justices to hold all assizes, juries and certifications within a group of specified counties usually coinciding with, or acting as, circuits.[19] Like the justices in eyre, the justices of assize visited the counties in succession, the first systematic assize circuits being set up in 1273.[20] The circuits themselves appear to have been fairly flexible during this early period and the configuration of counties varied.[21] In 1293, however, a rationalisation of the existing system took place and four assize circuits were established.[22]

Although commissions for gaol delivery were issued in circuits during the early 1290s and were recorded in chancery in 1294,[23] they did not necessarily coincide with the assize circuits, and for some years thereafter were usually issued singly for individual gaols. Like those given to assize justices, gaol delivery commissions may also be categorised as general and special. The former appointed justices to 'deliver' (bring to trial and judgment) all prisoners within a stated gaol or gaols, while the latter were concerned with the delivery of named persons or certain categories of prisoner.[24] Gaol delivery circuits differed from those for assizes until the two tasks were linked in 1299 by the Statute of Fines.[25] The justices of assize were now given responsibility for the delivery of gaols within the shires of their circuit.[26] In theory, the combining of assize and gaol delivery duties should have replaced single commissions for each gaol with commissions covering entire circuits. In fact, this practice was adopted only for the counties of the Midland circuit, and there only briefly; elsewhere in the country the old formula remained.[27]

The 1305 'trailbaston' visitations (see below) appear in some respects to have disrupted the assize circuits set up in 1293: in the wake of these visitations, the assize commissions were often fragmented to cover only single counties, pairs or groups of three.[28] This should not be taken to imply that the circuit system had completely broken down or dissolved, however, since the commissions for individual counties or pairs of counties can usually be pieced together to form a circuit group. Although their specific alignments were not always later observed, assize circuits clearly prefiguring those adopted in 1328 were outlined in a chancery document of 1310.[29] By the end of Edward II's reign, therefore, the configuration of counties within the assize circuits was gradually becoming standardised. Gaol deliveries, on the other hand, were being carried out on a single-county basis or in small groups of adjoining counties, with little or no reference to the assize circuits.

In the aftermath of the civil war of the 1320s and the deposition of Edward II, the early years of Edward III's reign witnessed a concern to regularise the administration of justice and return it to the paths envisaged by Edward I (see Chapter 4). There were particularly important clauses in the statutes of 1328 and 1330 relating to the assizes and gaol delivery sessions. The Statute of Northampton (1328) stressed that commissions should not be granted against the form of the Statute of Fines (1299), which had required the assize justices to deliver the gaols of the counties within their circuits.[30] The link was confirmed in the statute of 1330, which added that the justices should make their visitations at least three times a year, and more often if necessary.[31] Betraying a noticeable concern for standardisation, commissions covering all circuits were issued *en masse* following the promulgation of the statutes of 1328 and 1330.[32]

From 1344 the duties of the assize justices became entwined with the peace commissions. Initially these justices were attached to such commissions in an ad hoc manner in order to determine indictments, as specified by a statute of 1344.[33] From the 1350s, however, they were appointed, as standard practice, to the peace commissions in each of the counties forming their own assize circuits. The connection between the two agencies is demonstrated by the order in which the chancery enrolled peace commissions on the patent rolls, so that the counties were grouped according to their assize circuits.[34]

The establishment of regular visitations of the provinces during the central courts' vacations for the purpose of holding assizes and delivering the county gaols enabled a significant proportion of the civil and criminal work formerly undertaken by the general eyre to be performed in its absence. Fully integrated into the system of regional justice, the assize circuits maintained a vital administrative link between central and local justice. Since the circuit justices were primarily concerned with trying cases of felony at gaol delivery, they did not, however, fulfil the eyre's obligations regarding the crown's burgeoning jurisdiction over trespasses.

Commissions of Oyer and Terminer

The rise of trespass as a plea of the crown, and the government's perception of an increase in the level of disorder, influenced the development of a wide range of commissions to investigate alleged malefactors and to hear and determine (*oyer* and *terminer*) civil and criminal offences. Arising out of Edward I's programme of administrative reform of 1274, oyer and terminer commissions were initially intended to relieve some of the pressure on the general eyre by helping to deal with the flood of bills and plaints. They quickly proved their worth, however, and established themselves as a useful supplementary part of the judicial machinery.[35] Commissions of oyer and terminer could vary widely in type and scope. Although modern historians have labelled the two main categories as 'special' and 'general', these merely represent the ends of a much broader spectrum of judicial commissions.

Special commissions of oyer and terminer are discussed in more detail in Chapter 5. They could be obtained by private persons for specific incidents or disputes within a given area. Although felony was within the scope of these special commissions, their prime concern lay with cases of trespass. Such commissions were available from chancery in the same manner as original writs.[36] The volume of special commissions grew significantly over the early fourteenth century as a result of popular demand and the crown's willingness to supply them upon payment of a fee.

General commissions of oyer and terminer demand more extended treatment here. They could range over a circuit of counties and contain broad powers to punish an entire class of offences, as in the case of the powerful commissions popularly known as 'trailbaston' (from the sticks or 'bastons' that criminal gangs were reputed to use in acts of terrorism).[37] The Ordinance of Trailbaston of 1305 and the ensuing set of judicial commissions (1305–7) represented the first systematic attempt to confront the backlog of judicial business that had built up following the suspension of the general eyre in 1294.[38] Operating on five circuits of counties, the trailbaston justices received the power to hold assizes and deliver gaols.[39] Their main concern, however, was with organised violence and concerted abuse of legal procedure. The 'articles of trailbaston' contained in their commissions targeted areas beyond the traditional core of jurisdiction associated with pleas of the crown. Inquiry was to be made concerning those who seized lands by force and then escaped legal action by putting them in the hands of great lords; those who threatened jurors and litigants in the assizes; and those who impeded the administration of justice at the local level. Articles were also directed against assaults, burglary by night, and batteries; those who hired themselves out for such crimes; and those who coveted poor neighbours' lands.[40] Following the Ordinance of Conspirators (1305), a transcript of which was sent to the trailbaston justices, concerted judicial abuse through maintenance or champerty (the undertaking at one's own expense of another's suit in return for receiving a share of the subject in dispute) was established as a class of criminal trespass.[41] The justices were empowered to hear cases brought by the crown alone, serious or 'enormous' trespasses, and lesser offences brought at the king's suit and privately.

For a while, general oyer and terminer commissions in this mould became an established part of the judicial machinery and were often initiated as a result of law enforcement drives, as in 1314, 1321, 1328, 1331 and 1340.[42] While indictments and appeals of felonies continued to be heard at gaol delivery, the numerous cases of trespass coming before the oyer and terminer justices were turned to the crown's financial advantage through the imposition of fines for remission of imprisonment upon conviction.[43] Trailbastons, particularly the *novelles enquerrez* (new enquiries) of the 1340s, thus earned an unfavourable reputation for their heavy financial penalties.[44]

Although they proved useful options for law enforcement and dispute settlement, both special and general commissions of oyer and terminer should be viewed as only short term and mainly reactive expedients. The largest numbers of special commissions were issued during the 1310s and 1320s, when annual totals could rise to over 250; after the 1340s, however, the numbers dwindled rapidly (see Chapter 5).[45] General commissions also changed in character: now more often issued for single counties or pairs of counties, or even for particular groups of manors, they were often directed at specific concerns of direct interest to the crown such as counterfeiting or treasure trove.[46] Although extra-judicial factors such as the Black Death and new agreements on forms of taxation may have hastened the decline of oyer and terminer commissions,[47] the primary explanation for this can be found in the move towards a more specialised form of oyer and terminer proceedings: sessions held by justices of the peace.

Keepers and Justices of the Peace

The keepers of the peace came to the fore during the years of the baronial wars in the mid-thirteenth century. Appointed in areas where they already held authority as local lords, the keepers assisted the sheriff in his policing of the countryside by employing the shire militia, holding inquests and arresting peace-breakers.[48] However, the promulgation of the Statute of Winchester in 1285 offered a new direction to the office of keeper of the peace.[49] This statute was an amalgam of much older measures on the community's obligations regarding local defence and the maintenance of the king's peace. In particular, it defined two closely allied facets of government in the shires: local policing and military array.[50] Initially, the justices of assize were ordered to enforce the Statute of Winchester, but this arrangement does not appear to have provided the desired regularity, and the task became more naturally associated with the keepers of the peace.[51] In the years following the statute of 1285, commissions were generally issued to ensure the preservation of the peace during the king's periodic absence from the realm (see Chapter 4). The judicial potential of the system was further recognised when, following the Articles upon the Charters of 1300, the keepers of the peace were entrusted to hear and determine complaints of trespass against Magna Carta and the Charter of the Forests.[52]

In judicial terms, the keepers of the peace possessed powers of pursuit and arrest and were able to receive indictments of felony and trespass.[53] However, the power to determine those cases was not officially included in the peace commissions until Edward III's reign. In the preceding decades, indictments were determined at gaol delivery sessions by virtue of special mandates authorising the justices to try prisoners indicted before the keepers of the peace.[54] In 1314 and 1326, special commissions of justices operating on circuits were issued with the specific purpose of trying such undetermined indictments.[55] In 1320, trailbaston justices were also entrusted with the task.[56] The peace commissioners themselves were eventually awarded the right to try offenders in March 1329.[57] Eighteen months later, however, this concession was effectively nullified by the statute of 1330, which stated that the keepers' indictments were once more to be tried at gaol delivery.[58] The 1330 provision may simply have confirmed an existing practice, which would imply that at least some keepers of the peace were not using their determining powers. The power to try prisoners was similarly withheld in the commissions of 1331 and 1335; but those issued in 1332, 1336 and 1338 restored the keepers' power as justices.[59] From 1332, commissioners of the peace were generally empowered to enforce both the Statute of Winchester and the more recent Statute of Northampton of 1328, an act which confirmed the provisions of the 1285 legislation and prohibited armed riding by day.[60]

In 1344 the crown took a new step: it issued peace commissions 'afforced' with 'men of law' and empowered them to hear indictments when the latter were present. This foreshadowed the quorum for felony introduced officially into the peace commissions in 1350 (see below).[61] At first applied sporadically, such commissions were appointed countrywide in 1351, when the assize justices were for the first time appointed to the panels of all the counties within their circuits.[62] A decade later, the statute of 1361 granted the power to hear and determine felonies and trespasses at the king's suit without the need for the assize justices to be present.[63] Further legislation in 1362 extended to the justices of peace the requirement earlier set upon the justices of labourers in 1351 to sit at least four times a year, and specified the dates at which the sessions ought to be held. This explains why such sittings became known, in the course of time, as 'quarter sessions'.[64]

In 1364 there came a shift in policy reminiscent of the mechanisms adopted in 1329–30: justices of the peace were now told to send their indictments to the assize justices, who would determine them at gaol delivery. However, the justices of the peace 'afforced' by the assize judges regained their determining powers between 1368 and 1380. In the latter year the powers of the justices of the peace were significantly enhanced, enabling them to try cases of extortion, livery and maintenance and armed conventicles (see Chapter 4); the requirement that assize justices be present to determine all felonies was also relaxed. Determining powers were omitted from the commissions of 1382, but seem still to have been exercised in the localities. In 1389 they were formally revived; and in 1394 royal legislation confirmed the essential form of the peace commissions for the next two centuries, during which time only short-lived adjustments and minor variations were experienced.[65]

In military terms, the keepers of the peace retained responsibility for the view of arms carried out by their subordinates at the local level, as set out in the Statute of Winchester.[66] The task of supervising military array was usually entrusted to separate commissions, but these included many men serving also as keepers of the peace. During the civil war under Edward II, these duties were sometimes combined.[67] The power of array was specifically entrusted to the so-called 'keepers of the county' in March 1332, but was subsequently omitted from the 1335 peace commissions, although the responsibility was hived off to a separate series of commissions which included significant numbers of men also serving as keepers.[68] The men appointed as justices of the peace in 1338 were also to supervise the process of array and aid the wardens in maritime and coastal parts.[69] From 1340, when the threat of invasion subsided, this duty was no longer considered necessary, though some commissions during the later 1340s did contain the power of array.[70] The peace commissions of 1350 and 1351 also included array, but the military and judicial tasks were separated in 1359 when special commissions were issued once more to deal with local defence.[71] Although from this date the power of array was no longer part of the peace commission, the military importance of the office was maintained and many of its members continued to receive commissions as arrayers. Indeed, ability to supervise the array was still considered an important qualification in the selection of justices of the peace in 1372.[72] Responsibility for internal peace was a natural corollary of defence and the pursuit of war.

Enforcement of economic legislation was at times equally within the keepers' purview (see Chapter 4). The commissioners of the peace appointed in 1307, for example, were to ensure that the coinage and prices of Edward I's reign were observed and arrest forestallers (see Chapter 4); the power to arrest unjust purveyors was added a year later.[73] Similarly, in 1346 commissions concerning the circulation of false money in the counties of the Midland circuit were entrusted to the keepers of the peace and justices of assize (elsewhere this task was undertaken solely by the latter group).[74] In the aftermath of the plague of 1348–9, the crown brought in new legislation to deal with the economic emergency arising from an acute shortage of labour. The power to enforce the Ordinance of Labourers of 1349 was first included in the peace commissions of 1350 and duly incorporated in those issued a year later, following the promulgation of the Statute of Labourers (1351).[75] Between 1352 and 1359, the enforcement of the labour regulations was formally separated from the peace commissions, though the justices of labourers were in fact the same persons as the keepers of the peace (with the omission of the assize justices). From 1359, enforcement of the Statute of Labourers was once more carried out at peace sessions, though authority for the labour laws was not officially provided until the legislation of 1361–2.[76] Permanent jurisdiction came in 1368.[77] The association between the labour legislation and the peace sessions had the effect of further broadening the economic powers of the justices of the peace: in 1361, for example, they were given authority over weights and measures.[78]

The keepers of the peace played an important role in the new judicial system of the fourteenth century. Through their own seigneurial authority and private connections, they brought their personal influence to bear upon the administration of royal justice in the counties. As local agents functioning permanently within the shire, they were also ideally placed to receive the complaints of trespass which had tended to engulf the eyre and other irregular organs of justice. Endowed with powers to hear and determine offences, the peace commissions could be seen as a hybrid form of oyer and terminer given jurisdiction over felony and trespass within a whole county. Having acquired responsibility for economic offences and the enforcement of labour legislation, they emerged at the forefront of the local administration of justice and, in many respects, of the political life of the shires.

The early fourteenth century was a period of much judicial experimentation and improvisation. The agencies which had previously been used merely to supplement the general eyre now superseded it and emerged in the vanguard of judicial administration. Various strands of business and particular powers were devolved upon justices of assize and gaol delivery, special commissioners of oyer and terminer, justices of trailbaston, and keepers/justices of the peace. The jurisdiction of the court of king's bench was also enlarged. It played an important role in the trailbaston inquiries of 1305 on the home circuit (comprising the city of London, Middlesex, Surrey, Kent and Sussex), where the chief justice and his associates, in addition to hearing assizes and delivering gaols, continued to receive pleas *coram rege*.[79] More generally, it was also used for the suppression of disorder as an itinerant court of trailbaston between 1320 and 1360.[80] In the short term, indeed, the appointment of general commissions of oyer and terminer and the deployment of the king's bench as a 'superior eyre' seemed likely to form the foundations of the new judicial structure. They never materialised as such, however, since they were designed to cope with immediate problems of law and order and did not provide regular sessions.[81] In the longer term, much more significance attaches to the growth of the assize circuits and the development of the justices of the peace: it was these agencies that came to provide the twin pillars of judicial administration in the fourteenth century and beyond.

Personnel

The previous section treated the judicial agencies separately, as if they were discrete bodies, isolated from each other and non-interactive. While this seemed a suitable means of introducing the different types of judicial commissions and charting their development, its artificiality immediately becomes evident when one examines the names of those commissioned to act as the king's justices in the provinces. In contrast to much of the existing historiography of the fourteenth century, which emphasises the development of the justices of the peace and tends to ignore the wider judicial context, this study aims to explore the links, both jurisdictional and human, between the whole range of commissions that emerged from the period of judicial experimentation and evolution in the fourteenth century.

Our next task, therefore, is to examine who the recipients of different judicial commissions really were, and who actually sat at judicial sessions held under these commissions. This will reveal four important features of fourteenth-century English royal justice. First, the various types of judicial agency functioning in the regions were interconnected and (when they worked properly) genuinely integrated. The considerable overlap of personnel suggests in particular that the acquisition and loss of determining powers by the keepers of the peace should not receive the degree of emphasis placed upon it by Putnam: the men who occasionally exercised powers of oyer and terminer as justices of the peace often also enjoyed that responsibility in connection with their work for other judicial agencies.

Secondly, and by extension, in all aspects of regional judicial administration the story as revealed in the extant documents is not one of competition between rival judicial commissions, but rather one of shifting balances between differing, but complementary, agencies. This is particularly observable in the appointments to gaol delivery commissions over the first half of the century, in the commissions to determine indictments made before keepers of the peace issued to so-called 'supervisors', and later in the peace commissions themselves.

Thirdly, a re-evaluation of the composition of commissions provokes a re-assessment of the orthodox explanation for the emergence of the justices of the peace. Putnam placed great emphasis on a supposed tension between commissions staffed by local men and those dominated by magnates and/or lawyers from the central courts. For her, the appointment of 'supervisors' to determine indictments brought before the keepers of the peace (as in 1314 and 1326), or of 'keepers of the county' appointed (supposedly) over the heads of the peace commissioners (as in 1338) relegated the keepers of the peace to a 'subordinate position'.[82] In fact, a close comparison of the personnel of the various commissions indicates that the term 'supervisor' is something of a misnomer and is unjustified within the context of the peace commissions.

Finally, and more generally, analysis of a broad range of commissions reveals that many – perhaps most – of the men employed on the king's judicial business in the shires possessed a certain level of legal knowledge and a degree of administrative experience. In the case of the lawyers from the central courts seconded to local commissions, the expertise was the product of the formal legal training discussed in Chapter 2. Among the local men who featured on such commissions, most of the gentry tended to have some understanding of legal process, acquired either through personal experience of litigation or through regular attendance at the county court and service in other local offices such as that of sheriff. Another significant group, moreover, may be described as 'men of law'. These were trained and practising lawyers functioning in the shires who were co-opted by the crown to provide the necessary legal expertise on county commissions. The nature of the education acquired by these men of law, and the degree to which they participated in the broader culture of the legal profession, is discussed in Chapter 5. Here, however, it is worth stressing that there may have been as many similarities as differences in the perspectives of 'local' and 'central' lawyers. Onlookers in the localities themselves regarded the justices of the peace primarily as royal representatives, and only secondarily as especially 'local' figures: in 1374, one John Braundys, when informed of the coming peace sessions in Berkshire, was heard to utter, 'Iche defie alle the kynges justices'.[83] Equally, the great lords who sometimes featured on commissions occupied positions of authority within particular counties and were not there just as representatives of the great men of the realm or as close allies of the king. The logical corollary of this is that the men serving on royal commissions should be classified not primarily in terms of their allegiance to central government or the localities, but according to their legal experience and their relationship to, and status within, the county or counties forming their jurisdiction.

In the light of this, we should clearly avoid viewing the composition of peace commissions as static and fixed. The balance could vary depending on their size and importance and the reason for their appointment, as well as the geographical location, political requirements and traditions of each region and county. The commissions of the late thirteenth and early fourteenth centuries usually contained no more than three members per panel. During the 1330s there was an expansion to five or six (sometimes more in large counties), reflecting the enhanced powers of the peace commissions in 1332 and 1338; but there was a noticeable reduction in 1335 and again in 1344. There were no specific parliamentary requests regarding the composition of the peace commissions until the 1340s: a petition of 1344 dealt with the inclusion of 'men of law'; and in 1348 the commons proposed the appointment of two magnates, two lawyers and two knights (or more) in each county.[84] This was not immediately observed, and there were slight fluctuations both in the size and in the composition of the commissions. By 1360, however, it would appear that the peace commissions increasingly accorded with the view put forward over the previous decade and a half, that they should be a balanced, workable and sufficiently authoritative judicial body.[85] This consistency of approach was confirmed by the famous statute of 1361,[86] which set the membership at one lord, three or four of the gentry and some lawyers: this pattern was observed until 1364, and generally after 1368 – although again, the exact composition did not remain hidebound. To some extent, therefore, there was a tension between the statutory guidelines and reality. This was observable during the 1370s when, in spite of the commons' request for panels of six or seven men, the practice of associating additional members in existing peace commissions meant that the total number of commissioners in any county could reach as many as eighteen.[87] The panels were considerably enlarged in 1382 in the aftermath of the Peasants' Revolt and retained a membership of at least twelve per county until 1389, when they were reduced to eight (including two assize justices) in accordance with the Statute of Cambridge (1388).[88]

While it is important to keep the three emergent categories of magnates, gentry and lawyers in mind, it is also apparent that there was, in reality, a considerable overlap of expertise, particularly between the second and third groups. In 1352 it was suggested that the peace commissions in general should comprise loyal, local men who had knowledge of the law: in other words, it was assumed that the majority, if not all, of the king's justices should have some understanding of legal process and judicial administration.[89] It is significant, therefore, that an unofficial abstract of the first chapter of the 1361 statute, drawn up in about 1362, substitutes *sages de la ley* for *hommes de ley*:[90] it was not necessary to be a professional 'man of law' (*homme de ley*) merely to be 'wise' in the ways of the law (*sage de la ley*). Moreover, as the century progressed it is apparent that the judicial work involved in the peace commissions increasingly became an outlet for the experience of county-based lawyers. Analysis of the personnel of the peace commissions in Suffolk and Gloucestershire between 1382 and 1389 reveals that the commissions were expanded chiefly by the addition of lawyers active in local administration.[91] In 1389 and 1394, the same men were formally recognised as having a distinctive role by receiving statutory sanction to act in the place of the justices of assize when first trespasses and then all cases, including felonies, were brought to judgment. By the fifteenth century, therefore, the bulk of the work of the quarter sessions had fallen to this group, composed of the most substantial men of legal training resident in the county.[92]

Accordingly, the following discussion of the development of the personnel of regional justice uses the term 'men of law' specifically to refer to men with legal knowledge based in the shires. This is justified by contemporary practice: although the statute of 1344 and the petition of 1348 mentioned above used the phrase more ambiguously in apparent reference both to lawyers of the central courts and to county-based lawyers, the label tended to be increasingly applied only to those outside the circle of the assize justices. By distinguishing the men of law from the personnel of the central courts, the intention is not to set up a dichotomy or tension between the two groups but to identify the main strands of commissioner in royal service and, indeed, to emphasise their complementarity. Although they were employed alongside each other at times on commissions of oyer and terminer and at gaol delivery, the real and lasting interface between them lay in their mutual involvement in the peace commissions.

Judges and Serjeants of the Central Courts

The judges and serjeants of the central courts have traditionally been regarded as enjoying a monopoly over hearing assizes on circuit. In fact, this became true only during Edward III's reign, and was not a fixed policy during the late thirteenth and early fourteenth centuries. The assize justices of Edward I's and Edward II's reigns were by and large serjeants at law.[93] During the latter reign, however, this pattern changed: some local men were given assize commissions; and justices from the central courts also became involved in taking assizes. The inclusion of local men was common in special assizes (the Statute of York of 1318 itself condoned the association of 'discreet men of the county' for special assizes and *nisi prius* business),[94] but was virtually unprecedented for general ones, and may have been a concomitant of the issuing of assize commissions for individual counties and a consequent over-burdening of the existing personnel.

The promotion of a number of king's serjeants to the court of common pleas and their subsequent appointment as assize justices extended the involvement of central court judges in the holding of assizes begun during the trailbastons of 1305–7.[95] This trend was confirmed in 1328 with the Statute of Northampton, which envisaged that 'the assizes, attaints and certifications be taken before justices commonly assigned, which should be good men and lawful, having knowledge of the law, and none other'.[96] Accordingly, the assize justices appointed were all drawn from the central courts.[97]

The balance of personnel in the assize commissions was modified once more with the statute of 1330, which ordained that 'good and discreet persons, other than of the places, if they may be found sufficient, shall be assigned in all the shires of England to take the assizes.'[98] It is likely that the phrase 'of the places' refers not to the counties in the commissions,[99] but to the two benches of the central courts:[100] this is reflected in the sudden influx of local men into the assize panels.[101] By the mid-1330s, however, the practice of appointing local men of law to the assize circuits had disappeared and general commissions of assize became the preserve of the justices and serjeants of the central courts. Their effective monopoly of the circuits, mirroring the professionalisation of the judiciary, was confirmed in a statute of 1340 which required justices dealing with *nisi prius* business (usually the assize justices) to be judges of one of the benches or king's serjeants (in practice, this was also taken to include the other serjeants at law functioning in the central courts).[102]

The trial of prisoners held in the county (and town or liberty) gaols was entrusted to the justices of assize following the Statute of Fines of 1299, which linked the assizes with gaol delivery duties. As a result of a clause forbidding clerks in holy orders to sit on the panel, the assize justices were permitted to share the burden of gaol delivery commissions with local men – and in practice generally did so, even though increasingly few royal justices were in fact clerks. By 1316, although an assize justice was normally commissioned to deliver the individual gaols within his circuit, the task was invariably carried out without the presence of assize justices at the sessions. This was rectified as a consequence of the renewal of the link between assizes and gaol delivery under the provisions of the statutes of 1328 and 1330. The change in personnel envisaged by the statute of 1330 brought mixed panels once again, but the revival of the older system proved only temporary and by 1340 the assize justices once more held sway.[103]

Justices of assize were frequently appointed to circuits in which their own private interests lay. Geoffrey Scrope, for instance, possessed estates in Yorkshire, and William Shareshull had lands in Staffordshire; both men were regularly appointed justices of assize and gaol delivery in these particular regions.[104] A more unusual case is that of Thomas Sibthorpe, who as a chancery clerk was not part of the hierarchy of lawyers in the central courts, but who was regularly appointed to the Midland assize circuit from 1341 to 1350. It is interesting that Sibthorpe only ever acted in Nottinghamshire and Lincolnshire, the former being the county of his origin and the latter an area where he had secured ecclesiastical preferment.[105] The practice suggests that some local knowledge of the area under the justices' jurisdiction was deemed appropriate – and, indeed, that the crown was fully aware of the need to temper what might otherwise be seen as its 'centralising' tendencies. In 1375, there was a request from the parliamentary commons that lawyers should not be appointed as assize justices in their home county, as they were too closely associated with people there and their judgments might accordingly be biased. Specific complaints were invited on the matter, and a statute was later issued in 1384, but the provision was manifestly ignored and the circuit personnel remained virtually unchanged.[106]

Judges of the central courts and serjeants at law also monitored regional justice through their presence on commissions of oyer and terminer. As outlined above, the spectrum of oyer and terminer commissions ranged from 'special' to 'general' and thus varied in scope and importance across a wide range of offences and different geographical areas. Under the second Statute of Westminster (1285), appointment to commissions of oyer and terminer concerning civil trespasses was confined to justices of king's bench and common pleas and justices in eyre.[107] This proved impossible, since the comparatively small group of central court professionals in Edward I's reign was unable to sustain the rapid expansion in the number of oyer and terminer commissions issued by chancery.[108] Following the regularisation of the assize commissions in the period after 1340 and the appointment of the assize justices to the commissions of the peace, however, it became standard practice for the senior judges and serjeants at law to be nominated to special commissions of oyer and terminer relating to the counties in their assize circuit. General oyer and terminer commissions similarly tended to be staffed by a combination of central court lawyers and men with good local knowledge, the latter (in this case) often including quite substantial figures in the counties.[109] The continued presence of the justices and serjeants of the central courts on local commissions of oyer and terminer therefore provides a notable example of their emergent role in regulating the administration of an increasingly devolved judicial system.

It was in their role as assize justices that the lawyers of the central court came to be particularly identified with peace sessions. This involvement began as part of their work as gaol delivery justices commissioned ad hoc to try persons indicted by the keepers of the peace. The justices of assize (as justices of gaol delivery) were ordered by the statute of 1330 to deliver the gaols of persons indicted before keepers of the peace; some men had already been exercising this power before this date, either by virtue of special mandates or (unofficially, since 1329) in lieu of the justices of the peace.[110] Lawyers from the central courts also served on the panels for their home counties in the commissions of 1332 (issued first to keepers of the peace and then to keepers of the counties) and of 1336, both of which awarded oyer and terminer powers.

The inclusion of lawyers from the central courts in the set of appointments issued on 1 August 1338 is curious in that the commissions, although concerned with the defence of the realm, had no ostensible judicial powers.[111] This may have represented a pre-emptive move towards the practice of associating royal lawyers with peace commissions for the purpose of determining indictments. Certainly, the appointment of men 'wise and learned in the law' to hear and determine indictments made before the keepers of the peace was officially sanctioned in the statute of 1344. This foreshadowed a later characteristic of the peace commissions: the quorum. The quorum was a select group of named men within the peace commission whose attendance was required for certain reserved business. The lawyers named to 'afforce' the keepers of the peace regularly included assize justices of the circuit in which the given county lay. Commissions were issued on an ad hoc basis during the 1340s for single counties (or sometimes pairs), presumably whenever it was felt necessary for accumulated indictments to be determined.[112] From 1350–1 assize justices were appointed to all the peace commissions within their circuits and formed the quorum necessary for determining felonies. This ensured that such cases were not determined without the presence of one of the assize justices. In practice, the trying of felons indicted by the justices of the peace appears frequently to have occurred at gaol delivery sessions: this was a logical and time-saving move allowing the lawyers of the central courts to rationalise the various aspects of their work in the localities.[113]

The requirement for a quorum was removed in the commissions of March 1361, enabling any combination of those appointed as justices of the peace to try their indictments. Consequently, assize justices were not appointed *en masse* to the counties of their circuits as before. Virtually all of them, however, continued to operate in a private capacity as members of the peace commissions in their home shires.[114] A further change in government policy in 1364 meant that assize justices were empowered to try offenders in their capacity as gaol delivery justices, and in most counties there was a dramatic reduction in their inclusion on the peace commissions. In 1368, however, with the restoration of the quorum for felonies, justices of assize were once again appointed to the commissions of the peace in the counties within their circuits, and they continued regularly to determine indictments made before the justices of the peace at their gaol delivery sessions.[115]

Significant changes appeared in the 1380s with regard not only to the work of the quorum but also to its apparent exclusivity. In 1380 the presence of the assize justices was made a prerequisite for difficult cases of extortion, but was no longer required for determining cases of robbery and homicide. Then, in 1382, the assize justices were included in a quorum specifically for inquiring of felonies, but the quorum for determining was omitted altogether. Although this may at first appear a strange move, it should be seen in the context of the general oyer and terminer commissions of December 1382, with which there was a substantial overlap in personnel: this administrative integration enabled the assize justices to oversee (if they were not themselves directly involved in) the taking of indictments and the punishment of offenders. The 1389 peace commissions gave birth to two quorums. One, charged with determining felonies, comprised the assize justices on their own; the second, employed for all other offences, consisted of a mixture of assize justices and local men of law. This method of judicial administration only lasted for five years, being replaced with a single mixed quorum of assize justices and men of law in 1394. The working relationship between these two groups therefore continued after receiving statutory confirmation, as a means of avoiding unnecessary delays in the trial of offenders.[116]

On the eve of Henry IV's reign it is apparent that, by a process of professional demarcation, the justices and serjeants at law from the central courts had gained a monopoly over the assize and gaol delivery circuits and had come to be closely associated in the trying of offenders at peace sessions. They maintained a presence on commissions of oyer and terminer, but these particular judicial agencies were no longer employed as regularly as had been the case earlier in the century. It is also important to remember that the assize justices had private local interests and so were not divorced from county society or the prevailing concerns of the regions. As such, they represent another line of argument against the alleged division between centre and locality.

Men of Law

The early fourteenth century was a period of transition in many aspects of English government. The rapid expansion in the scope of royal administration was inevitably accompanied by the need for a corps of government officials who were able to put the king's wishes into effect. In the absence of a paid bureaucracy, the maintenance of law and order, the administration of royal estates, the raising of troops and the collecting of taxes all required the co-operation of men whose knowledge and influence within the local community could be put at the crown's disposal. It is within this context that we should view the employment on royal judicial commissions of local men of law: those whose profession was the law or whose involvement in judicial and administrative affairs enabled them to acquire some legal knowhow. Through the crown's willingness to use them, and the advantages they in turn derived from the exercise of jurisdiction, these men facilitated the growth of royal justice and carved out a niche for themselves in the local administration of criminal justice. To describe this group as part of the 'gentry', as is conventional practice, is certainly correct in the sense that most such men came from the lesser aristocracy or (in the case of the practising lawyers) aspired to a place in the county elite. The following analysis, however, resists the use of that terminology on the grounds that it does less than credit to the expertise and experience that most, if not all, of these men brought to their role as royal judicial agents and, in particular, underrates the active role played by provincial members of the legal profession in the development of a county-based judiciary.

For obvious reasons, most historians have tended to focus on the keepers and justices of the peace to the exclusion of other commissions involving such local men of law. The orthodox view has been that in the early fourteenth century the pursuit, arrest and indicting of offenders was undertaken by a different set of officials from those trying them (that is, that the latter task was left to the justices of gaol delivery and of oyer and terminer).[117] Despite some vague foreshadowing under Edward II, the keepers of the peace first became justices only at the beginning of Edward III's reign; and even these advances were short-lived or compromised by resort to 'supervisors'. Only following the Black Death, it is argued, was local judicial authority firmly vested in these officials.[118] However, the 'transformation' of the keepers into justices can be reinterpreted along more evolutionary lines by taking into account the significant changes in the scope of the keepers' jurisdiction occurring before the 1330s and the considerable duplication of personnel in overlapping judicial agencies. This is important in explaining the development of the local judiciary, since local men would thus have been quite familiar with the task of hearing and determining complaints within the county. The following discussion aims to show that men of law were not only involved at all stages of the judicial process, but also served on a variety of complementary commissions. Three types are worthy of attention: special oyer and terminer, gaol delivery, and peace commissions.

Special oyer and terminer commissions provide the most straightforward example of the integration of men of law into the judicial system: as was indicated above, the lawyers of the central courts found it impossible to deal with the growing amount of business undertaken through such commissions under Edward I and Edward II, so that by the second decade of the fourteenth century the majority of commissioners tended to be drawn from the gentry and men of law in the localities.[119]

The role of county-based lawyers in gaol delivery business is less well established and requires fuller treatment. From the suspension of the eyre in 1294 until the withdrawal of the trailbaston commissions in 1307, a higher proportion of ordinary gaol delivery commissions went to local men than to lawyers from the central courts – and this in spite of the legislation of 1299 which associated the delivering of gaols with the assize justices. This may have been possible because of the loophole in the law which allowed for 'one of the most discreet knights of the shire' to be seconded to sit in judgment at gaol delivery if one of the assize justices was a clerk.[120] Surviving records of judicial sessions confirm that local men of law were not simply commissioned, but actually served: Robert Holand, for example, is known to have delivered gaols in Lancashire in the years 1300–4.[121]

After the trailbastons were ended in 1307, men of law retained a place on gaol delivery commissions alongside the assize justices. By 1316, however, a distinct change is observable: local justices carried out all the deliveries, and the lawyers of the central courts, though named in the commissions, rarely sat at actual sessions. Up to 1328, therefore, local men played a significant role in trying offenders, and worked virtually independently of their professional colleagues. Despite the statutes of 1328 and 1330, it is noticeable that local men once more featured in commissions during the early 1330s;[122] and on the Midland circuit at least, local justices can be shown to have continued to deliver gaols until 1335.[123]

Thirdly, and finally, there are the peace commissions. Throughout the opening decades of the fourteenth century a considerable overlap is observable between men commissioned as gaol delivery justices and as keepers of the peace. Indeed, in the years before 1305 keepers of the peace from no fewer than twenty-four counties were commissioned to deliver gaols. Furthermore, many are recorded as sitting at sessions, although there is no direct evidence that they were determining their own indictments at this stage. The first unequivocal evidence of keepers acting as *de facto* justices of the peace comes from a series of gaol delivery sessions held in Kent and Surrey at the beginning of

Edward II's reign.[124] Moreover, this phenomenon was not restricted to the home counties: it is also observable in Northamptonshire, Nottinghamshire and Yorkshire.[125]

The overlapping duties of keeper of the peace and justice of gaol delivery increased when the crown began to issue special mandates permitting delivery of persons indicted before the keepers of the peace. In the majority of these cases, one of the current keepers of the peace was appointed to the gaol delivery panel. In 1314, as a logical extension of this practice, commissioners (whom Putnam labelled 'supervisors') were appointed to travel on circuits, grouped mainly into three or four counties, and were empowered to inquire of felonies and trespasses and to hear and determine them.[126] Of the fifty-six persons named on 18 June, half were already keepers of the peace under the commissions of 5 June, and consequently determined their own indictments.[127] Following this watershed, there was considerable activity amongst keepers of the peace not only in Kent (as Putnam noticed)[128] but also in many other counties, where they were involved in trying their own indictments at gaol delivery. The experiment or administrative convenience of employing the trailbaston justices in 1320 to determine the keepers' indictments was necessarily restricted to the life of the relevant trailbaston commission. Gaol deliveries therefore continued to be the forum for trying such indictments, even though the special mandates were not always recorded on the patent rolls.[129]

In 1326 oyer and terminer commissions on circuits were issued once again in order to try the keepers' outstanding indictments. Analysis of the personnel of the commission of 8 June makes it apparent that the existing keepers of the peace were once again allowed to determine their own indictments in their capacity as justices of oyer and terminer. Cross-referencing with the order to keepers issued on 28 February 1326 indicates that, of the thirty-seven people known to have been commissioned for various counties on 8 June, no fewer than eighteen were also keepers of the peace.[130] The surviving rolls of proceedings once more provide confirmation of their role: in each county one of the keepers of the peace was present at these oyer and terminer sessions.[131]

The 1330s were particularly formative years in the development of the peace commissions.[132] The commissions of 1332 and 1338, which included determining powers, are indicative of a significant change in the nature of the peace sessions. First, the commissions were larger in size than any that had been issued previously, accommodating as many as six men on each county panel. Secondly, their personnel was mixed, including earls and other prominent lords as well as the usual gentry and men of law. Although Putnam asserted that the commissions of March 1332 were quite distinct from the peace commissions issued a month earlier,[133] a comparison of the personnel of the two 1332 commissions actually reveals that there was scarcely any difference between the keepers of the peace and the keepers of the counties.

The relationship between the various sets of peace commissions issued in 1338 also requires some re-assessment. The first set of commissions (6 July) was sent out to all counties except Cumberland and Westmorland,[134] and seems to have contained representatives of the local landed and professional elite: substantial figures such as William la Zouche of Harringworth (Northamptonshire) and Robert Colville (the Kesteven division of Lincolnshire) and lawyers such as William Cheltenham (Gloucestershire) and Henry Hillary (the Lindsey division of Lincolnshire).[135] It is true that the men commissioned as justices of the peace on 6 July were to be 'assistant and attentive' to the magnates and others assigned as supervisors in the subsequent commissions of 7 July and 1 August 1338 (see below). It would be wrong, however, to imagine great lords breathing down the necks of gentry and men of law and pushing them into a position of impotence in the peace sessions. The judicial authority of local justices was emphatically not being overridden or infringed by representatives of central government.

While men of law would therefore appear to have been able to exercise their oyer and terminer powers unfettered at this period, this was not necessarily the case: we have already outlined the evidence for the increasing involvement of the assize justices in the work of the peace commissions after 1338. The emergence of a *de facto* quorum for peace sessions after the statute of 1344 should not, however, be regarded as a threat to the interests of those members of the commissions resident in the shires. It is interesting to note that petitions to parliament in 1346 requested that the justices of the peace should have concurrent jurisdiction with the assize justices.[136] This suggests that an alliance with the lawyers of the central court was regarded as the proper (if not the most streamlined) way of organising peace sessions. There are, nevertheless, several questions which are provoked by the personnel of the peace commissions after 1350, when the quorum was first formally introduced. Did the presence of assize justices after 1344 necessarily curtail the powers which men of law had exercised previously as gaol delivery justices or as justices of the peace? To what extent, if at all, were they able to try offenders on their own? Was there a move to gain admittance to the quorum?

The quorum established in the 1350s was officially confined to assize justices, who usually determined felonies. But men of law such as Thomas Musgrave, who sat with the assize justices William Wichingham and William Skipwith at York in 1360, might also try cases coming before them.[137] Following the statute of 1361, the men of law who continued to be appointed to the peace commissions exercised determining powers for three years, unrestricted by the quorum.[138] And even though the authority to try offenders was temporarily transferred to the gaol delivery justices between 1364 and 1368, the peace commissioners in some counties, such as Staffordshire, clearly ignored the directive and carried on using their oyer and terminer powers.[139]

The criminal jurisdiction of the local men of law was significantly augmented in 1380 when a statute laid down that the lawyers from the central courts were no longer required to be present for determining the felonies of robbery and homicide or cases of extortion, livery and maintenance, and armed conventicles heard before the justices of the peace. The role of the quorum was, therefore, effectively limited to other common law felonies and difficult cases of extortion.[140] The 1382 peace commissions also witnessed some changes: a quorum for inquiry was specified, and was to consist of five or six men of law (including, in this case, the justices of assize). Although determining powers were omitted, probably as a result of the general oyer and terminer commissions issued a day after those of the peace (in a move reminiscent of 1331), it is apparent that men commissioned as justices of the peace continued to exercise the right to try offenders throughout the 1380s.[141] In 1389, men of law were formally included (alongside the assize justices) as part of a second quorum initiated solely for trespasses. They had still not gained permanent admittance to the inner sanctum, the quorum for felonies. But this was eventually remedied in 1394 by a statute enabling two local men of law to be appointed to an extended quorum having jurisdiction over all offences.[142]

It can therefore be seen that men of law had a discernible role to play in royal judicial administration throughout the fourteenth century. They were not simply promoted from a subordinate to a primary role by being 'transformed' from keepers to justices of the peace, but emerged from a whole series of experiments as an important and recognised part of the judiciary, and already had considerable experience as royal justices before the rapid expansion in the competence of the peace commissions from the 1350s. Although there was inevitably always something of a gap between the established members of county society appointed to commissions because of their status and the local lawyers drawn in for their expertise, the distinction between 'amateur' and 'professional' is not particularly meaningful during the first half of the century. Indeed, it was probably only the association of local men of law in the quorum for the peace sessions after the 1380s that created a clear distinction between those who viewed their place on the bench as a mark of political status and those whose presence was required to expedite business. The rapid and inexorable growth in the size of the peace commissions during the late fourteenth and fifteenth centuries is itself a mark of this process: many of the new recruits were members of the gentry who regarded their appointments to the bench simply as a sign of honour and favour and had no intention of becoming involved in the tasks undertaken by the 'working' justices selected from among the men of law.[143] The clear line of development that links the men of law on late thirteenth-century and early fourteenth-century assize, gaol delivery, oyer and terminer and peace commissions to the working justices of the peace of the fifteenth and sixteenth centuries is surely one of the most striking examples of the evolutionary processes that shaped later medieval English justice.

Landed Society: Gentry and Magnates

It has already been remarked that the expansion in the scope of royal jurisdiction during the course of the thirteenth century depended to a large degree on the existence of a body of men able and willing to participate in the administration of the shires. The commissions upon which these men served were not large, often comprising no more than two or three members in the first half of the fourteenth century; consequently, such men had little choice but to take an active role in the business that resulted. The idea that the members of landed society who participated in such commissions were necessarily 'amateurs' has therefore to be questioned. The description has conventionally been used to distinguish the gentry who served on judicial commissions from the 'professional' lawyers of the central courts. However, by identifying local 'men of law' as an important component in the personnel of provincial justice, the foregoing discussion has already challenged the supposed dichotomy between the 'professional' element drawn from central government and the 'amateur' contingent recruited from the shires. In this section, we have to confront a further blurring of categories: for whereas the organisation of this chapter supposes a reasonably clear distinction between 'men of law' and 'landed society', in reality there existed a considerable overlap between the two groups. In part, the blurring represents the shortcomings of existing knowledge: we simply do not know enough about the families and careers of those who made up the local element in royal judicial commissions. Ironically, however, our uncertainty also arises from the deliberate efforts of 'men of law' to disguise the fact they owed their status to their professional knowhow and to present themselves publicly as part of gentry society.

The appointment of members of the gentry to judicial commissions in the shires obviously reflected a desire and need that local landed society be properly represented in the prosecution of the king's business.[144] The inclusion of substantial knights and esquires in the county peace commissions, or on the panels of justices enforcing the labour laws, represented a natural extension of this norm. The gentry undoubtedly regarded inclusion on a royal commission as an indication of status, a marker which might vary with the relative importance of the commission, the nature of its powers and jurisdiction (for example, whether it operated at shire or provincial level), and its general size and composition (especially if the other members of the panel were significant figures). This did not mean, however, that the peace commissions immediately took their later characteristic form, consisting of a body of landed society whose presence was purely honorific and a smaller group of 'working justices' who conducted the bulk of the business of the sessions.[145] Although the post of keeper of the peace was not an unattractive appointment, the small size of the peace commissions in the late thirteenth and early fourteenth centuries, their somewhat ad hoc nature and their relatively limited judicial powers militated against the keepership being regarded as much more than a functional office, and certainly one less prestigious than the shrievalty.[146] In the first half of the fourteenth century, only the commissions of 1332 and 1338 merited real political significance – and accordingly contained a slightly greater level of gentry representation. By contrast, in the later part of the century, when the commissions of the peace had become the premier judicial agency in the shires and the position of justice of the peace had established a prominent place in the *cursus honorum*, it is noticeable that the size of the commissions increased at least partly to accommodate more members of local landed society.

In the first half of the fourteenth century there were already a number of substantial men who played a leading role in local judicial administration. John Thorpe, for example, was regularly employed for assize and gaol delivery work, sat on peace commissions and acted as a trailbaston justice in Norfolk and Suffolk. Edmund Deyncourt had a very similar career based in Lincolnshire.[147] Interestingly enough, both these men – and a significant proportion of their colleagues – received personal summonses to parliament and thus, in a formal sense, moved up from the gentry to the baronage. While this in part reflected their status as wealthy and powerful landholders, some of these new recruits to the parliamentary peerage may have owed their summonses less to their personal authority and influence within the shires and more to their knowledge and experience in local administration. Indeed, in terms of contributions to local judicial administration, the real distinction in this period is to be drawn not between the gentry and the baronage, who fulfilled very similar roles on royal commissions, but between the baronage and the titled nobility, since the latter operated on an altogether different level.

The involvement of the magnates in the administration of justice varied according to the nature of the judicial agency and the intention behind the commission. Great lords were often employed on general commissions of oyer and terminer (as in 1328 or 1340), and were regularly appointed to special commissions of oyer and terminer, on account of their personal standing and political authority within a county. Their appointment to commissions of the peace often reflected the need to include, and have the co-operation of, those with the greatest landed wealth and political authority; this trend became especially noticeable during the 1320s and culminated in the commissions of 1332.[148] It was the military functions associated with the keepers and justices of the peace, however, that seem to have been primarily responsible for drawing the great lords of the realm into regular involvement with judicial administration in the shires.

The commissions of 7 July 1338, which appointed magnates as 'supervisors' of the commissioners of the peace, mark a particularly important stage in this process.[149] Significantly, the new commissioners enjoyed jurisdiction over groups of counties rather than single shires.[150] They appear to have had no actual judicial powers.

Subsequent commissions, issued on 1 August, not only amplified those of 7 July, but also added lawyers of the central courts to the personnel. Even then, however, there is nothing in the commission to suggest that the powers of the keepers were in effect 'nullified' by the new appointments: Putnam's notion that the 'supervisors' effectively subordinated the peace commissioners is erroneous.[151] The 'supervisors' may have had peace-keeping duties, but there is no general indication that the crown expected them to act as justices and to hear and determine felonies and trespasses. The magnates, in other words, were primarily intended to fulfil a military function in organising the array of the shires.[152] There is only one example of indictments coming before such 'supervisors', when in December 1338 the magnate Anthony Lucy and the king's serjeant Robert Parving (appointed for the border regions of Cumberland and Westmorland) sat at Carlisle.[153] The supervising committees were not renewed after 1340, which suggests that, after the initial anxieties and setbacks of the war, they were no longer considered a necessary part of defence strategy. What did survive was the perception that the great lords of the realm might continue usefully to assist in the ancillary task of keeping the peace.

The increased size of the peace commissions and the greater social range of their personnel reflected the new importance they acquired during the mid-fourteenth century, particularly after the Black Death. The inclusion of magnates as a vital element in the peace commission was first explicitly proposed in the parliamentary petition of 1348.[154] While the commons may not have influenced the selection of justices of the peace during the 1350s,[155] their request regarding the composition of the peace commissions was answered to some extent in the personnel of 1350 and 1351. Even in 1351, though, there was not an enormous influx of magnates: most of those appointed – men such as the earls of Arundel, Warwick, Devon and Stafford – were familiar names on such commissions. It was in 1352 that the commons actively encouraged the king to involve 'the great men of the realm, earls and barons, each in his own region' in the peace commissions; thereafter the magnates regularly headed the county benches in the areas where they had landed interests.[156] For example, both of the later fourteenth-century dukes of Lancaster, Henry of Grosmont (d. 1361) and John of Gaunt (d. 1399), were regularly included in the peace commissions for those counties (such as Yorkshire, Lincolnshire, Leicestershire and Derbyshire) in which they had important landed interests. In 1389 great lords were deliberately excluded from the county commissions, but this was a comparatively short-lived and overtly political phenomenon. It was duly reversed in 1397, when it was considered expedient to renew the aristocratic presence (see Chapter 4).[157]

The formal integration of the baronage and titled nobility into the peace commissions during the second half of the fourteenth century reflected the gradual emergence of the justices of the peace as the primary agency of royal justice in the provinces. Given contemporary perceptions of society, it would indeed have appeared anomalous had the peerage not been included in a function that gave such obvious prominence to men of lesser status among the gentry and the legal profession. (It was for similar reasons that senior churchmen were also sometimes appointed to commissions of oyer and terminer and of the peace.) That said, it is also clear that the magnates did not, by and large, consider themselves to be working justices. This was partly a matter of practicality and partly one of dignity: a figure such as John of Gaunt, who headed thirteen peace commissions in 1382, nineteen in 1394 and twenty-two in 1397, and whose political career had a national and international perspective, was neither able nor inclined to spend his life touring the shires *en route* to the next quarter sessions. There is at least one recorded instance when Gaunt himself sat as a member of the Warwickshire bench; but this was undoubtedly a rare event.[158] Lesser noblemen and barons with interests restricted to one or two counties may have been more inclined at least to attend the peace sessions. The earls of Stafford, for instance, were among the working justices in Staffordshire, while the earl of Angus is known to have acted in Lincolnshire (and was even keeper of the rolls for the Kesteven peace commission in 1372).[159] Even so, the participation rates of the peerage remained strikingly low throughout the later fourteenth and fifteenth centuries. In the long term, then, by far the greatest burden of royal judicial administration in the shires was borne by the lawyers of the central courts sitting at assizes and gaol delivery and, ultimately, by the local men of law working as justices of the peace.

A careful study of the personnel of regional justice acts as an important corrective to existing historiographical traditions in both judicial and political terms. In particular, it suggests that Putnam greatly exaggerated the supposed tension between centre and locality in the evolution of a successful judicial system. In the early fourteenth century, it was simply not possible or practical to appoint completely separate groups of men for each and every type of judicial commission; and since there was already a considerable overlap in the essential tasks undertaken by these various agencies, it was only reasonable that the same people should be employed in several different spheres of law-keeping. The employment of local men of law, sometimes working in tandem with lawyers from the central courts, on commissions of gaol delivery and oyer and terminer and (more occasionally) at the assizes, not only points towards the versatility of the system but also emphasises the frequent blurring of distinctions between a 'central' and a 'local' personnel. Nor did pragmatism and overlap entirely disappear in the more settled judicial structure that emerged by the 1360s. The judges and serjeants of the central courts still regularly toured the shires in their capacity as justices of assize and gaol delivery. The peace sessions were not infrequently timed to coincide with these visitations, in order that the senior lawyers could assume their role as the quorum for determining serious offences brought before the locally based justices of the peace. This integrated and complementary system seems to have survived even beyond the reform of the quorum in the 1390s, when the local men of law were theoretically allowed more autonomy in the trial of felonies. The particular professional associations built up between two key groups – the personnel of the central courts and the county-based men of law – was probably of particular importance in guaranteeing and perpetuating this integrated system. We shall have more to say on the significance of this subject in Chapter 5.

Conclusion

This chapter has challenged the traditional account of judicial evolution in the regions during the fourteenth century on three fronts. First, it has demonstrated the multiplicity of agencies that emerged to replace the eyre and has emphasised the long-term importance of the assize and gaol delivery commissions as well as the historian's more usual focus of attention, the keepers and justices of the peace. Secondly, it has indicated that, both in the period of experimentation in the first half of the century and in the more settled structures that emerged after the 1350s, there was considerable overlap and/or co-ordination between these agencies and the personnel appointed to them. In this respect, in particular, it has argued that the emergent judicial system, operated by a combination of specialists from the central courts and generalists in the shires, was much less obviously and self-consciously 'devolved' than has usually been assumed. Finally, and by extension, it has suggested that the judicial system that emerged during the second half of the century was more coherently organised than ever before, and that it retained a strong sense of identity and unity that owed much to the powerful influence of common lawyers from both the central courts and the shires. The justices of the peace therefore emerge from this analysis not as an isolated agency of royal justice operating a semi-autonomous regime in the provinces, but as part of a much more elaborate and co-ordinated system which for the first time provided the crown with a permanent judicial presence in the localities.

4
EXTERNAL INFLUENCES ON THE EVOLUTION OF JUSTICE

Chapters 2 and 3 examined the evolution of justice during the fourteenth century primarily in a descriptive manner, without directly engaging with the various influences that acted upon that process. In the next two chapters, we shall analyse these influences, distinguishing between external or 'exogenous' factors and internal or 'endogenous' forces for change. In order to do so, we must remember, as in the example given in Chapter 1, that exogenous factors may *accelerate* change, but do not necessarily change the pre-existing *pattern* of development. It is also important in this context to remember the distinction between law, which may be seen as an organic form of social organisation capable of developing from within, and the judicial structure for the enforcement of that law, which is more often shaped by external forces. Because it focuses on exogenous factors, this chapter is principally concerned with structural issues, and specifically with the various influences that determined the hierarchy of courts and jurisdictions analysed in Chapters 2 and 3.

In treating exogenously induced change before endogenous development, it might be thought that this study puts the proverbial cart before the horse. There are two reasons for proceeding thus. First, it is reasonably obvious that changes provoked by external influences inevitably tend to be more conspicuous. It is therefore helpful to put those structural 'transformations' into their economic and political contexts before examining the degree to which the law itself adapted to longer-term changes in the way that society used and regarded the courts. Secondly, as we have seen, the historiography of the fourteenth century places great emphasis on the twin exogenous forces of war and plague and their impact upon the judicial system. By making a critical re-assessment of these and other external influences, we shall show how the economic, demographic and political upheavals of the period only partly explain why the legal system and the king's courts developed in the way that they did, and thus set the scene for the complementary discussion of endogenously induced change that follows in Chapter 5. For the purposes of the ensuing analysis, exogenous influences may be grouped under three headings: war; economic crises and popular disturbances; and constitutional conflicts.

Before we proceed to that analysis, however, it may be helpful to provide some further clarification on some of the specific issues that are addressed in this and the next chapter. In particular, it is necessary to address the impressionistic nature of contemporary comment on law and order. No efforts were ever made in the Middle Ages to produce statistics of reported or convicted crime. Although this does not necessarily invalidate the use of such techniques in historical research, any attempt to apply quantitative methods to fourteenth-century records is necessarily fraught with problems. First, there is the incompleteness of the evidence: although the plea rolls of king's bench and common pleas survive in virtually complete series for this period, there are comparatively few extant records of the county sessions – assize rolls, gaol delivery rolls, peace rolls – and those that we have are not always necessarily representative.[1] Secondly, the raw statistics derived from a run of judicial records, no matter how complete, remain fundamentally ambiguous: depending on one's position, a peak in the data can be employed either to prove an increase in lawlessness or, ironically, to demonstrate the greater success of government in bringing its subjects to account for their misdemeanours. Consequently, while the quantitative approach may be useful in testing contemporary perceptions and in demonstrating long-term trends in rates of litigation,[2] it has been particularly criticised during recent years as a means of measuring the real extent of criminal activity and general lawlessness in medieval England.[3]

The alternative, qualitative, approach places much more reliance on medieval political discourse and judges the 'success' or 'failure' of a given judicial policy not in statistical terms but in reference to how contemporaries perceived the achievements or shortcomings of the courts. The danger with this approach, of course, lies in assuming that, if contemporaries thought there was a crisis of justice, there must have been one: it is surely one of the historian's responsibilities to assess whether such notions had real validity. But the qualitative approach also lays great stress on the *context* in which complaints about the system of justice were made, and recognises that lawlessness in the Middle Ages (as, indeed, today) was often assumed to be the result, or the symptom, of underlying political or social upheaval. Consequently, a tailing off of complaints during periods of relative stability may not indicate any absolute change in the techniques and success rate of law enforcement, but simply reflects a greater sense of wellbeing and confidence on the part of the political community.[4] This in turn provides strong justification for a critical discussion of such external influences and their impact not only on real or perceived fluctuations in lawlessness but also on the evolution of the judicial system itself.

War

The military enterprises undertaken by the English state in the century between the 1290s and the 1390s were of a scale and duration probably unparalleled in its earlier history. The Anglo-French peace ushered in by the treaty of Paris of 1259 was broken, temporarily, in the wars of 1294–8 and 1323–5 and then, more decisively, in the three sustained bouts of hostility – 1337–60, 1369–89 and 1415–53 – which historians call the Hundred Years War. The Scottish succession crisis of 1290–1 also precipitated long periods of war between 1296 and 1328, and again from 1333 to 1357; although these were followed by a series of truces only briefly interrupted by official military campaigns in 1384–5 and 1400, the peace was a fragile one, and the northern border remained in a permanent state of defence. These major hostilities also bred lesser ones: the English crown and/or English forces became involved in wars in the French provinces, in the Iberian peninsular, and in Italy, not to mention the military interventions that were latterly launched by Richard II and Henry IV, respectively, into their own dominions of Ireland and Wales.

War and Disorder

It was widely believed in later medieval society that war outside the kingdom bred disorder within it.[5] It will be helpful at the outset to identify the particular symptoms of this problem, since these inevitably shaped both political attitudes and royal policy. Three such issues are especially relevant here: lawlessness on the frontiers; the corruption of crown officials involved in the administration of war; and the criminal tendencies of the military.

The first of these problems is the easiest to comprehend. Frontiers always had a reputation for lawlessness, and it was natural to suppose that they might become ungovernable when they turned into war zones. The Welsh border was theoretically relieved of its frontier status as a result of Edward I's conquest of the principality in the late thirteenth century, though the continued exemption of the native inhabitants of Wales from English royal courts inevitably compromised the crown's ability to deal with the cross-border cattle-rustling that was such a regular feature of life in Herefordshire and Shropshire.[6] The situation on the Scottish borders was, for obvious reasons, a great deal more problematic. Organised raiding by the Scots was most prevalent in the 1310s and early 1320s, when it proved a substantial threat to the security of many northern English communities stretching down into Lancashire and the vale of York.[7] In the wake of the defeat at Bannockburn in 1314, some members of northern society took matters into their own hands: the treasonous activities of Sir Gilbert Middleton in 1317 and Sir Andrew Harclay in 1322–3 highlighted the degree to which the north had fallen beyond the effective reach of the crown.[8] Although the threat of large-scale, systematic raiding was much reduced after the 1330s, the north had gained a permanent reputation for disorder exacerbated, if anything, by the presence of unruly English garrisons in the border strongholds.[9]

The Hundred Years War had the effect of opening up yet another frontier, this time on the English Channel. Already during the Anglo-French hostilities of 1294–8 and 1323–5 coastal communities had experienced problems both from cross-Channel raiding and from the behaviour of English troops gathering for overseas campaigns.[10] Rumours of full-scale French invasion plans and reports of destructive raids abounded in the late 1330s, the mid-1370s and the mid-1380s; and the most dramatic outbreak of disorder witnessed in fourteenth-century England – the Peasants' Revolt of 1381 – may be explained in part by the dissatisfaction felt by coastal communities in Kent and Essex with the crown's policy for domestic defence.[11] War and its aftermath had therefore created a series of frontier zones within England where the threat of external attack created an understandable neurosis about public order.

The belief that the king's peace was also jeopardised by the activities of officials involved in the administration of war is perhaps rather less obvious. War created an enormous amount of business in local government: troops had to be recruited and marched to the muster; victuals and arms had to be requisitioned or purchased; and special taxes had to be assessed and collected. The principal officials charged to undertake this work, and the numerous assistants they commissioned in order to fulfil their duties, were inevitably tempted to abuse their authority and indulge in oppressive and corrupt practices – not least, it must be said, because they received no formal payment from the crown for what were often time-consuming, difficult and even hazardous tasks. The very application of government policy therefore tended to generate discord: the king's subjects, singly and collectively, flung accusations of corruption against officials who, in turn, claimed to have suffered intimidation and physical violence while going about their lawful duties.[12] Moreover, as the crown's commitment to war grew, particular concern arose that the king's departure from the realm would encourage officials in local – and, indeed, central – government to take the law into their own hands, threatening the domestic interests of those who had departed the realm with the army and leaving the non-combatant population with no effective means of redress.[13]

The third symptom of lawlessness on which contemporaries tended to concentrate was the criminal tendency within the king's own armies. From the 1290s, the crown began to make much more extensive use of its prerogative of pardon as an inducement to undertake military service.[14] The political community was greatly concerned about the way in which this practice seemed to condone lawlessness: in 1311, the Ordainers actually attempted to deprive the king of his right to dispense mercy to hardened criminals, and the crown agreed to statutory limitations on pardons in 1328, 1330, 1336 and 1340.[15] Neither Edward II nor Edward III felt particularly constrained by such measures, however, and complaints were still being made in parliament in the 1350s about the way that pardons for military service had the effect of emboldening criminals and threatening public order.[16] The statistical approach, if it proves anything, appears to corroborate these concerns by suggesting that peaks in criminal activity tended to occur just after, rather than merely during, major military campaigns.[17]

What particularly unnerved contemporaries was the highly organised nature of some of this criminal action. The trailbaston inquiries of 1304–5 were set up in part to counter disquiet about demobilised soldiers who pursued profitable careers as bandits.[18] It has to be said that the most striking examples of organised crime in the early fourteenth century were the product more of the disturbed state of domestic politics in the 1320s than of the crown's war policies: the Folville and Coterel gangs, which stood at the centre of an elaborate web of criminal bands operating in Leicestershire, Rutland, Nottinghamshire and Derbyshire, were only subsequently drawn into royal service in Scotland and France during the later 1330s – when, perhaps significantly, their local criminal activities declined.[19] Somewhat ironically, however, the apparent decline in banditry during the middle decades of the century coincided with the emergence of the 'indenture system', a new form of military recruitment based on contracts. In order to guarantee willing recruits for the forces which they agreed to bring to the king's army, the greater lords of the realm increasingly tended to retain men for service in peace as well as in war.[20] Consequently, the belief that those involved in legitimised violence on campaign abroad might also be employed at home to prevent the due process of law remained strong.[21] Out of a combination of fear, impressionistic evidence and logical argument, the fourteenth-century polity had therefore created a lasting political agenda founded in the notion that the pursuit of foreign war challenged the state of public order within the realm.

The Royal Response

How did kings answer such arguments? To say that the 'law state' of the thirteenth century was simply replaced by the 'war state' of the fourteenth, and that the crown was sufficiently distracted by its military enterprises to leave the judicial system in a state of limbo, fails adequately to represent the realities of fourteenth-century governance. In some senses, indeed, as the previous discussion has intimated, the challenges of war heightened, rather than diminished, the king's responsibility for the administration of the law.[22] A closer study of royal policy during periods of warfare in the fourteenth century will help to demonstrate that war could have a dynamic, as well as a merely inhibiting, influence on the development of the English judicial system.

It is undeniable that war necessitated certain compromises in the administration of justice. The calling off of the general eyre and the *quo warranto* inquiries in 1294, which is so often taken as a symbolic turning-point from law state to war state, was a deliberate incentive to the landed classes to participate in the impending campaign in Gascony: by abandoning the most politically sensitive elements within the articles of inquiry of the eyre – concerning the king's feudal prerogatives and the rights of franchise-holders – the crown sought to persuade noblemen and knights that they would not jeopardise their interests by departing the realm.[23] It was for similar reasons that Edward I and his successors often granted licences to members of the aristocracy suspending assizes in which they were involved, or halting proceedings in the exchequer on their debts to the crown, for the duration of a military campaign.[24] Consequently, when Edward III contravened this tradition by forbidding respites of debts, ordering investigations into his feudal revenues and attempting to revive certain communal fines specifically associated with the eyre during the preparations for war with France in 1337–8, he faced considerable criticism and was quickly induced to abandon the policy.[25] Later, indeed, Edward extended the range of immunities and quasi-legal privileges offered to those taking service in his armies: following up on his grandfather's policy of consenting to the permanent alienation of lands held in chief of the crown, he also began to license enfeoffments to use, which guaranteed that, should a tenant in chief die on campaign, his lands would not be taken over by the crown but be held in trust for the heir.[26] One of the most striking – and neglected – cases of these necessary compromises of war was the withdrawal of the special commissions of labourers on the eve of Edward III's expedition to Rheims in 1359, which was occasioned partly by the concerns of franchise-holders over their rights to the financial profits of the labour sessions, and partly by the need to free the gentry commissioners to take up their places in the cavalry section of the king's army.[27] If even such a major law-enforcement drive as that led by the justices of labourers could be called off pending a campaign, then the war state must be acknowledged to have created a whole series of interruptions and disruptions in the regular workings of the royal courts.

Whether such measures actually provoked broader and lasting crises of justice is, however, quite another matter. As we have seen in Chapter 3, the work of the eyre was already being taken over by the justices of assize and gaol delivery before 1294; and the labour laws were revived, under the jurisdiction of the justices of the peace, in 1361–2.[28] Even pardons, which were undoubtedly abused from time to time by notorious criminals and were so much criticised in parliament, nevertheless had a recognised place in the judicial and political process. This is demonstrated by the development of the general pardon, an amnesty granted, in theory, to all the king's subjects as a mark of gratitude and good faith.[29] The first comprehensive general pardons, issued in 1377 and 1381, offered indemnity from all felonies and trespasses (except treason, murder, larceny and rape) and a wide range of offences against the king's feudal, statutory and administrative rights.[30] In reality, however, these pardons, like those granted in 1398 and at fairly regular intervals during the fifteenth century, were only available to those who purchased copies of the royal grant from the chancery. At 18s. 4d., these were a comparatively cheap investment for the landed and mercantile classes: over 10 000 such pardons were issued between 1377 and 1399.[31] On the other hand, as the parliamentary commons pointed out in 1382, they were beyond the resources of a large proportion of the lower orders.[32] Their comparative exclusivity may also be a clue to their real intention: the suing out of a general pardon was, in fact, part of a more subtle process of negotiation in which the beneficiary of the royal grace was expected to offer some return favour – including, when appropriate, the agreement to provide military service. General pardons, then, far from representing the failure of the judicial system, became an effective means of reconciling the king's greater subjects to their public obligations and offered them the opportunity to express their loyalty and commitment to the regime.[33] Here, in turn, lay a powerful royal argument on the positive political benefits of war.

Such an appeal to honour and to the mutual advantages that flowed from war could certainly do much to encourage good behaviour among the elite: it was, after all, on this basis that Edward III, and later Henry V, built their reputations as effective managers of aristocratic society. But it was hardly sufficient to guarantee good order in the realm at large. Royal judicial policy had to respond, directly and explicitly, to public worries about the supposedly inexorable decline into lawlessness during periods of active warfare. The measures undertaken to secure the defence of the Scottish border and the coasts and to re-establish order in the north of England provide one index of the manner and extent of this royal response. Faced with major threats from foreign enemies, the crown began, from the 1290s, to appoint wardens and admirals of the coasts with special responsibility for local defence by land and sea; although the keepers of the peace were already by that point moving away from their earlier role in the organisation of the local militia, both they and their successors, the justices of the peace, continued to play an important supplementary role in measures for national defence, by being empowered between 1332 and 1359 to array and lead forces in the event of imminent invasion (see Chapter 3).[34]

In the north, there was also a more specific issue arising from the need to resolve cross-border disputes. During the years of war between 1294 and 1328, and to some extent from 1332 to 1357, the Scots were simply treated as rebels and enemies, and could be dealt with summarily in English courts. After the peace settlement of 1357, however, it was necessary to acknowledge that English common law courts had no formal jurisdiction over subjects of the Scottish crown, and the English government therefore sanctioned the revival of the thirteenth-century laws of the march, a series of judicial conventions specifically designed to deal with private disputes between parties from different sides of the border. The wardens of the march, who had emerged during the first half of the century to organise the defence of the northern frontier, now became the presidents of the 'days of march' at which such cases were heard, and thus took on an important judicial role which further enhanced their status as the effective rulers of the border shires.[35] For all its shortcomings, the law of the march demonstrates two very important features of relevance to the present study: the capacity of the fourteenth-century state to supplement the common law where the latter proved inadequate; and the crown's awareness of, and responsiveness to, the public order issues arising out of war.

The clearest and most assertive expression of the crown's commitment came, however, at the beginning and end of royal campaigns. The notion that the king's absence imperilled the realm was taken seriously by all rulers in this period, and a royal departure on a diplomatic or military mission normally occasioned special peace-keeping measures. The trend was already set, indeed, before the starting point of our study. The appointment of keepers in 1287 during a royal absence in Gascony was especially important, however, since it marked the beginning of their particular association with the enforcement of the Statute of Winchester.[36] Thereafter, the pattern became a familiar one. On the eve of a royal departure, the crown would normally issue special peace commissions or, at the very least, issue proclamations exhorting the king's subjects and judicial agents to be diligent in upholding the peace during his absence.[37]

The return of the king similarly tended to trigger a particular response: the inquiries into the infringement of franchisal rights and administrative abuses launched by Edward I on his return from two lengthy absences in 1274 and 1289 set an important precedent for his own and his successors' governments.[38] If visitations of the localities were also deemed necessary, the usual procedure until 1360 was to send powerful commissions of oyer and terminer into the shires to hear the indictments pending before the keepers of the peace and others, and to make general investigations of local administration during the king's absence: such commissions were set up in 1298, 1304–5, 1314, 1340 and 1343.[39] In 1361, however, the crown chose to use the justices of the peace for the task of post-war reconstruction, by giving them jurisdiction over 'all those who have been pillagers and robbers in parts beyond the sea, and have now returned and go wandering and will not labour as they were wont to do in times past' – a clear reference not only to the disruptive activities of demobilised soldiers, but also to the peace commissioners' newly emerging responsibility for economic regulation.[40]

This brief review of the policies adopted by the crown at the beginning and end of royal absences serves to demonstrate two important features of the administration of justice between the 1290s and the 1360s. First, as is often highlighted in the historiography, the crown's approach undoubtedly tended to be short-term and reactive. These measures were merely intended to deal with special circumstances, and were often withdrawn as soon as the emergency was perceived to have passed. Furthermore, there was no absolute guarantee that the king would even take such measures: Edward III actually called off a number of important judicial initiatives on the eve of campaigns, claiming somewhat disingenuously (as in 1332) that they had already fulfilled their function or, more blatantly (as in 1337), that the commissioners were needed for the campaigns in Scotland and France.[41] Secondly, however, and in contrast to the usual picture of random experimentation, it is evident that when the crown *did* act in response to the pressures of war, it followed a remarkably consistent line. Down to 1360, this involved the appointment of commissioners of the peace (sometimes with, sometimes without, determining powers) at the king's departure, followed up by more powerful commissions of oyer and terminer (with powers of inquiry) upon his return. After 1360, the two functions were united in the responsibilities of the justices of the peace. This is important, because it demonstrates that the commissions of the peace, although not necessarily the only agency of law enforcement employed by the crown in the period down to the 1340s, had already by that date come to fulfil a recognised role in the maintenance of public order.

The foregoing survey of royal judicial responses to the pressures of war has, very consciously, accentuated the positive. It is foolish to deny either the public order problems that were perceived to emerge from the making of war or the obvious limitations of the policies adopted to counter those problems. But the standard accounts of the period from the 1290s to the 1340s have placed such emphasis on highly sensationalised reports of criminal behaviour and on the supposedly wilful and irresponsible behaviour of war-mongering kings that we are in real danger of forgetting the creative and formative nature of the changes wrought in the judicial system during these years.[42] To argue that contemporaries were dissatisfied with the judicial measures taken by the crown in response to the challenges of war is not, in itself, to eliminate the importance of those initiatives: indeed, even tentative and short-lived judicial experiments could set new benchmarks against which contemporaries judged the success or failure of subsequent regimes. In particular, we have emphasised how close and consistent is the correlation between the public order issues raised by war and the early development of the keepers and justices of the peace. So far, however, we have not directly addressed the issue as to whether this new trend in judicial policy represented the preferred option of the crown or of the political community. To assess the range of influences behind the evolution of royal justice it is therefore necessary to examine the special political dynamics that arose from the war state of the fourteenth century.

The Politics of War

Medieval royal policy was never made in a vacuum: sensible kings always responded to the demands of their subjects. Those subjects, however, became particularly vocal in the period covered by this book, for two reasons. First, the barons who led opposition to Edward I and

Edward II increasingly claimed to speak in the name of the 'community of the realm' and often articulated the grievances of the polity in terms of the inadequacies of royal justice: in 1311, for example, the Lords Ordainers somewhat sanctimoniously expressed the hope 'that the king's peace be firmly kept throughout the realm so that every one can safely go, come and abide in safety according to the law and usages of the realm'.[43] Secondly, when the tradition of complaint was taken up by the representative element in parliament from the 1320s and 1330s, the commons attempted to use their control over taxation as a bargaining position to secure concessions from the crown. As Edward III became increasingly reliant on parliamentary subsidies to fund his expensive wars, he therefore encountered growing political pressure for the improvement of justice and the reform of the judicial system.[44]

This pressure was recognised by Putnam, who regarded it as one of the primary influences in the emergence of the justices of the peace: according to her thesis, the crown was hostile to judicial devolution, and it was the commons, as representatives of the localities, who kept up the pressure for the creation of permanent judicial tribunals in the shires.[45] The resulting tensions that she perceived, and her belief that the commons emerged victorious as a result of their control over fiscal and legislative processes, have had a powerful impact on historical writing.[46] But given the argument outlined above, that the crown in many ways supported the development of the peace commissions as part of its strategy for wartime government, it is necessary to test the validity of Putnam's thesis. Two issues in particular arise. How close is the correlation between grants of taxation and major changes in judicial administration? And how close is the correlation between the common petitions and the legislative remedies offered by the crown?

On the first of these issues, there is comparatively little to be said before the 1330s.[47] Even in the early years of Edward III, finance and justice rarely overlapped: neither the peace commissions of 1327, for example, nor the judicial reforms instituted by statute in 1328 and 1330, arose from tax-granting parliaments. By contrast, the commissions to keepers of the counties in 1332 may be so linked, as may the statute of pardons of 1336, the 1336 oyer and terminer commissions and the 1338 'supervisors' of the peace commissions. Clearly, the frequency of the Scottish and French campaigns mounted from the mid-1330s created a pattern: the peace commissions issued in 1344, 1351, 1364 and 1380, and important programmes of legal and judicial reform such as those enacted in 1351–3, 1362 and 1388–90, all emerged from parliaments in which the commons gave their consent to grants of direct and indirect taxation. In particular, we may note that the crown's attempts to extend its fiscal base by negotiating various types of taxation during periods of peace in the 1360s and after 1389 made it vitally important to pacify the commons with concessions: the release of the realm from the penalties of the eyre in 1362 and the general pardon of 1398, both purchased by parliament with promises of new subsidies, are especially relevant in this respect.[48]

In a general sense, then, we can agree that the course of justice was influenced by the fiscal imperatives of war. When we come to match the crown's actions against the parliamentary agenda as set out in the common petitions, however, a less coherent picture emerges. It is important to remember that throughout the fourteenth century the knights and burgesses in parliament felt it their primary duty simply to request remedial action: while they were perfectly capable of recommending a particular course of action, they recognised that it was the crown, and not the commons, that made and implemented policy through statutory legislation.[49] This is reflected in the admittedly imperfect evidence from the first half of the century: while the commons frequently complained about endemic lawlessness, there was no consistent request for the appointment of commissions of the peace in the 1320s and 1330s, and when specific preferences were expressed or can be inferred – for justices of the peace (in 1327 and 1339), for keepers of the counties (in 1332, 1333 and 1334), or for commissions of trailbaston (in 1337) – they actually tended to follow recent or existing government initiatives rather than recommending changes in policy.[50] This passivity is also evident in the commons' attitude to the nomination of peace commissioners: it was only after the crown had consulted with the county communities in the spring of 1338 and issued powerful peace commissions on the eve of the king's departure for the continent in July that the commons in parliament began to express an interest and claim a part in the selection of local justices. 'It was typical of the commons' attitude down to the early 1340s that judicial innovations by the king and council were subsequently taken up by them and applied more broadly.'[51]

It is somewhat ironic, then, that when the commons' attitude to peace keeping did become rather more coherent from the 1340s, it also tended in certain respects to deviate from royal policy. The particularly intrusive inquiries of the early 1340s and the financial penalties associated with these visitations had the effect of alienating the county communities from general commissions of oyer and terminer, and the parliamentary commons thereafter developed a consistent hostility to such measures.[52] In the two parliaments of 1348, they outlined in some detail their own preferred model: the appointment of permanent commissions, comprising nobles, lawyers and gentry (who might be selected locally or nominated in parliament), with comprehensive powers to receive indictments and hear and determine felonies and trespasses, to be sworn in parliament to hold their sessions three times a year and to receive wages for their work as the king's justices.[53] This provided a template upon which the commons based similar petitions in 1352 and (probably) in 1361.[54] Some of the suggestions were fairly quickly incorporated into royal policy: regular sessions, for example, were laid down by statute in 1351 and 1362 (though these specified four meetings a year, rather than the three of the petition).[55] Other recommendations were taken up only after some delay: although the justices of labourers appointed in the 1350s received payment for their work, it was not until 1388 that the crown finally instituted a system for paying expenses to those who sat as justices of the peace.[56] Similar delays and vacillations were encountered, as we shall see below, in the development of the economic jurisdiction of the peace commissions. And some of the measures advocated in 1348 were never, in fact, adopted: the crown, for example, retained the right to nominate commissioners, and although it may have allowed parliament to approve lists of names in 1362 and 1363, it refused to permit this practice when petitioned by the commons in 1365, 1376, 1379 and 1390.[57] It is apparent that, while crown and commons seem to have agreed on the notion of creating permanent judicial tribunals in the shires from at least the mid-1340s, there remained discrepancies on sometimes quite fundamental points of detail for the next twenty to forty years.

It would therefore appear that any attempt to explain the rise of the justices of the peace in terms of a coherent parliamentary agenda for devolution successfully forced upon an unwilling government as the price for wartime taxation tends to break down when examined in detail. The keepers of the peace were already recognised by the crown as a reasonably well-established part of wartime administration before the opening of the Hundred Years War, and the commons showed no consistent preference for such agencies until the government-inspired commissions of 1338 had proved the general utility of the peace commissions. By extension, the argument that the conflict between crown and commons was resolved through tax bargaining only goes part way towards explaining how things developed as they did: in fact, the commons achieved very few effective concessions from the crown on *any* issue before the 1340s, and it was only during the 1350s and 1360s, in a new atmosphere of co-operation, that they began to find their developing agenda more adequately reflected in parliamentary statutes and government policy.[58] Finally, the latter point reminds us that the debate over the judicial structure was part of a larger political dialogue on effective governance: correspondingly, the commons' complaints on legal matters encompassed a broader spectrum of issues merely than the powers of the justices of the peace, ranging over the length and cost of legal process, the problem of corruption at all levels in the judicial administration, and a host of technical matters relating to customary, common and statute law. The emergence of the justices of the peace may seem to some historians as a victory for the devolutionists in a state driven by the politics of war, but to contemporaries the new judicial structure emerging by the 1340s may well have marked an uncertain beginning, rather than an end, to the process of reform.

Economic Crises and Popular Disturbances

Next to the man-made pressures of war, it is the natural disasters of the fourteenth century that present the most obvious exogenous influences upon justice. We have already seen how legal historians tend to present the Black Death as a great turning-point in English governance and, specifically, as the major determinant of change in the late medieval judicial system. The plague was not, however, the only natural disaster to hit England in this period: the first half of the fourteenth century was also marked by serious economic crises, particularly the series of severe famines that struck in 1315–22. It is helpful to examine the responses to these earlier crises in order to establish the degree to which the initiatives taken during the second half of the century were actually conditioned by pre-plague precedents. After reviewing the economic challenges to public order before and after 1348, we shall also discuss the judicial response to popular disturbances by focusing on the background and response to the Peasants' Revolt of 1381.

The Great Famine and its Aftermath

It is now generally agreed that the economic and demographic expansion which had been such a feature of the high Middle Ages came to an end half a century before the arrival of the Black Death. Agricultural productivity declined in the last decades of the thirteenth century, perhaps as a result of the over-exploitation of natural resources and long-term climatic changes. When harvests were relatively poor – as they were in 1308–10, 1314 and 1320 – prices for foodstuffs rose markedly. When they failed – as in 1315, 1316 and 1321 – they generated a veritable famine, in which significantly large sections of society suffered hunger, malnutrition, disease and death: between 10 and 15 per cent of the population may have died during the sustained economic crisis of 1315–22.[59] Although harvests improved somewhat in the following quarter-century, the damage to the agrarian infrastructure was profound: livestock holdings were seriously depleted, and by 1340 there were reports of large tracts of land which lay waste and uncultivated.[60] Nor did famine prove the only exogenous blow to the pre-plague economy. The export of large amounts of English silver coin in the form of war subsidies during the 1290s, coupled with the drying up of the normal sources of silver bullion in central Europe during the early fourteenth century, had the effect of reducing the currency by anything up to a half: during the 1330s there is evidence that the lower orders suffered some hardship, and the economy in general stagnated, for lack of ready currency. The situation was further exacerbated by the high level of war taxation, especially after 1337. Consequently, the low prices that were a feature of the 1330s and 1340s, rather than denoting a period of plenty, are actually a measure of a deep economic recession.[61]

These miserable conditions created two challenges for central government: they generated public fears of increased lawlessness; and they forced the state to take a more assertive role in the regulation of the economy. The first challenge was met partly through the existing structures for law-keeping and partly by ad hoc measures. Modern quantitative research has indicated, for example, that large numbers of economic-related crimes – specifically thefts of livestock and grain – were brought before the keepers of the peace and justices of gaol delivery, and that such business increased notably during periods of dearth and hardship.[62] The central government also granted special powers of arrest to tax collectors and other fiscal agents, and issued commissions of arrest, inquiry, and oyer and terminer to deal with specific outbreaks of criminal activity brought to its attention by urban authorities or feudal lords.[63] The piecemeal nature of this response may seem inadequate. But it should also be acknowledged that the contemporary fear of economically induced lawlessness was rather greater than the reality: given the scale both of the economic recession and of the crown's fiscal demands, for example, it is remarkable how infrequently the king's agents actually encountered co-ordinated resistance in the years before the plague.[64] As with the threats posed by war, the crown tended to believe that short-term, economic-related problems were most appropriately dealt with by temporary, pragmatic measures.

On the issue of economic regulation, the crown's response was also essentially reactive. Clearly, it was beyond the powers of the medieval state to develop and enforce a comprehensive 'economic policy'.[65] There were, however, a number of very notable developments during this period which suggest that central government was already beginning to make assertive use of the judicial system as a means of enforcing its economic initiatives. The second half of the thirteenth century had already witnessed a move towards government supervision on matters such as weights and measures and market regulations. Then, in 1307–8, the commissioners of the peace were empowered, through a network of lesser officials at work in the towns, to deal with cases relating to the coinage, prices, weights and measures, and forestalling (the practice of intercepting produce on its way to market in order to maximise profits). Although these economic provisions were not specified in the terms of later peace commissions, and enforcement continued, as before, in the customary courts of manor and borough, the commissions of 1307–8 were subsequently believed to have turned at least one economic offence, forestalling, into a statutory trespass.[66] In the spring of 1315, furthermore, when shortages of various provisions were already becoming evident, the crown took the remarkable step of fixing a series of maximum prices for some livestock and foodstuffs (though not for grain).[67] No special means of enforcement was specified; and when, early in 1316, it became evident that the ordinance was merely encouraging traders to withhold their supplies from markets, the government quickly withdrew it.[68] These early ventures into economic regulation therefore tended, not surprisingly, to be short-lived and sometimes abortive – though they undoubtedly provided important precedents for subsequent policies in the reign of Edward III.[69]

Nor should it be assumed that more ambitious strategies emerged only in the aftermath of the plague. One particular case in point is the maintenance of weights and measures. The crown had stood as the guarantor of standard weights and measures since the late twelfth century – its obligation in this respect was enshrined in Magna Carta in 1215 – and had used the eyre and other judicial agencies to launch periodic investigations into local practice on this vital issue.[70] In 1324, however, the crown took a new approach by setting up special standing commissions in the shires to survey measures of wine, ale and corn.[71] While this and subsequent initiatives cannot immediately be explained in terms of exogenously induced economic crises, it is quite possible that the shortage of food and money, coupled with the unscrupulous activities of royal purveyors (who had a particular reputation for falsifying the true weight and value of grain taken from the king's subjects) helped to drive government policy on the matter, particularly after the late 1330s.[72] Accordingly, although the 1324 tribunals do not appear to have survived the change of political regime in 1327, parliament was again able to provoke the government into action in 1340, when new county commissions were appointed to arrest those who used illegal weights and measures, to determine such cases, and, significantly, to take a quarter of the profits of their sessions as wages.[73] The commissions were formally withdrawn in 1344, possibly because of the parallel reform of the peace commissions, which placed new emphasis on the need for royal judges to be present in the localities when felonies and trespasses were brought to trial.[74] But there is some evidence that the structure of 1340 survived at least to the end of the decade;[75] and after the royal confirmation of standard weights and measures in 1352 and a vigorous policy of local enforcement by the king's bench, it was indeed briefly revived in 1356.[76] More significantly, these county tribunals set a significant precedent, not only for the unusual procedure adopted in 1349 and 1351 for the payment of the justices of labourers, but also for the inclusion of weights and measures jurisdiction, first into the labour commissions in 1357 and subsequently into the peace commissions from 1361.[77] The weights and measures commissions of 1324 and 1340 therefore stand as examples of the manner in which royal government was already being encouraged to involve itself in economic regulation, and to create permanent mechanisms for the local enforcement of its policies, in the two generations preceding the Black Death.

The Plague and its Aftermath

The Black Death arrived in England in the summer of 1348 and raged throughout the following year, subsiding only towards the end of 1349. Mortality rates varied considerably from area to area, but recent research has tended to emphasise the impact of this epidemic and suggests that between 30 and 40 per cent of the population was wiped out in little over a year. The plague returned, with somewhat reduced virulence, in 1361–2, 1368–9, 1371 and 1375. The cumulative impact was astounding: between 1348 and 1377, the population of England was virtually halved.[78] The short-term disruption and long-term effects upon the economy and society were undoubtedly profound – even though historians are now more disposed to see the plague as accelerating existing trends rather than altering their pre-existing course. The judicial response was inevitably conditioned by the immediate threat which this natural disaster posed to public order and by the longer-term issue of how the legal system might be used to deal with the special challenges of the post-plague economy.

Contemporaries were quick to point out that the loss of such a large proportion of the population had given the advantage to the lower orders, who, using their scarcity value as leverage, were able to push down rents and, in particular, push up the price of labour in the agricultural and manufacturing economies.[79] The crown responded on the latter point with national legislation in the form of the Ordinance of Labourers of 1349. This was principally concerned to peg wages at their pre-plague levels and to force able-bodied men and women to accept and fulfil contracts of labour in the countryside and the towns. Following the precedent of 1315, however, it also attempted to fix prices at reasonable rates according to local conditions.[80] The legislation was supplemented by the Statute of Labourers of 1351, which specified the maximum wages to be paid for different types of work, extended the range of commercial activities subject to price regulation, and established more precise mechanisms for the enforcement of the new laws, including the systematic use of financial penalties.[81] In 1361, just prior to the second outbreak of the plague, a more elaborate scale of punishments was issued: imprisonment was introduced, and those outlawed under the labour laws, when caught, were in theory to be branded on the forehead.[82] The epidemics of the 1360s and 1370s ensured the legislation a permanent part in the judicial structure. In 1378 the original ordinance of 1349 was re-issued as a statute;[83] and in 1388 the list of fixed-rate wages was extended still further and servants and workers were required to seek written licences if they wished to leave their customary place of residence.[84] In the wake of this legislation came other coercive measures obviously responding to the economic problems arising from the plague: the church instituted its own scale of maximum wages for stipendiary priests;[85] the crown helped lords to enforce their rights over defiant and rebellious villein tenants;[86] tax collectors were given powers to distrain, arrest and imprison those who refused to pay the king's subsidies;[87] an ordinance of 1363 attempted to impose restrictions on the manner of dress and diet of various orders of society;[88] and a series of supplements to the labour legislation aimed to control vagabondage, to prevent begging, and to prohibit peasants from carrying weapons or indulging in idleness and riotous games.[89]

How were such elaborate measures enforced? The answer is, sporadically. The sumptuary legislation of 1363, for example, proved quite impractical and was actually abandoned within a year.[90] In theory, the labour legislation was more rigorously applied, at least during the first decade after the plague. In 1349–51 and 1352–9 it was enforced by special standing commissions in the shires, selected from the very class that was most likely to benefit from the new legislation – the landholders and agricultural employers among the country gentry. Throughout the 1350s these commissioners received wages from the profits of their sessions, on the model previously established for justices of weights and measures; down to 1354, furthermore, tax collectors were allowed to use the rest of the fines from the labour sessions to offset the burden of the king's subsidies. These features of the system obviously proved a powerful incentive to effective enforcement.[91] After 1359, however, they no longer obtained. It is true that the commissioners of the peace, who took over *de facto* responsibility for enforcement of the labour laws in 1359, were still drawn predominantly from the proprietary classes; and the crown's decision formally to confirm their responsibility for the legislation in the statutes of 1362 and 1368 is certainly explained by the renewed fears of labour shortages following the second and third outbreaks of plague.[92] On the other hand, the justices had no particular interest in maximising profits from labour offences since these were no longer used to provide tax relief or to pay commissioners' expenses. And by the time that the justices of the peace were allowed wages in 1388, they had also taken on responsibility for weights and measures (1361) and forestalling (1364), and were therefore generating judicial revenue from a much wider range of economic-related offences. In terms of its real effectiveness, the labour legislation has therefore to be regarded as at best a temporary and modest success: the thousands of cases brought before the justices of labourers in certain counties during the 1350s declined to hundreds in the 1360s and 1370s, and to a mere trickle by the early fifteenth century. Meanwhile, manorial accounts reveal that all across the country, employers of labour were regularly ignoring the legislation and responding actively to the realities of the market: between the 1340s and the 1390s, average wages for craftsmen rose by nearly 50 per cent in real terms, and the increase was even higher for unskilled labourers.[93] In 1390, interestingly enough, the crown made a significant concession to the realities of local enforcement (though one that was not, apparently, applied with any regularity before the 1420s) by actually allowing the justices of the peace to fix wages according to the relative scarcity of labour within their areas of jurisdiction.[94]

Wherein, then, lies the true significance of the labour legislation?[95] First, it undoubtedly represents a landmark in the attitudes of the crown towards social regulation, setting in motion a legislative tradition that would culminate in the Statute of Artificers of 1563 and the Tudor poor laws. Secondly, when it was applied, it was used chiefly to enforce the terms of labour contracts and thus to preserve the interests of employers (litigation of this kind had only previously been possible in the customary courts). This point does much, in turn, to explain the sporadic nature of its enforcement in the peace sessions. The nobility and, to some extent, the gentry had sufficient clout to ensure themselves a reasonably ready supply of labour – particularly when they offered terms in excess of those officially allowed by royal legislation. As a parliamentary petition of 1368 indicated, it was lesser landholders and employers (including many leaseholders within the upper ranks of the peasantry) who really encountered problems in securing and retaining household servants and agricultural labourers.[96] This leads to a third point: namely, that the litigation which emerged from this legislation could not in itself have created the more general antagonisms that are often perceived to have arisen between lords and peasants in the so-called 'feudal reaction' after the plague. Instead, that litigation reflected the multiplicity of employment practices across the whole social spectrum. Fourthly, and finally, the true significance of the labour legislation actually lies not in the comparatively modest number of cases it generated in the sessions of the peace, but in the more subtle forms of social control that it created at the most basic levels of local government. The statute of 1351 required domestic servants and wage labourers to make regular oaths before the constables and bailiffs of their vills obliging them to observe the legislation. Like the Statute of Winchester of 1285, which required the same officials to review the able-bodied males available for military service, this legislation therefore bit deep into the constitutional structures and political attitudes of peasant society. Consequently, while the labour legislation alone need not necessarily be accorded quite the significance that Putnam gave it in the establishment of the peace commissions, its psychological and social impact is not to be minimised, and seems to have contributed, as Palmer has argued, to a more general emphasis on obligation and obedience evident in both the law and the political culture of the second half of the fourteenth century.[97]

The Peasants' Revolt and its Aftermath

The fear of organised resistance to seigneurial and royal authority, which we have already noted as a feature of political life in the early fourteenth century, obviously intensified after the plague. Although the more sensational examples of brigandage tended to subside, there is plenty of evidence to indicate that the economic and social dislocation created by the plague found expression in acts of passive defiance, labour strikes and physical violence.[98] In response to these problems, the parliament of 1380 sought and obtained a notable extension to the authority of the peace commissioners, who were permitted to hear and determine a range of new cases including armed confederacy; they were also empowered to determine the culpable felonies of notorious larceny and murder without waiting for the justices of assize to come into the county, thus significantly reducing the emphasis on a professional quorum for the trial of serious offences.[99]

Shortly afterwards, in the summer of 1381, the collective fear of lawlessness and insurrection evident behind such measures was dramatically realised in the series of regional risings and local outbreaks of disorder that historians call the Peasants' Revolt. No attempt is made here to provide a generalised history of the rising: what is important for present purposes are its implications for, and impact upon, royal justice. For that reason, too, the following account is very largely restricted to the revolt in the south-east, specifically the risings in Kent and Essex that culminated in the march on London and the meetings between the rebels and the youthful Richard II at Mile End and Smithfield. It is in the chronicle accounts of this rising, rather than in the somewhat laconic official records generated in the subsequent campaign of repression, that we find the clearest evidence of the important part played by judicial issues in motivating the rebels and conditioning their demands.[100]

It is a commonplace of historical writing that the Peasants' Revolt was precipitated by a fiscal issue in the form of the 1380 poll tax. However, it must be stressed that what really caused offence in the localities was not the actual assessment and collection of this tax, iniquitous though that process may have been, but the arrival in the shires of supplementary *judicial* commissions empowered to make far-reaching inquiries into the administration of the levy.[101] It is possible that these were seen as a revival of the earlier trailbaston and general oyer and terminer commissions: unlike other commissions of inquiry into taxation, they included a strong representation from central government;[102] and their efforts to extract more revenue for the crown were reminiscent of the cynical money-making exercises earlier attempted by the *novelles enquerrez* and the itinerant king's bench in the 1340s and 1350s.[103] Certainly, the demand of the rebel leader, Wat Tyler, for a return to the 'law of Winchester' chimes well with this interpretation: Alan Harding has suggested that Tyler was referring to the arrangements for local self-policing enshrined in the Statute of Winchester of 1285, and thus to the desire of peasant communities to organise their own systems for dealing with public order without interference from central government.[104]

However, as Harding has also argued, the growing association of such peace-keeping responsibilities with the keepers and justices of the peace since the late thirteenth century, and the emergence of the latter group as agents of a coercive programme of social and economic legislation after the plague, meant that the rebels of 1381 were also generally opposed to the gentlemen-justices who had now emerged to replace trailbaston-style visitations in the shires.[105] Such antagonism, furthermore, had emerged not simply among the victims of that legislation, the wage labourers, but also among the more substantial peasants whose role in the government and policing of the localities required them to conspire with the justices of the peace over local law enforcement. Although, as we have noted, there were significant numbers of prosperous peasants prepared to use the labour laws to protect their own interests as employers, there were also others who, in their capacity as bailiffs and constables of hundreds and vills, found it embarrassing, not to say sometimes hazardous, to participate in the application of this legislation. In the latter respect, it is striking that the rebellions in the south-east and East Anglia seem to have been organised and led by men who had regularly served as bailiffs, constables, jurors, reeves and tax collectors in their villages and hundreds in the years before 1381.[106] Far from being simply a rebellion by the under-class, the Peasants' Revolt also represented an opportunity for a sophisticated, articulate and experienced section of the peasantry to express its frustration at the infringement of its traditional rights of self-government.

It is hardly surprising, therefore, that representatives of the royal judicial system should have featured prominently among the victims of the rebellion. Three members of the gentry currently serving as peace commissioners were killed (all in East Anglia); many others justices of the peace were subjected to violence and harassment, including a number of those who had also been appointed to serve on the special commissions of inquiry into the administration of the poll tax. John Bampton, one of the most controversial figures on the peace commission in Essex, survived an attempted ambush at Chelmsford only to die, perhaps from his injuries, a few months later.[107] Sir John Cavendish, the chief justice of king's bench, was murdered at Lakenheath (Suffolk) and his head was set on a spike at Bury St Edmunds alongside that of another victim of the rising, the abbot of Bury.[108] In London, the agenda was set by John Ball, who apparently called on the rebels of Kent to kill all judges, lawyers and jurors.[109] In the event, they were rather more selective: Richard Imworth, the marshal of the king's bench, and Roger Legett, a notorious 'questmonger' (one who corruptly procured indictments, writs and commissions instigating malicious litigation) were the only representatives of the judicial system to be murdered in the capital. It may be that Wat Tyler was more concerned to target the heads of government departments, and that the rebels' thirst for blood was assuaged by the murder of Chancellor Sudbury and Treasurer Hales. It is also true, however, that the central courts were shut down for the Trinity vacation at the time the rebels arrived in London, and that their own principal officials could simply not be found. (This explains why Cavendish's murder took place in Suffolk, where, as usual during the legal vacations, he was fulfilling his function as a justice of assize.) The highly unusual decision to call off the Trinity term sessions of king's bench and common pleas was a striking indication of the state of emergency that existed in the capital and the very real fear felt by judges and lawyers for their personal safety.[110]

If grievances about justice therefore stood at the heart of the rebels' aims in 1381, it is interesting to ask whether the crown's response to the rising did anything more than mobilise the existing system for the purposes of suppression. Despite Richard II's initial offer to meet the rebels' demand and issue letters of freedom and pardon for villeins,[111] the central government took a stern view of events and for some months was preoccupied with a series of punitive measures. The royal household itself undertook a quasi-military tour of the home counties; assistance was provided to landholders who were experiencing difficulties in reasserting their rights over disobedient peasants; and, above all, general commissions of oyer and terminer staffed by royal judges and landholders, complete with their own military forces, were despatched into the shires to quell the rebellion and punish the insurgents.[112] Ironically, the last of these policies represented a repeat of those intrusive inquiries that had sparked the revolt in the first place: contemporary chroniclers, who were generally prejudiced against the rebels, commented critically on the severity of this campaign, no doubt because they feared that it might simply provoke further uprisings.[113]

There followed an abrupt change of policy. In August and September 1381, both the peace commissioners and the justices of oyer and terminer were ordered to send records of all indictments and pleas to the chancery and to suspend all current proceedings until further notice.[114] This may have been intended as a means of transferring overall responsibility for suppression to the king's bench, which briefly visited Kent at the beginning of the Michaelmas term.[115] But it may also have been done in preparation for the parliament that eventually convened in November to discuss the resolution of the crisis. The remarkably measured response adopted on this occasion by the commons – who were much more inclined to ascribe the revolt to the corruption of royal officials than to the malice of the peasantry – seems to have persuaded the crown that conciliation was the most appropriate policy. Accordingly, the king issued a general amnesty to all lords who had acted oppressively in putting down the rebellion, and allowed indicted rebels (with some exceptions), together with any other of the king's subjects who wished to indemnify themselves in this way, to purchase general pardons from the chancery releasing them from liability to prosecution for misdemeanours committed during the period of the revolt.[116] In 1382, furthermore, when the commons in parliament commented that many of those indicted for participation in the rising could not afford to sue out pardons in this manner and had therefore taken to the forests and other places for fear of exigent and outlawry, the crown granted a comprehensive general pardon (again, with some named exceptions) which, for the first time ever, did not require the purchase of letters patent but automatically extended the king's mercy to all his subjects.[117] This was a remarkable concession. Although it may have demonstrated the limitations of the judicial system as much as the perils of a highly repressive regime, it also had the desired effect: while isolated outbreaks of disorder were encountered in the years following the revolt,[118] such a restrained response undoubtedly assisted the processes of social and political reconstruction after 1381.

There remained the broader issue of whether or not the judicial system should be reformed to accommodate the criticisms either of the rebels or of parliament. While there are some signs that the crown attempted to answer public disquiet over the operation of justice in the shires, it has to be said that its initiatives were only fumbling and faltering. In December 1381 all separate commissions of the peace for towns were suspended and new commissions of oyer and terminer were issued for the shires.[119] Although the county peace commissions continued in force for another year, they lost their determining powers in December 1382 and formally reverted to their earlier supporting role in receiving, but not trying, indictments; the right to give judgment was now reserved to commissions of oyer and terminer which, while incorporating many members of the county benches, also included a quorum of royal lawyers.[120] This strategy seems to have represented a specific reaction on the part of the government to the recent relaxation of the quorum on felonies in 1380, and a more general attempt to tighten up central supervision of proceedings in the peace sessions: there may have been real concern on the part of the crown to prevent provincial landed society and urban oligarchs from taking over the structure of royal justice for the pursuit of their own interests.[121] Such a modest move, however, had very little discernible impact. Commissioners of the peace continued, despite the restriction on their powers, to hold trials.[122] Parliament itself was uneasy about the new prominence accorded to the justices of assize acting on the oyer and terminer commissions, and played the government at its own game by arguing that, since the royal lawyers were sent into shires where they had personal interests, they were just as susceptible to corruption as were the local gentry.[123] Accordingly, separate urban peace commissions began to be appointed again after 1385; and in 1389 the crown restored to the justices of the peace powers to determine all offences, with more flexible rules on the operation of the quorum.[124] In the longer term, then, it would appear that the Peasants' Revolt had negligible impact upon the structure of English justice.

In one sense, of course, this is hardly surprising: the rebels' anti-establishment stance and their resort to violence effectively eliminated the possibility that any of their own judicial demands might be considered or adopted. On the other hand, it remains striking that the official response to the revolt did not, in fact, precipitate more reactionary policies that played into the hands of the county elites by persuading the crown to use the commissions of the peace as the sole or primary agency of repression. In 1381–2 – as, indeed, after subsequent fifteenth-century insurrections such as the Lollard Revolt of 1414 and Cade's Rebellion of 1450 – the justices of the peace played only a supporting role, and the principal responsibility for quelling uprisings and restoring law and order lay with extraordinary general commissions of oyer and terminer and/or the king's bench.[125] The resulting prominence of the justices and serjeants of the central courts in the suppression of rebellion demonstrated the enduring determination of the crown to retain a transcendent authority within the realm and to modify the standard judicial apparatus when extraordinary conditions demanded. In this sense at least, the response to the Peasants' Revolt provides a powerful reminder both of the integrated nature of the judicial system and of the continued ability of the central government to direct the course of English justice.

Constitutional Conflict

The third and last of the external influences on justice that we have identified for discussion is constitutional conflict. This is not intended as an opportunity for a general analysis of fourteenth-century politics: many of the political pressures that helped shape royal justice in this period arose from general concerns about effective governance, and are more appropriately dealt with as endogenous influences. Here, the focus is on those extraordinary political conflicts that were capable of provoking civil war and palace revolution. Two particular periods of sustained or repeated crisis present themselves in this respect: *c.* 1321–32, and *c.* 1386–99.

The Tyranny of Edward II and the Minority of Edward III

In 1321–2 a section of the English aristocracy led by the king's cousin, Thomas of Lancaster, took up arms against the crown, arguing that Edward II's closest allies, Hugh Despenser the elder and younger, had persuaded the king to govern in arbitrary fashion against the laws of the land. The revolt was of only brief duration, since the rebels were cornered and crushed by the king in the battle of Boroughbridge in March 1322. The repercussions, however, were considerable. Edward's enemies were imprisoned, executed or forced into exile; the restrictions that the Lancastrians had attempted to impose upon the king since the time of the Ordinances of 1311 were rescinded in the Statute of York (1322); and the victorious royal regime became increasingly dominated by the ambitions of the Despenser family. In the winter of 1326–7, Edward's own estranged consort, Queen Isabella, invaded the country with a small army; despite the outbreak of disorder this provoked in London, there was no armed confrontation and the king, who had fled into Wales, was simply taken prisoner and induced to abdicate. But the use or threat of violence for the pursuit of political ends did not end with the unexpected accession of Edward III. The minority government, increasingly dominated by Isabella's unpopular lover, Roger Mortimer, in turn had to quash an attempted rebellion by Henry of Lancaster in 1328 and a rumoured revolt by the earl of Kent in 1330. Finally, the young king asserted his right to rule in reality, as well as in name, by ambushing Mortimer in a military-style operation at Nottingham late in 1330.

This series of civil wars, rebellions and political coups left their mark on the politics of justice in two ways. The first we have already touched upon in Chapter 2: namely, the debate over how the crown ought properly to deal with acts of treason perpetrated by peers of the realm. The manner in which Edward II went about suppressing the rebellion of 1321–2 implied that he ruled the country not with the rod of justice but with the sword of tyranny. His deposition certainly helped to discredit arbitrary treason trials; thereafter the general practice, as we have seen, was for such proceedings to take place in parliament. This, however, did not prevent the crown from using treason to suit its own purposes: in the 1340s the courts are known to have been extending the definition of this crime to include private war and the offence of 'accroaching' the king's authority. Although these cases did not involve members of the peerage, they highlighted the need for vigilance against the extension and abuse of royal power. Accordingly, in 1352, the regime of Edward III agreed to narrow the definition of high treason to a few specific crimes: planning and attempting to kill the king, his consort, or his heir; raping his consort, his eldest unmarried daughter, or the wife of his heir; raising war against the king or allying with his enemies; counterfeiting the great seal or the currency; and murdering the senior officials of state when in session.[126] The statute provided an important confirmation of the good faith that Edward III had kept with the nobility since the condemnation of Roger Mortimer in 1330. Indeed, the reversal of the judgment upon Mortimer and the restoration of the latter's grandson, another Roger, to the earldom of March in 1354 may have been calculated, in the context of the Statute of Treasons, as a way of contrasting Edward II's arbitrary treatment of the families of aristocratic rebels with the more conciliatory attitude of Edward III.[127]

The second issue arising out of the political disturbances of the 1320s, and the one demanding more extensive investigation here, is that of public order. The early phase of the civil war of 1321–2, which was concentrated in the Welsh marches, generated a wave of private feuding and violence that spilled over into the counties of south-western England. The later stages of the war, in the north, provoked similar reports of criminality in areas such as Lancashire and Yorkshire. Meanwhile, other regions were subjected to the depredations of rival armed retinues as they moved around the country.[128] Queen Isabella's invasion in 1326 and the resulting crisis of central authority similarly encouraged outbreaks of lawlessness in the localities, especially in the towns of Bury St Edmunds, Abingdon, St Albans and Northampton.[129] Meanwhile, the high nobility's claim to represent the interests of the king's subjects began to ring hollow when so many of the magnates appeared to be taking advantage of the political situation to subvert royal justice. An extant common petition of 1322 and a letter from the archbishop of Canterbury in 1328 both refer directly to the king's coronation oath and make thinly veiled allusions to the failures of Edward II and III to uphold the law and protect the poor against the rich.[130] Indeed, they differ little in this respect from the articles of deposition, which directly accused Edward II of breaking his vow to do right to all.[131] And despite efforts by the new regime in 1328 and 1331 to secure promises from the magnates that they would not go armed about the kingdom, protect criminals or disrupt the due processes of the law, the early years of Edward III's reign witnessed numerous examples of unruly aristocratic behaviour, not least among the close friends of the king such as Sir John Molyns and Sir Thomas Bradeston.[132] While historians may have sensationalised the activities of some of these 'robber barons',[133] the bad example set by them was undoubtedly deemed to have serious repercussions.

It is this perceived political and social crisis that provides the essential background to the bewildering series of judicial experiments of the 1320s and early 1330s. Many of these measures have been referred to in Chapters 2 and 3; here it is necessary to draw them into a chronological sequence and assess their general significance. The crown responded to public order issues raised during and immediately after the civil war by issuing peace commissions to selected counties (1321–3) and despatching the king's bench on an itinerary that took in Yorkshire, Lancashire, the north midlands and the counties bordering the Welsh marches (see Appendix).[134] The murder of the royal judge Roger Bellers by the Folville gang in 1326 also prompted Edward II's increasingly beleaguered government to take firm action: the peace commissioners were sent supplementary instructions charging them to disperse unlawful assemblies, arrest malefactors, and report the names of those who maintained criminals to the king; and commissions were appointed to hear and determine the indictments collected by the keepers.[135]

The new regime of Mortimer and Isabella made some effort, especially in the parliaments of 1327, 1328 and 1330, to convince the political community of its commitment to law and order, and operated a three-pronged policy. First, large numbers of special commissions of oyer and terminer were issued to deal with the demands for justice coming in from the provinces. Secondly, keepers of the peace were appointed in each county in 1327. They were followed by general commissions appointed on circuits to serve at least sixteen shires in 1328; in May 1329, the functions of receiving and hearing indictments were combined in new commissions to *justices* of the peace. Thirdly, the general eyre was revived in September 1329 and launched into what was reputedly the most lawless region of the country, the midlands, with two separate agencies being appointed to operate, in the first instance, in Northamptonshire and Nottinghamshire respectively. After Edward III's coup of October 1330, the eyre was withdrawn, and it was laid down by statute that keepers of the peace be appointed in all shires; early in the following year, new commissions of peace were issued, but instead of relying on the justices of gaol delivery to determine the indictments brought before the keepers (as the statute had required), the crown chose to appoint complementary general commissions of oyer and terminer to serve in the shires. In February 1332 the powers of the keepers and the justices of oyer and terminer were amalgamated in new commissions to justices of the peace, reinforced a month later by newly appointed keepers of the counties with full powers to pursue malefactors and to hear and determine felonies and trespasses. These commissions were subsequently withdrawn in October, prior to the opening of war with the Scots and the resulting new pressures of war on the judicial system.

What are we to make of this complicated chronology? Putnam, who wanted to trace the emergence of the justices of the peace, saw it as a series of disjointed experiments in which the various elements were often in conflict with each other: the keepers of the peace briefly achieved determining powers in 1329 and 1332, only to lose out to the eyre and the keepers of the counties.[136] In fact, as we have seen in Chapter 3, analysis of the personnel of the various county-level commissions and of the extant records of their sessions reveals a much more coherent and co-ordinated system at work: there was no competition between keepers of the peace on the one hand and commissioners of oyer and terminer or keepers of the counties on the other. Moreover, the revival of the eyre was clearly not designed to put the clock back to the thirteenth century. In some respects, it was merely another way in which to despatch royal justices into the localities, along the lines that the king's bench had adopted since the 1310s and was to continue to do until the 1350s. Furthermore, it was *only* in the counties where the eyre was actually sitting – in the first instance, Nottinghamshire and Northamptonshire – that the work of the peace commissions and the justices of oyer and terminer (like that of all lesser judicial agencies) was suspended in 1329.[137] This would also indicate that the abandonment of the eyre late in 1330 was a lot less disruptive than might at first be thought: the crown was, after all, only reverting to the system of parallel peace and oyer and terminer commissions that had operated in 1327–9.

What is perhaps most remarkable about the judicial measures adopted in the decade *c.* 1322–32, then, is the general *consistency* of approach: in response to major political pressures and civil disturbance, the crown generally maintained the line that local law-keeping was best done through standing commissions in the shires. It was only when exceptional situations arose – as in the north in the aftermath of the civil war of 1321–2 or in the midlands as a result of the exploits of the criminal bands in the later 1320s – that extraordinary measures were needed and the king's bench or the eyre were sent out to enforce the king's justice. It is clear that certain policies *were* compromised as a result of changes in the political regime during these years: the outstanding example is Edward III's decision following the coup of 1330 to call off the eyre, thus releasing two county communities (Derbyshire and Bedfordshire) from their visitation and ultimately relieving the whole realm from these unpopular inquiries. However, the prevailing trends identified above are relatively easily rationalised when we remember that the senior judiciary remained remarkably stable throughout: Sir Geoffrey Scrope held office as chief justice of king's bench from 1324 to 1338.[138]

The real reason why the state repeatedly revised its policy during these years was not, in fact, the successive changes in political regime, so much as the continuing need to find an *effective* mechanism to counter lawlessness: changes were made when initiatives failed, not simply when governments fell. So far as the commissions of the peace are concerned, this reinforces a point already made about the 1330s: although keepers of the peace were already a well-established part of the wider judicial structure, neither the crown nor parliament had a particularly dogmatic approach to how the judicial system should develop. Close study of judicial changes in the period *c.* 1322–32 therefore reveals, once again, that exogenous shocks – in this case from civil war and palace revolutions – only partly explain the way in which the system developed, and did comparatively little to alter the direction in which that system was already moving.

The Personal Rule and Tyranny of Richard II

The second cluster of constitutional crises that demands our attention is the series of events between Richard II's first great political crisis in 1386–8 and his deposition in 1399. The 1380s witnessed a number of attacks on the court and challenges to the king's prerogative, culminating in the appointment of a reform commission in the Wonderful Parliament of 1386. When this commission's term expired late in 1387, a group of magnates, including the king's uncle, the duke of Gloucester, and his cousin, Henry Bolingbroke, took up arms and made appeals of treason against five of the king's supporters, including Michael de la Pole, Robert de Vere and Sir Robert Tresilian, the chief justice of the king's bench. Richard's attempt to pre-empt the situation through a show of military strength failed when his Cheshire supporters were defeated by the Lords Appellant at Radcot Bridge; thereafter, there was little he could do to prevent the parliamentary condemnation of the appealed traitors and other courtiers and the appointment of a standing council early in 1388. But the Appellant regime was discredited by the failure of its foreign policy: a campaign against the French failed, and the Scots defeated an English army at the battle of Otterburn. Consequently, during and after the Cambridge Parliament of 1388, the king undertook a series of reforms – including important judicial changes – deliberately designed to undermine the Appellants and bring credibility to his own regime. In 1389 he formally declared himself free of the constraints of continual councils and agreed to the terms of a new Anglo-French truce. The early 1390s marked a period of relative calm. But in 1397–8, the king launched a renewed attack on the former Appellants, either (as he alleged) because they were plotting to overthrow him or (more likely) as vengeance for their earlier attack on his authority. Of the five, Bolingbroke was singled out for preferential treatment: he was exiled for ten years (subsequently reduced to six) and accorded the right to enter into the title and estates of his father, John of Gaunt, duke of Lancaster, should the latter die during the period of the sentence. On Gaunt's death in 1399, however, the king reneged on his promise. Bolingbroke's subsequent invasion, though ostensibly launched to reclaim the Lancastrian inheritance, rapidly turned into a direct challenge to the king's authority; Richard II was constrained to renounce his royal title and Henry IV claimed the throne as his own.

Out of this complex story emerge the same two essential issues that we identified for the period 1322–32: the politics of treason and the administration of justice. The period after 1386 witnessed a revival of politically motivated treason trials and a renewed concern among the nobility at their new vulnerability to arbitrary judgments. Richard II's attempt to discredit the reform commission of 1386 rested on the opinions expressed by a group of senior judges, including Sir Robert Belknap, chief justice of common pleas, in two meetings at Shrewsbury and Nottingham in August 1387.[139] The parliamentary commission was declared contrary to the royal prerogative, and the process of impeachment was pronounced invalid; more controversially, the king's legal advisers stated that those responsible for such challenges to royal authority ought to be punished as traitors. This theoretically meant that the act of accroaching the king's power, which had not been included in the Statute of Treasons of 1352, could again be interpreted by the courts as a treasonable offence.[140] Ironically, the very group that had gained most from the guarantees provided in the 1352 legislation – the peerage – was now forced to use arbitrary methods of its own in any attempt to assert its traditional function of protecting the king from evil counsel. The appeals of treason lodged against Richard's supporters in the Merciless Parliament of 1387–8 resurrected the idea that judgment could be passed simply on the basis of notoriety (though in other respects they held firm to the statute of 1352 by arguing that allegations of serious crimes by peers of the land should be heard in parliament).[141] In the parliament of 1397–8, it was the turn of the king's friends to appeal three of the Appellants – Arundel, Warwick and Gloucester – on similar charges of accroachment: establishing the commission in 1386; riding in warlike fashion against the king in 1387; and effecting the sentences of treason in 1388.[142] Not only did Richard II secure these convictions, he also excepted from the general pardon of 1398 all those implicated in the armed rebellion of 1387. The latter point was applied so rigorously that a number of commons' members were forced to submit, on behalf of their constituents, to the king's pleasure and to put their seals to documents declaring that Richard had the right to deal with them and their property in any way he deemed fit (this royal *carte blanche* explains why the documents were referred to as 'blank charters').[143]

The last development in particular helps to explain why the issue of aristocratic treason became of more general concern to Richard II's subjects towards the end of his reign.[144] The judgments passed by the lords in the Merciless Parliament of 1388 had already overridden the restriction, implicit in the statute of 1352, on what the crown could seize from condemned traitors: entailed lands (those which formed an inalienable endowment) and enfeoffments (those subject to trusts), which had previously been immune from forfeiture, were then made liable to permanent confiscation. Not surprisingly, both commons and lords had taken fright. The parliament had ended with a declaration that its proceedings were not to be taken as a precedent, and that in future the act of 1352 would hold firm; a statute had also been issued re-affirming the immunity from forfeiture of entailed estates (though not those enfeoffed to use) and extending such protection to the widow's inheritance and jointure (a life interest in a portion of her husband's estates). In imposing penalties upon the former Appellants in 1397-8, however, Richard II once more made entailed lands liable to forfeiture for treason. This was not without justification, since process brought by appeal of treason was not formally bound by common law conventions. But these measures, coupled with the king's refusal to deliver the Lancastrian estates to their rightful heir in 1399 and the atmosphere of fear engendered by the 'blank charters', created increasing disquiet about Richard's commitment to the law of property – the law that lay at the heart of contemporary notions of justice. The so-called 'Record and Process', the list of the king's offences placed before parliament in 1399 to justify the removal of Richard II, contained not simply a series of allegations about his arbitrary treatment of the Lords Appellant, but also more general accusations about his belief that the king was above the law, his refusal to abide by common law process, and his determination to subject the lives and possessions of his people to his will.[145] In this sense, the deposition of 1399 represented a decisive condemnation of the politicisation of the law during the last years of Richard II's reign.

The more general issue of how the administration of justice was affected by constitutional crisis after 1388 revolves, not surprisingly, around the justices of the peace. In the aftermath of the Peasants' Revolt the crown, as we have seen, had attempted to establish parallel commissions of the peace and of oyer and terminer and to stress the need for the presence of officials from the central court when serious cases were brought to trial in the shires. There the matter rested until 1388-90, when Richard II instituted three important changes. Each of these we have touched upon in other contexts: it is necessary here to draw them together in order to establish their particular contribution to the politics of the late 1380s.

First, there was the campaign against maintenance. Earlier in Richard II's reign the commons' petitions in parliament had begun to draw an explicit link between the corruption of the courts and the granting of livery: consequently, in 1380 the justices of the peace had already been empowered not only to deal with cases of extortion and maintenance but also specifically to enforce a statute of 1377 regulating livery of hats.[146] From the mid-1380s, the commons began to identify the great lords of the realm as the principal perpetrators of maintenance, precisely because the latter usually had the largest numbers of liveried retainers. In the Cambridge Parliament of 1388, the commons demanded nothing less than the abolition of all liveries. Although the king balked at this, he clearly perceived that the commons' hostility to the magnates might usefully be mobilised to discredit the aristocratic regime of the Lords Appellant and win him a new power base in the localities.[147] Accordingly, one of his first actions on assuming full power in 1389 was to issue new commissions of the peace which excluded the great lords from their now accustomed position as presidents of the county benches.[148] In 1390 he followed this up by issuing a proclamation concerning the grants of liveries by lords, with the explicit intention of eliminating the evil of maintenance from the courts.[149]

That these were politically motivated measures designed to appease the commons is evident from their short lifespan. The ordinance of 1390, although apparently given statutory authority in 1393, was neither enforced nor, probably, enforceable. Although the king was not restricted by the legislation, he set no standard of behaviour for the aristocracy: indeed, his earlier offer of 1388 to cancel his own grants of livery began to ring ironically hollow in the 1390s with the widespread distribution of his personal livery of the white hart. Similarly, the exclusion of the nobility from the peace commissions proved not only temporary, but blatantly reversible: in 1397, after instituting his programme of revenge against the Appellants, Richard issued new commissions whose presidencies were dominated by his own aristocratic creatures and allies. By its nature, then, the campaign against maintenance could not outlive the political circumstances in which it had been conceived.[150]

The other two changes instituted in the peace commissions after 1388, however, proved more enduring. The new labour laws of 1388–90 reinforced the role of the peace commissions in economic and social regulation by giving them new powers to coerce recalcitrant labourers (1388) and allowing them to set their own scales of maximum wages according to local conditions (1390). Much of this new legislation apparently reflected the agenda of the commons, and several matters – such as the payment of expenses to justices of the peace – clearly acted to the advantage of the county gentry represented on the bench and in parliament.[151] So too did the final reform, of the quorum. Local men of law were introduced into the quorum for trespasses in the peace sessions in 1389, and into that for felonies in 1394. As the statute of 1394 made clear, this was done to speed up the process for trying prisoners in the shires, and therefore allowed judgments to be given in the absence of the central court lawyers who had dominated the quorum for the previous fifty years.[152] After 1388 the crown therefore appears to have set out deliberately to placate the county communities by confirming and enhancing the power of the peace commissions. The result was remarkable. 'In the course of this unprecedented process of constant review the judicial authority of the justices [of the peace] had been raised to its highest point and the terms of the commission itself had been developed to the form it was to retain throughout the following century.'[153]

The successive constitutional crises of the period 1386–99 therefore appear to have had a good deal more impact on the course of justice than might at first be supposed – and more impact, in certain respects, than the events of 1322–32. The renewed use of treason trials as a means of acting out political disputes between crown and nobility opened up new sensitivities about the form of trial and the extent of the penalties imposed. This spread to a more general paranoia about the king's disregard for the due processes of the law and the threats that this posed to the property rights of his subjects. Beyond these concerns, however, the political conditions of the years immediately after 1388 also left an enduring mark on the judicial system. Richard II's conscious strategy of undermining the lords and creating a new support base among the provincial gentry had a decisive impact on the personnel and powers of the justices of the peace. Indeed, the influence of Richard's political ambitions on the reform of the peace commissions in the years immediately around 1390 is one of the most striking examples of exogenously induced change in the judicial system during the whole of the fourteenth century.

Conclusion

The foregoing analysis has suggested that it is no longer adequate to explain the various changes encountered in the judicial system during the fourteenth century simply in terms of the logistical and political challenges posed to the English state by the onset of the Hundred Years

War and the advent of the Black Death. The keepers and justices of the peace were a well-established part of the judicial system *before* parliament began (itself somewhat belatedly) to use the new political dynamics arising from the French wars to advocate the employment of such commissioners as the primary agency of law enforcement in the localities. Furthermore, it needs to be stressed that it was during periods when England was at *peace* with the Scots and French (as in 1328–32, 1361–8, and 1389–94) that there occurred some of the century's most influential experiments and changes in the administration of justice. This is perhaps an obvious point: programmes of reform and reconstruction are much more likely to occur outside, rather than during, periods of intense military activity and national emergency.[154] However, the fact that the first and last of these bursts of creativity coincided with, and were occasioned by, major upheavals in the *domestic* regimes of Edward III and Richard II provides an important reminder that there was a whole series of other exogenous political 'shocks' which, particularly in the short term, could have as much influence on the judicial system as did the so-called fourteenth-century 'war state'. Indeed, it has been suggested in this chapter that the causal link between constitutional disruption and judicial reform was actually considerably closer than that between military–fiscal considerations and the long-term evolution of the peace commissions.

A similar conclusion emerges from the expansion of jurisdiction over economic matters in the fourteenth century. There was nothing new about the way in which the crown intervened in economic regulation immediately before and after the Black Death: the programme for the enforcement of uniform weights and measures discussed earlier in this chapter, for example, was itself part of a much longer tradition of state intervention stretching back to the Assize of Measures of 1196.[155] What *was* novel in the fourteenth century was the degree to which the state provided its own semi-permanent mechanisms for the enforcement of such regulations. Whereas both local and national ordinances on prices, wages, supply, weights and measures, quality control, and so on, had earlier been left largely to the responsibility of the county, borough and manorial courts, the fourteenth-century initiatives – the keepers of the peace in 1307, the justices of weights and measures in 1340, the justices of labourers in 1352 and, ultimately, the justices of the peace from the 1360s – provided an efficient judicial framework in which to undertake an increasing range and proportion of such business. The important point to stress here is the degree to which such initiatives had become a recognised part of the system of royal justice *before* the arrival of the Black Death. The process was certainly accelerated by the exogenous shock of the plague, but its general direction had already been fixed before 1348 and was not in fact to be greatly altered by the challenges posed even in the new economic environment of the second half of the century.

This leads to our second principal conclusion, this time about politics. The increasing emphasis on the use of royal justice as a means of economic regulation calls into question the notion that the delegation of judicial responsibilities to the localities represented a political concession or defeat on the part of the crown. Down to the 1340s the politics of justice was to a large degree the politics of crime: it was to counteract a supposed increase in lawlessness (itself in part perceived to be a consequence of war) that many of the judicial reforms of this period were devised. After the middle of the century, however (and despite the continuing military activity against Scotland and France), there was rather less overt concern about violent criminal activity, at least among the parliamentary commons.[156] The crown and its subjects now became more interested in minor misdemeanours – most obviously, breaches of the labour laws – and sought to establish a judicial framework better able to encompass this new range of business. Far from hindering the development of the state, the emergence of the peace commissions therefore opened up the possibility for the implementation of government policy on a range of issues that had previously been beyond the conceptual or logistical scope of the central government. Even vested interests in the localities, such as franchise-holders and urban corporations, who might have been initially suspicious of certain of the activities of the new sessions of the peace, were quick to recognise their advantages: for example, the separate urban peace commissions issued from the 1320s and the process of allowing town officials to act *ex officio* as justices of the peace, which became the norm from the 1390s, helped considerably to reinforce the authority of urban administrations in a time of economic and social uncertainty.[157]

Consequently, it becomes apparent that the crown, far from merely reacting to economic crises and to pressure from below, found the new legislative and law-enforcement programmes of the fourteenth century to be a liberating and empowering experience. If it was sometimes slow or reluctant to follow the line of the parliamentary commons and devolve general responsibility for all these initiatives onto the justices of the peace, this was not because of some fundamental suspicion about a consequent loss of authority to the provinces, so much as a timely reminder that the king and council retained the initiative in shaping the judicial system and could at any time alter it to suit the needs of the state. In particular, the special arrangements made for the administration of provincial justice in the aftermath of the Peasants' Revolt served as an important reminder that this transcendent authority still existed and could be mobilised in times of crisis. It also highlighted the great range of judicial agencies upon which the crown could draw as a result of the previous century of experimentation: the commissions of the peace, far from assuming a monopoly over the administration of royal justice, had emerged as a truly integrated part of a much larger and more elaborate whole.

5

INTERNAL INFLUENCES ON THE EVOLUTION OF JUSTICE

Chapter 4 highlighted the role of politics, war and the economy in bringing about changes in the legal system. This chapter aims to complement its predecessor by examining the internal dynamics of the law: forces for change that were already at work as part of a pattern of internal development and would have been observable irrespective of any externally induced 'shocks'. A consideration of endogenously induced changes therefore allows us to discern the direction and implications of judicial evolution unfettered by the more pronounced, short-term exogenous factors with which historians have normally been preoccupied.

The fourteenth century witnessed an enormous increase in the scope of the common law, both in the range of civil and criminal actions and in the persons who were influenced by it and took advantage of its remedies. The system of courts designed to enforce the law and administer justice was required to adapt, improvise and experiment in an attempt to accommodate the rising tide of business, while at the same time seeking efficient, flexible and more permanent methods of providing for justice. It should be remembered that alterations in the methods used to administer that justice did not automatically trigger changes in the law itself: indeed, the body of customs and processes which comprised the common law remained largely immune to such interference. That is different, however, from saying that the law remained rigid and immutable. Where necessary, new doctrines and legal fictions were created to override previous tenets. These modifications, often judicial reactions to clever arguments made by legal counsel, were the product of the intellectual processes of those who made and practised law, the judges and pleaders. Equally, it would be a mistake to regard endogenous influences as occurring purely 'internally', within the courts.[1] Legal change did not occur in a vacuum; nor did lawyers operate in one. In reshaping aspects of legal procedure and redefining areas of law, practitioners were responding both to the practical requirements of litigants and to the exigencies of law enforcement – that is, to a series of general and specific influences arising out of the society of which those lawyers were themselves a part.

For the purposes of analysis, the internal influences on judicial evolution can be characterised under three separate headings, although their obvious thematic links should be kept in mind and will be drawn together at the end of this chapter. The first area to be considered can somewhat anachronistically be termed 'consumer demand': in other words, the capacity of the judicial system to stimulate and accommodate the litigiousness of medieval society. This involves an examination of both civil and criminal justice and of the procedural advances associated with particular actions. The role of the judicial profession is explored, next, in the context of its own expansion, definition and specialisation. The extent to which lawyers devised and implemented the new common law processes from within the system will also be addressed. Thirdly, and finally, the spotlight is turned on the development of statute law, legislation parallel but complementary to the common law, and the importance of parliament in providing a focus and forum for new legal thinking.

'Consumer Demand'

Medieval society has been characterised variously by historians (whether rightly or wrongly) as both exceptionally lawless and highly litigious.[2] To some extent this is confirmed by the volume of legal records – although we should be careful not to attribute too much to what may equally reflect an expansion in record-keeping, as well as a greater awareness and availability of the legal processes themselves. Accordingly, this section argues that the actions offered by the king's courts were determined by, and in turn responded to, the society they served. This manifested itself in the continued need for dispute settlement and for more effective enforcement of criminal justice.

At this point, it is worth reiterating that this chapter (and indeed this book) addresses the entire scope of the law: not just the prosecution of criminals, but the range of civil litigation that stemmed from the crown's obligations to defend the rights both of persons and of property. Politically and economically, medieval society was underpinned by the ownership of land. Land determined people's standing in society and provided both physical security and income.[3] The use and enjoyment of land was duly preserved and regulated by the law, and most of the legal processes undertaken before royal justices were disputes concerning land and property. The relative importance of civil litigation, however, is not mirrored in the existing literature on medieval justice. The sheer number of records and their intricate legal technicalities, which can daunt all but the most erudite and persistent of scholars, have led to a disproportionate emphasis on the more accessible and sensational criminal side of judicial business. As a consequence, the role of the legal system, and indeed its very success in resolving disputes and containing private violence, has been skewed towards one element at the expense of the other.

It is more appropriate to view the two areas as complementing each other. Criminal prosecution, which at this time relied on the active role of the victim, had many aspects of procedure in common with civil suits. This is particularly noticeable in procedure by bill, which began as a way of allowing individuals or communities to bring complaints before the justices in eyre. Bills combined civil and criminal elements: they offered injured parties a means of obtaining damages, but they also potentially formed the basis of indictments.[4] A similar dovetailing of civil and criminal procedure can be found in the labour legislation of 1351 with regard to provisions for breach of covenant (a civil action): it was now possible for masters to arrest employees who had broken contracts of service and forcibly bring them back to serve (as if in response to criminal proceedings).[5] Civil actions could also be used in tandem with indictments as complementary devices in the same dispute.[6] It is obvious, then, that the interplay of the rules of law and legal remedies (either as part of complex litigation strategies or as complementary methods of enforcement) in itself proved a catalyst to legal development. Where it is possible to view this happening, it provides us with a considerably more holistic appreciation of the range and purpose of the late medieval judicial system.[7]

An initial appreciation of the relative volume and frequency of recourse to the law over an extended period of time can be gained by examining the contemporary registers of writs (which contain examples of the chancery documents initiating legal actions) and from the fluctuating size of the common plea rolls. The provision of remedies through all manner of writs, and their acceptance by litigants, increased exponentially. In the early thirteenth century some fifty actions were in use. By the early fourteenth century, the figure had risen to nearly 900. Large numbers of writs were added to the registers during the reigns of Edward III and Richard II; and by the early sixteenth century the total number of common law writs stood at 2500.[8] The development of new writs to cope with the fresh situations in which litigants found themselves, and indeed the form of these writs, were important determinants of legal change and proved particularly influential in the advancement of trespass law.[9] But the evolution of new forms of action and their active exploitation by a more litigious society was also matched by an increase in the use of older actions and, in particular, by the instigation of an enormous number of debt proceedings in the court of common pleas. The consequent expansion in the business of that court can be measured, albeit crudely, by the sheer bulk of the common plea rolls. Despite a dip in litigation during the plague years of the mid-fourteenth century, the rolls doubled in size over the course of the fourteenth century as a whole.[10] In the two-year period 1327–8 alone, it has been calculated that there were just over 13 000 cases in process in the court of common pleas, of which no fewer than 6500 were new suits (though, in the light of the political upheavals of the period, this figure may not be completely typical).[11]

There is also quantitative evidence to prove that the arrival of the court of king's bench within a particular county could generate a large amount of civil and criminal litigation. The *rex* section of the king's bench plea rolls, for instance, considerably swelled in size during certain of these visits, as exemplified by sessions at York and Wigan in 1323, at Canterbury in 1337, at York again in 1343 and 1348, and at Norwich in 1352.[12] On such occasions the major increase in trespass litigation is even more striking. This is obscured in the plea rolls themselves, since they record only those cases brought by bill that were successfully concluded by trial and judgment. Other evidence, however, demonstrates that, whereas the king's bench rarely dealt with more than a hundred bills of trespass a year when sitting at Westminster, it handled over a thousand such cases in the course of just three terms when sitting at York and Lincoln in 1348–9.[13] In contrast to the physical appearance of the *de banco* rolls, which provide a rough index of the business of the court of common pleas, the actual size of the *coram rege* rolls therefore offers comparatively little clue as to the dramatic fluctuations in the civil side of king's bench proceedings and seriously underrates its role as a court of first instance for trespass litigation in the period between the 1320s and the 1360s.

The invisible nature of much of the king's bench business serves as a timely reminder that recourse to the law and the performance of the legal system cannot and should not be measured solely on the basis of recorded proceedings. This is partly owing to the relatively poor survival rate of the records of judicial sessions held in the counties, and is partly a reflection of the fragmentary or rudimentary nature of the material contained in the plea rolls. The clerks who compiled these records intended only to provide an *aide memoire* of a case or a confirmation of a decision. The rolls can provide a useful tool for the limited purpose of gauging general trends, but only in so far as they reflect the process of cataloguing the appearance or non-appearance of litigants and the orders and judgments of the court. More importantly, records of proceedings rarely provide evidence for dispute settlement in the form of 'lovedays', the method frequently employed to reach out-of-court settlements.[14]

Special Commissions of Oyer and Terminer

Having taken a general introductory view of 'consumer demand', it is necessary to focus more distinctly on gauging society's influence on the judicial system. This can best be appreciated through a closer examination of certain remedies or legal devices commonly employed during the fourteenth century and, in particular, by considering the essential characteristics which gave rise to their popularity, their receptiveness to change, and their capacity to meet increases in demand.

'Popular pressure was undoubtedly the most significant factor in the expansion of special commissions of oyer and terminer.'[15] Charting the issue of these commissions over the century or so encompassing the reigns of the first three Edwards, Kaeuper found that there were significant peaks and troughs of activity. After a fairly modest beginning in the 1270s, there was a spectacular escalation of demand in the first decade of Edward II's reign, with 270 commissions being issued in a single year in 1318. This was only to be equalled by another great flood of activity in 1327, immediately following Edward's deposition. Although the output of commissions remained high in the later 1330s, at around 100–120 per year, there was a slow decline during the 1340s and 1350s, interrupted briefly during the 1360s but confirmed over the course of Edward III's final years. Political factors were clearly at work here: commissions were issued at the whim of the Despensers during the 1320s, and were subject to some statutory restrictions under Isabella and Mortimer. But the general trends were not determined by the government. The popularity of special oyer and terminer commissions and their consequent importance within the judicial system can be related to the wider history and practice of *querelae*, bills and petitions: three-quarters of the commissions issued during Edward II's reign emanated from private petitions detailing complaints of trespass. Once the crown had indicated a willingness to provide special oyer and terminer commissions in sufficiently large numbers, a popular demand grew of its own accord. The ups and downs, therefore, should be perceived as fluctuations in demand, signifying an increase or decline in the total number of petitions received by the central administration and a longer-term shift of attention towards other judicial agencies. The crown itself did not seek to check the growth in these special commissions, because they actually served as a useful means of relieving pressure on the existing royal courts.

The popularity of special commissions of oyer and terminer is explained by the swiftness of their proceedings, the good prospects of success they offered, and their particular effectiveness within a wider litigation strategy. Once a commission had been obtained, the process was comparatively quick. The justices could be sitting within a couple of weeks – or even, in the right circumstances, a few days. The proceedings might be concluded in the space of about a year, though sometimes settlements were achieved in a matter of months. The complainant's ability to select the justices to try the case, either by providing a list of suitable names in the petition or by specifying them through personal communication with the chancery, may have had considerable bearing on the eventual outcome. While there may have been some bias on the part of nominated justices, the real advantage in exercising a choice of personnel lay in the fact that the justices could set the venues and dates for sessions in a manner that might advantage the plaintiff and inconvenience the defendant. The plaintiff's participation in the selection of justices did not guarantee success, and in 1360 it was, in any case, forbidden by statute;[16] but it may have helped while it was available. Finally, a special commission may have commended itself to potential litigants as an ideal vehicle for putting pressure on difficult adversaries. The threat of a commission could lead to an out-of-court settlement or (if the case was successfully prosecuted) to a sizeable sum being extracted from the defeated opponent in the form of damages.

Disappointed parties were rarely able to obtain their own special commissions in response, but this did not necessarily bring an end to the litigation. There were two further options open: to rely on an independent suit before some other court (such as common pleas) or to bring an appeal to a higher court (by transferring the record and process of the case to king's bench). Either route provided additional momentum to a dispute without allowing it to degenerate into outright violence; both routes also, significantly, served to increase the business of the royal courts.

The demand for special commissions of oyer and terminer, and their consequent importance in the development of the legal system, sprang from their flexibility, the swiftness of their proceedings, their ability to achieve satisfaction or compromise, and their capacity to absorb a significant swathe of trespass litigation. Why, then, did they decline in popularity? The downward trend noted by Kaeuper continued into the reign of Richard II: in the later 1370s and 1380s there were sometimes twenty or thirty commissions issued each year, and by the 1390s the annual figure had dropped to between half a dozen and a dozen.[17] This was undoubtedly a reflection of the increased use of the peace sessions as the courts of first instance for trespass litigation. The change is well reflected in the business of the king's bench: whereas in the early fourteenth century many of its cases had begun as suits before general and special commissions of oyer and terminer, by the early fifteenth century the majority were referred from the justices of the peace.[18] The enhanced powers accorded to the peace commissions during the second half of the fourteenth century, and the regularity and frequency of their sessions, persuaded most litigants to opt for this route, though some members of society still considered special oyer and terminer commissions to be effective for their purposes. The decline in resort to special oyer and terminer commissions may also reflect changes in the nature of trespass litigation itself: by the end of the century a wider variety of trespass actions could be sued by writ, and other forms of remedy, such as novel disseisin, became more accessible and 'user-friendly'.

The Assize of Novel Disseisin

An action for novel disseisin was a means of recovering land from which the occupier had been ejected (disseised) without due process of law, or as part of a genuine disagreement about ownership or the right to occupy. The attractiveness of novel disseisin was its comparative simplicity, its speed and its versatility. The only judicial action capable of matching a special oyer and terminer commission for efficiency, it was described by Henry Scrope in 1316 as 'the quickest and most expeditious action which exists'.[19] A tenant ejected from his land might be able to recover it by judgment about six months later, but there were occasions on which the timescale was much shorter: a month, twenty-four days, or even an astonishing twelve days.[20]

While swiftness was undoubtedly a major attribute, it was not the main reason for the action's popularity. Unlike some of its close relatives, such as the assize of mort d'ancestor, novel disseisin survived into the fifteenth century because it was capable of being adapted to serve the requirements of a rapidly changing society. Although it remained entrenched in twelfth-century doctrines for nearly a century after its inception, the assize was greatly extended during the later thirteenth and early fourteenth centuries, and by the 1380s it had emerged as a fully comprehensive action capable of satisfying the needs of the majority of eager litigants. This process of emancipation involved an expansion of existing concepts and a redefinition of the action itself, in order to fit in with contemporary needs. The evolutionary path was neither wholly consistent, nor constantly ascending towards some distant ideal. There were blind alleys, and some persistent stumbling blocks. Nevertheless, as the old rules were gradually eliminated, so the ability of the assize to act as a general remedy for the recovery of freehold rights was established.

Until the thirteenth century, there were a number of restrictions involved in bringing a case under the assize. The action was concerned only with ejectment; the business had to be 'novel' in that it was originally bound by a seven-year limitation date; the action had to lie between the original parties; and it was a remedy that confirmed possession of, rather than rights to, land. The straitjacket which bound the action was first loosened by changes in the reasoning behind time limits. In the thirteenth century the limit of legal memory was fixed in general at 1189, and for the assize of novel disseisin specifically at 1242; thereafter, in spite of recommendations for further up-dating, it remained unchanged.[21] As the limitation dates receded into history and became meaningless, they were ignored, and the action was effectively released from arbitrary time constraints. There was also a corresponding expansion of the definition of a free tenement, which came to cover 'officers in fee' (such as wardenships of parks and forests) and common rights of every kind (including rights to woodland products). This relaxation reflected the growing corpus of rights surrounding possession of land: the new definition also included merchants who gained income from debtors by holding their lands, persons who were tenants 'for another's life', and mortgagees (lenders of the money for which land was offered as security).

These developments were mirrored by alterations in the rules as to who could be sued and how many times the same set of facts could be disputed at law. By the fourteenth century it was recognised that, because one or other of the original parties may have died in the intervening years, the current tenant and anyone alive who had been engaged in the disseisin could now be named as defendants. This was a significant advance on an earlier ruling that the current tenant should be named, along with the disseisor (if they were different) and everyone who had held the land since. The new ruling simplified matters greatly and helped the plaintiff by restricting the number of defendants to those who were actually connected with the disseisin and who could readily be sued. The tenant was further aided by rulings on the possessory nature of the assize. Originally judgment in the assize was not definitive and it was possible to resort to an action of a higher nature using a writ of right or a writ of entry. In the 1290s an unsuccessful defendant was able to issue a counter-claim under the assize in an attempt to correct earlier disseisins by his or her opponent. By the middle of Edward II's reign, however, it was resolved that the assize could only be used once on a given set of facts: matters between the same parties, therefore, could not be tried again.[22]

It was a requirement of the action of novel disseisin that plaintiffs prove they had genuine control of the tenements (they were 'seised') and had been wrongfully ejected (they had been 'disseised'). The concept of disseisin and the means whereby seisin itself could be established changed dramatically towards the end of the thirteenth century. The two ideas were stretched and reformulated so as to provide more practical solutions at law. Disseisin came to imply any interference with a freeholder's use and disposal of his own property. It could include dispossessing anyone who held land in the occupier's name (his wife, bailiff or the guardian of a minor), putting cattle on his pasture, harvesting his crops, or forcing enfeoffment by threats to his personal safety. Anyone with good title and a right to possession who openly entered the property and took control was deemed to have legally effective seisin. This was increasingly tested in ritualistic forms. In 1300, for example, a baby (the rightful heir) was positioned at the entrance to a house until his uncle, who was occupying it, came home. In the 1330s it was enough to be halfway through a window. In other words, in the eyes of the law it was sufficient to establish purely nominal seisin. By the later fourteenth century it was further conceded that, if the disseised did not dare to approach the property for fear of his own safety, it was enough to get as near as he could and then state his claim in front of witnesses.

The redefinition of what it meant to be seised greatly widened the scope of the assize and significantly altered the pattern of litigation. The majority of rules which had blocked entry by an owner, including the stipulation that a right of entry must be exercised without delay or be lost, were also set aside. Recognition of a right of entry enabled a wife to enter and regain land after her husband's death, especially where the husband had released her right to a rent to another party or set up a charge (mortgage) on her lands. Moreover, other forms of action such as mort d'ancestor became obsolete since an heir who was prevented from taking over his inheritance could now make a formal entry, claim disseisin and thus take advantage of the assize of novel disseisin. Irrespective of the circumstances, a writ of entry was frequently recognised whenever a valid claim could not be pigeon-holed into one of the existing forms of action.[23]

The new form of the assize overlapped (in the sense that it covered a similar legal area) with trespass actions, especially those spawned as a result of the enforcement of a statute of 1381.[24] In the thirteenth century it was well established that in order to ensure an effective entry, a group of supporters could be brought along to back up the claim. The techniques used by such 'heavy mobs' are obvious. However, the legislation of 1381 (which may simply have enacted a previously held rule) declared that entries on disputed lands were to be effected without such gatherings, and prohibited displays of violence in the course of entries. Private persons claiming property now had to ensure that their acts were entirely peaceful. Remedies were provided to make the new legislation stick: under the terms of the statute, an action for forcible entry could be brought following illegal and violent entries and might result in imprisonment and/or a heavy fine for offenders. If it was found that a defendant had entered where there was no right of entry, the plaintiff could claim damages. Since it was only damages (and not the property itself) that could be claimed in a trespass action, the assize of novel disseisin retained its usefulness and remained an important partner with actions for trespass to lands into the fifteenth century.[25]

Other Manifestations of 'Consumer Demand'

The above discussion has provided two detailed examples of how judicial agencies and legal remedies were capable of responding to the changing demands of litigants. It should be emphasised that special oyer and terminer commissions and the assize of novel disseisin represent two areas that are well documented and have benefited from systematic historical research. They are, however, not the only examples of endogenously induced evolution. The capacity of the law to reflect changes in society – whether by altering its erstwhile procedures, by varying its previously held tenets, or by executing a sudden *volte face* – extended into all areas in which there was existing consumer interest, and even helped to stimulate new growth areas.

The problems encountered by merchants arising out of non-payment of debts is a case in point. The inadequacy of the existing common law procedure based on the Statute of Merchants of 1285, highlighted in several test cases,[26] encouraged the mercantile classes to push for legislative change. The Ordinance of the Staple of 1353 (confirmed as a statute in 1354), which came to provide the legal framework for most debt recovery processes undertaken by merchants, offered a number of advantages over the older system. Those who defaulted on debts registered in the new English staples were, as in 1285, subject to imprisonment; if that did not suffice to secure full repayment, however, the process could now be transferred into the chancery, which could take immediate action to seize the person and property of the defendant, thus avoiding the three-month delay built into the Statute of Merchants. The legislation of 1353 also altered the basis of liability for debt by giving merchants exemption from forfeiture on account of their servants' misdeeds (in the absence of collusion). From the crown's point of view, these and other concessions were directed at foreign merchants, as an incentive for them to exercise their trade in England. But the remedies were also eagerly taken up not simply by merchants operating inside, and outside, the staples but also, in fact, by a whole range of people seeking recovery of debts.[27] A reduction in the number of actions to recover unpaid debts under the Statute of the Staple, observable in Yorkshire in the 1370s and slightly later in London and other counties, may at first appear to signify that demand for such legal remedy had actually dropped;[28] on a deeper level, however, this evidence points towards changing patterns of credit and how existing legal concepts and procedures could come to incorporate new definitions of the 'ownership' of debts.

A further example of the adaptability of the law can be seen in the growth, during the period after the Black Death, of the writs of assumpsit and trespass on the case, which offered remedy on a range of situations (such as the transport of goods or persons, medical treatment, the provision of agricultural work, or horse-shoeing) where a breach of duty had been alleged. Palmer has argued that these writs were essentially a by-product of the plague, representing as they did an attempt to rebuild a sense of personal and professional obligation in a society rendered temporarily dysfunctional by demographic crisis and economic disorder.[29] It would be strange, however, if the law was suddenly providing completely new remedies after 1348, since the situations covered (defects in goods or their loss at sea; builders' undertakings; the death of a patient at the hands of a doctor; a sheep in the custody of a shepherd; the laming of a horse in the hands of a farrier; and so on) were neither new nor rare. What seems more likely, in fact, is that matters already regularly pursued in local courts were now being transferred into the king's courts, and that the development of new writs to cover breach of contract reflected not so much a substantive change in the law as a simple transfer of jurisdiction. Indeed, some similar cases had already been remedied in the royal courts before the mid-fourteenth century. Non-admissible forms of writ had been 'smuggled' into court by skilful lawyers able to argue the special nature of a case.[30] The application of the writ of trespass *vi et armis*, which covered forcible trespass and wrongs in a broad sense, had also become more flexible, as the allegation of physical violence became a fictitious assertion employed simply as a means of getting the case into court, thus enabling cases involving non-malicious, negligent wrongdoings to be brought. Fashioned to enable them to meet the legal obligations posed in a variety of common situations and incorporating ideas from other already established actions, such as detinue (the remedy for recovery of movable property) and covenant (a remedy for the enforcement of written agreements), writs of assumpsit (regulating the performance of persons in occupations) and trespass on the case (concerned with wrongs inflicted indirectly or consequentially) were themselves merely variants of the older *vi et armis* writs.[31]

If the chronology of development therefore militates against a simple link between the Black Death and the emergence of the writs of assumpsit and trespass on the case, this does not necessarily mean, of course, that the new social and economic environment prevailing after the plague did not encourage and accelerate the take-up of such actions. There is an interesting correlation, for example, between the ending of the special commissions of labourers in 1359 and a bout of activity on the 'new' writs in the central courts, suggesting that assumpsit and trespass on the case came to be seen as a means of compensating for, and supplementing, the types of business pursued under the Ordinance and Statute of Labourers.[32] Even so, the plea rolls do not suggest that there was an overwhelming body of litigation using such writs in the later fourteenth century. The comparatively modest scale of such activity may also suggest something about the dynamic forces behind this development: while the needs of society were obviously relevant, the writs of assumpsit and trespass on the case may also exemplify the desire of the crown to turn the economic situation to its own advantage and attempt to attract new business into the royal courts. The evolution of writs of assumpsit and trespass on the case therefore appears primarily to represent an endogenously driven reformulation of the way in which (and the level at which) breaches of duty were handled at law (see also Chapter 6).

The Inclusivity of Royal Justice: Justice for All?

It has been established that there was a relentless growth in the scope and scale of civil actions undertaken in the royal courts over the course of the fourteenth century arising out of the judicial system's responsiveness to public demand. Such a discussion has so far avoided analysing the consumers of the law. Who were the litigants in the king's courts?

Did they form an elite or self-contained social group? How accessible was royal justice? To what extent did the litigants themselves influence the changes in the legal system?

Examination of the patterns of litigation can throw light on the accessibility and inclusivity of justice, the degree to which recourse to the law permeated every level of society, and the extent to which there were appropriate remedies available. Taking the court of common pleas, it has been calculated that in the early 1330s there were 15 300 different persons involved in lawsuits; this represented somewhere in the region of 0.5 per cent of the population, or one in every two hundred people. This is a remarkable statistic, especially when it is remembered that married women, children and villeins had no independent status at common law.[33] Given the fact that the population fell by anything between a third and a half as a result of the plague, the increase in the size of the common plea rolls during the later fourteenth century, discussed above, suggests either that a larger cross-section of society was making active use of this court or that those sectors particularly inclined to use the common law as a means of dispute settlement were seeking its remedies more frequently than ever before – or, indeed that both processes were at work.

An analysis of recourse to special commissions of oyer and terminer provides some indication as to the social status of litigants and the frequency with which they obtained commissions. On the basis of samples taken during the reigns of all three Edwards, it appears that about 15 per cent of commissions were issued in favour of great secular and ecclesiastical lords. Merchants and other townsmen quickly realised the potential of special oyer and terminers, since a quarter of all commissions were initially issued to them (although the proportion declined to around 10 per cent in the early fourteenth century). A third group, more amorphous, consisted of heads of religious communities, holders of ecclesiastical benefices, middle-ranking knights and esquires and those sophisticated, upwardly-mobile peasants just below the ranks of the gentry. This group received around 45 per cent of commissions issued in Edward I's early years and 50 per cent in 1300. During Edward II's reign, its share increased rapidly to over two-thirds of all commissions issued; by the late 1350s, the proportion tailed off slightly to the level observable at the beginning of the century.[34]

Clearly, at first blush, the 'market' had expanded in favour of the gentry and greater peasantry. They were the sector of society to which special commissions of oyer and terminer were particularly attractive options. The fee paid to the chancery for the issue of such commissions under letters patent was a sizeable sum: it could vary from half a mark (6s. 8d.) to £2 or more, with the normal charge being £1; it was therefore considerably greater than the 6d. charged for an original writ, though it was also, of course, a one-off payment and no follow-up charges would accumulate for the issue of judicial writs. It is also important to stress that due allowance was made for the relative poverty of applicants: the fee for a special oyer and terminer commission was not infrequently reduced or waived altogether 'for God' (that is, as an act of Christian charity).[35] Justice therefore appears to have remained accessible for those who could demonstrate 'poverty', even though it may still have been difficult at times for gentry families, let alone members of the peasantry, to raise the actual sums demanded by the chancery.

It was not just special oyer and terminer commissions to which those members of society below the ranks of the gentry had access. The increased volume of litigation encountered by the court of king's bench when it visited the shires reflected to a considerable extent the large number of lawsuits initiated by peasants: certainly in Lincolnshire, the one area for which such a social analysis is available, 'villagers' seem (in a quantitative sense at least) to have dominated the proceedings of this court.[36] In a selection of king's bench plea rolls from the period 1291–1339, new cases brought by this group never accounted for less than 70 per cent of the total business generated in the shire, and averaged an impressive 81 per cent. Privileged groups – nobles, gentry, ecclesiastics – may have preferred to pursue their own litigation strategies through special commissions of oyer and terminer and by bringing civil suits in the court of common pleas, with the result that they made comparatively modest use of the king's bench when it visited their 'home' shires. This should not, however, diminish the overall totals of villagers using king's bench in any one year. Indeed, the comparative frequency with which this court sat in Lincolnshire, especially in the period 1323–39 when it visited the county on average once every eighteen months (see Appendix), may have been a relevant factor in encouraging peasants to use the court – and, indeed, to *continue* using it after its departure. (These special conditions need also, of course, to be taken into account when applying the Lincolnshire model to the country as a whole.)

The immediate experience of litigation may also have impressed upon the more prosperous members of peasant society the fact that suits in the king's courts were not, after all, so expensive as the proverbial evidence would have had them believe. Here, the process of retaining an attorney was crucial: the ability to employ a local man expert in the law to manage the complexities of litigation and steer the case through court was a powerful means of overcoming both the technical and the psychological barriers to litigation. The increasing numbers of men so retained not just in Lincolnshire but throughout the realm testifies to the prevalence of locally based attorneys (see also below) and raises the possibility that the cost of their services was not, after all, exorbitant. Indeed, it has been suggested that the standard fee charged by a late medieval attorney operating in the localities was in the region of 3s. 4d.[37] Moreover, if the case was brought by bill (as was possible when the king's bench sat in the relevant county), then there would be no 'hidden extras' involved in purchasing original writs from the chancery.

If access to royal justice did indeed rely so much on the advent of the king's bench and the ability of the lower orders to take advantage of its right, inherited from the general eyre, to hear cases brought by bill, then the abandonment of the provincial sessions of the king's bench and the increasing reliance on the commissions of the peace to act as courts of first instance during the second half of the fourteenth century might at first appear to have restricted access to royal justice. Certainly this is the inference to be drawn from Putnam's statement, followed by a number of other historians, that the justices of the peace were forbidden after 1332 from accepting bills relating to common law offences.[38] Yet the argument is unreliable on three fronts. First, the peace commissioners appointed in 1338 were allowed to accept private suits of trespass.[39] Secondly, although the justices of the peace were not supposed to accept bills for common law trespasses after 1350, they continued sometimes to do so. Thirdly, and most importantly, they were still formally empowered to receive bills relating to the labour legislation and other statutory offences; and there is evidence, as Putnam herself admitted, that the audience of such bills formed a significant part of the business of the quarter sessions in the late fourteenth and fifteenth centuries. The main difference from the earlier practices of the eyre and king's bench was that such bills were not normally accepted immediately by the justices but were now sent to be tested and approved by juries of presentment.[40] The degree to which the jury thus acted as an effective block either against malicious accusations (the real intention of the procedure) or against the ability of a plaintiff of low status to secure justice (a possible by-product of the procedure, given the susceptibility of jurors to outside influence) has never been systematically analysed.[41] However, if we set aside for the present the notion that some form of inherent class bias may have operated in the sessions of the peace (discussed further in Chapter 6), it remains very striking just how many of the plaintiffs to cases accepted in the peace sessions were outside the ranks of the privileged elite. Viewed alongside our admittedly impressionistic surmise from the increase in litigation in common pleas during the course of the century, the evidence of the peace sessions can indeed begin to provide some sense of the way in which individuals from a great variety of social levels and backgrounds were able to employ the crown's judicial agencies for their own benefit.

Their expectations of success depended, of course, on a whole range of variables, of which relative social status was inevitably perhaps the most important. One modern study of fourteenth-century litigation found that the gentry were more frequently at law with those lower down the social ladder than with each other.[42] The same point emerges, as we have seen, from an analysis of proceedings under the labour legislation, in which substantial landholding peasants frequently took actions against poorer, landless workers. In such cases the system was clearly biased in favour of the plaintiff. That is not to say, however, that the law simply endorsed the social hierarchy. A significant proportion of private litigation was between social equals, such as fellow citizens or rival towns; and there was nothing in theory to prevent those of lesser social status taking proceedings against their superiors, whether they were employees wishing to sue their masters under the labour laws, townsmen challenging the rights of their feudal lords, or gentry seeking recourse against aristocratic oppressions.[43]

Traditionally, the remedies provided by royal justice and participation in judicial processes were available only to free subjects. The unfree, or villeins, who at the end of the thirteenth century comprised as much as a third of the population in certain parts of England, technically had no rights to sue in the king's courts. It is apparent, however, that villein status did not amount to a total exclusion from service on juries, nor access to royal justice. Outside the royal courts, there is evidence that unfree peasants regularly served on juries in manor courts, and possibly also at the county court and in coroners' inquests. Some villeins were even employed in the king's courts. The 1298 investigations held in Lincolnshire unearthed the case of a hundred bailiff bribed by a villein not to place the latter on the assizes or juries. Those villeins who removed themselves from the control of their lords often used service in the royal courts as an indication of their 'freedom' when challenged to prove their status.[44] Villeins frequently invoked protection (albeit unsuccessfully) under the assize of novel disseisin as if they were freemen.[45] There is also evidence of villeins obtaining special commissions of oyer and terminer. In 1306, for instance, five servile tenants of the prior of Ogbourne sought relief through the royal courts in this manner, as did a villein of the prior of Takeley in 1336.[46]

Both the ambiguities of villeinage and the debilitating impact of its invocation in the courts are observable in a dispute between Thomas Lisle, the bishop of Ely, and Richard and William Spink, which began in 1346 when Richard purchased a special commission of oyer and terminer against the bishop.[47] The Spink brothers were prominent citizens of Norwich, and Richard in particular was a man of wealth and power. In 1348, however, in a petition to parliament, Lisle tried to challenge the commissions ranged against him by claiming exception of villeinage: that is, that the Spink brothers had no right to sue since they and their ancestors had been villeins on the bishop's manor of Doddington in Cambridge. Richard Spink countered with another petition claiming that the bishop was unjustly trying to prevent his trial. The case was complicated by the fact that the original commissions of oyer and terminer had been brought in Norfolk, whereas the bishop naturally insisted that the jury summoned on the naifty (deciding whether the brothers were of villein or free status) should be brought in Cambridgeshire, the county in which villeinage was claimed. Meanwhile in Norfolk, where the Spinks' free status was readily apparent and not disputed, the brothers nevertheless attempted to gain a writ *de libertate probanda* to prove their free status in court. In his petition, Richard also invoked the principle of *favor libertatis*, claiming that the law favoured liberty above putting someone in servitude. In the end, the council ruled in 1348 that, since Spink did not deny his place of birth as Doddington, the exception of villeinage had to be decided by a jury from Cambridgeshire. Inconsistencies were also found in the facts stated in the oyer and terminer commissions, which were accordingly rejected as being maliciously conceived.

Although Bishop Lisle never pressed home his advantage and submitted to arbitration with the Spinks in 1352, the case became something of a *cause célèbre*, especially given the heightened concerns expressed by landholders over the enforcement of traditional rights after the plague. In 1352 the parliamentary commons pressed for the tightening of the appeals procedure arising from writs of naifty. It was argued that villeins were obtaining writs *de libertate probanda* in order to delay action on the writ of naifty until royal justices arrived in the county, and that this was detrimental to the interests of feudal lords. The resulting statute removed the protection hitherto afforded to villeins by the crown, enabling lords to reclaim their villeins even if a writ to prove liberty had been sued out.[48]

At first sight, this statute appears to provide powerful evidence that royal justice was becoming more exclusive in the face of the particular economic and political pressures brought on by the Black Death. However, there is no evidence that the statute was ever enforced, and it would seem that its intention was not to abolish the writ *de libertate probanda* but simply to prevent its abuse.[49] Other evidence also demonstrates that villeins continued to have access to a range of remedies provided in chancery. The appeal of ancient demesne was a well-established process by which those holding in servile tenure could claim royal protection and win special privileges, ranging from protection against increases in services to actual free status. To achieve this, they had to prove that their manor had once been part of the royal estate (or 'ancient demesne'). Throughout the fourteenth century peasant communities were employing lawyers to attend the chancery and purchase copies of the relevant entries in Domesday Book on which claims to ancient demesne status would be judged and the ensuing complaints accepted by the crown. Between 1376 and 1378 there was a particular flurry of activity in this respect, as the villeins of no fewer than forty villages in south-west England sought to use appeals of ancient demesne as a means of protesting against the unjust exactions of their current lords. Such was this activity, indeed, that in 1377 the parliamentary commons complained bitterly about the manner in which the preliminaries to appeals of ancient demesne were effectively allowing villein tenants all across the country to go on strike pending the king's intervention and judgment.[50] The fact that the system was so obviously stacked against the unfree, and that so many such appeals failed, does not in itself mean that the judicial system was perceived as a closed shop: access to the royal courts was clearly regarded as an important advantage to be preserved or acquired by whatever means available.

New Methods for Prosecuting Crime

In the criminal branch of the law, the crown was the interested party. It was the king's duty to maintain the peace of the land and punish wrongdoers. Crown pleas were thus concerned with prosecuting felons and upholding public order. While the crown's success in meeting its obligations depended on the scope and jurisdiction of a particular judicial agency, the relevant statute or the articles of inquiry contained in the operating commission, a defendant's actual appearance in court was secured mainly through the mechanisms of appeal and indictment operating at the local level.

The lack of a public prosecuting agency and a corresponding reliance on the wronged individual and the local community for the identification and prosecution of offenders has been seen as symptomatic of a judicial system that was 'reactive' rather than 'pro-active'.[51] While there was no attempt to imitate the inquisitorial procedure in use on the Continent,[52] it is possible to observe (or to interpret certain developments in terms of) a more active role on the part of the English crown during the course of the fourteenth century. This is apparent in the emergence of 'triers' (grand juries) and the increased attention afforded to 'approvers' (criminals who turned king's evidence).

Despite their name, 'triers' were concerned with presenting rather than trying offences. The system of triers originated in the age of the eyre, but the first datable appearance of a jury named as such occurs only at the very end of that period, in the rolls of the 1292–3 Cumberland eyre.[53] Following the demise of the general eyre, triers were commonly employed at trailbaston and peace sessions. The triers themselves comprised a jury of twelve men representing the county as a whole. As such, they usually formed a separate group from the hundred juries that presented offences, though there were instances where the membership of the two groups overlapped. They were men of some eminence in local society (including a healthy sprinkling of knights) who served in various key administrative and judicial capacities. Evidence from surviving peace sessions indicates that they not only confirmed the findings of the hundred jurors, adding their considerable weight to them, but were also concerned to put forward particularly serious crimes occurring within the county, including allegations of homicide, rape, robbery and counterfeiting. Considering the personnel of the 'triers', it is interesting to note that they also involved themselves in charges brought against persons impeding the work of the coroner and for armed disturbance of peace sessions.[54]

Knightly juries of presentment were particularly important in enabling accusations against their peers or social superiors, officials and great lords, to be prosecuted more resolutely (even if they did not result in convictions). An illuminating example of how serious crimes were tackled is provided by a study of the presenting juries for the various judicial sessions in Leicestershire following the murder of the royal judge, Roger Bellers, in 1326.[55] The Folville brothers, who were assumed to be responsible, were never brought to trial; but it became apparent that they were only ancillary to the murder, which had actually been perpetrated by members of another gentry family, the Zouches. The latter were duly accused by other leading members of county society. The various juries included a total of thirteen knights, and one of the juries labelled as 'triers' (two-thirds of whose members had previously presented Bellers' murder) contained seven knights and one of the county coroners. The fact that both the Folvilles and the Zouches escaped the clutches of the commissions of oyer and terminer set up to investigate this notorious case cannot therefore be put down simply to a local conspiracy by the landed classes to protect their own; indeed, it is explained largely by the political disruptions resulting from the collapse of Edward II's regime in the winter of 1326–7.[56]

The system of triers may not have engendered a wholly objective approach to the reporting of crime, but whenever and wherever the prototype grand jury did operate it is apparent that the knowledgeable and influential men empanelled were able to provide a co-ordinating role in the prosecution of serious criminal offences. The development of the grand jury, however, is obscured to some extent by the nature of the records. Even in the second half of the fourteenth century, a period for which there are a number of surviving rolls of peace sessions, the proceedings which include jury lists rarely mention triers. Nor do they record presenting juries drawn from the whole county. The role of this crucial mechanism of criminal justice in the age of the justices of the peace therefore still awaits proper evaluation.

The approver's appeal had long been recognised as the procedure whereby a man accused of a crime could confess his guilt and turn king's evidence.[57] As a method of prosecution, it has been looked upon with suspicion by historians, who believe it fell into disrepute and have highlighted the apparent ease with which it was abused.[58] Approvers' appeals are afforded renewed attention here for two reasons. First, in terms of sheer volume they take up a considerable amount of membrane space in the extant gaol delivery rolls: indeed, by the mid-fourteenth century, they take up proportionately more than normal indictments – which in itself would seem to suggest that the forces of demand were at work. Secondly, re-examination of the use of approvers' appeals as a method of prosecution yields the hypothesis that turning king's evidence was not only popular with felons but also actively encouraged by the crown.[59] The success of the approver's appeal as a method of prosecution is explained, of course, by the crown's ability to barter for information by offering the hope of discharge. Far from demonstrating the weakness of the judicial system, however, this practice proved remarkably efficient: for any such offer of freedom was usually a fiction.

For the approver, there were at least two incentives to turn king's evidence: procedural delay, which allowed the possibility of making an escape; and the prospect of freedom itself, which could only, however, be secured through the arrest and successful conviction of his alleged accomplices. The approver was spared from immediate trial because it took time for the coroner to take his confession (officially, this delay was limited to three days). During this confession, some men appealed two or three associates; but others might reel off as many as thirty or forty names. William Rose of Hampshire was something of a 'supergrass', naming an incredible fifty-four of his former partners in crime in 1389.[60] It might also take the sheriff and his staff some time to locate and extradite the accomplices named in the appeals. Consequently, there was plenty of opportunity for duplicity and further delay. John Kyroun of Norfolk sent the king's representatives on a wild goose chase: two years later, the sheriff finally had to acknowledge that the persons and places in Kyroun's appeal were fictitious.[61] A further advantage to the approver when turning king's evidence was the possibility of deciding the guilt of his appellees in battle rather than submitting himself to a jury. Trial by battle was an archaic procedure in other areas of the law (and in private appeals) by the fourteenth century, but was allowed to live on in this situation. If the approver was successful in battle or secured the conviction of probably at least six of his appellees, he was to be rewarded with his freedom. The down-side, however, was immediate execution should he fail on a single count.

For the crown, the approver offered the means of prosecuting crimes which might otherwise have gone undetected. The information provided could be most useful in breaking up professional criminal gangs and putting the finger on highway robbers and their confederates. An astronomic rise in the number of appeals can perhaps be linked with the crown's law-enforcement drives during the early fourteenth century. The overall total of approvers' appeals at Norfolk gaol delivery sessions in the years 1310–14 was thirty-four; this figure increased to 258 during the next five years (1315–19), reaching 420 in the period 1320–4 before dipping back to 213 in 1325–9. There was a corresponding increase in the number of approvers making appeals over the same twenty-year period: there were just nine approvers in 1310–14, but thirty-seven in 1315–19; the figure rose to fifty-four during the first half of the 1320s before settling at a figure of forty for 1325–9.[62] Similar numbers of appeals from approvers have been found in other counties.[63] In the first half of the fourteenth century alone (1299–1349), 193 Norfolk approvers are recorded as betraying 1560 alleged criminals. Since the latter figure represents those people actually located and prosecuted, it is clear that the approvers' appeals cannot have been entirely fictitious and must have made some contribution towards policing the countryside.

The sting in the tail of the crown's operation was the execution of the approver when he failed to secure the requisite number of convictions. Although some appellees might be convicted by the jury or vanquished in battle, the low rates of such activity meant that the approver himself was very frequently liable to be hanged. Even those, such as Walter of Mendham from Norfolk in 1312, who claimed release on the grounds that all their appellees had already been hanged or were dead, do not seem to have escaped execution.[64] This strongly suggests that the crown had no intention of giving approvers their freedom. Their elimination undoubtedly helped in the maintenance of law and order: a fifth of all convictions in early fourteenth-century Norfolk were a result of the approver system, and in the years 1325–9 the level of such activity amounted to 41 per cent of all convictions.[65]

Obtaining approvers' appeals and prosecuting individuals named in them was one thing; getting convictions on the basis of the appeals was quite another. Convictions solely on approvers' appeals were rare, amounting to 4 per cent of all convictions in Norfolk during the first part of the century and less than 1 per cent of all jury verdicts rendered. Indeed, there appears to have been a fundamental difference between the crown's encouragement of information on criminal activity and the localities' treatment of persons brought to court on approvers' appeals. Despite the volume of appeals, the procedure produced far fewer convictions than prosecution by private appeal or indictment: 98 per cent of those appealed by Norfolk approvers in the years 1299–1349 were acquitted.[66] This may reflect the low esteem in which approvers were held, and general public concern for abuses in the system: common petitions in parliament not infrequently complained of false and malicious appeals and the undue pressure thus exerted on innocent people. Nevertheless, the verdicts rendered by trial juries in such cases should not necessarily be taken at face value. It has been suggested that appellees who were acquitted may not really have been innocent of the crimes alleged and that, even in cases where there was strong suspicion against the supposed accomplice, a verdict of 'not guilty' was normally returned.[67] It is accordingly clear that the approvers were the victims of the system and the ones who came off worst all round.

The approver's appeal survived into the fifteenth century because of its continuing usefulness to both king and felon. Turning king's evidence continued to appear attractive: judging from the large numbers of criminals that consistently tried to take advantage of it, the system could obviously be regarded as a rather clever 'honey-trap'. For the government, which did not have the benefits of the lengthy analysis and array of statistics presented here, approvers were rightly considered to be a major source of information on the whereabouts and activities of criminals. The degree to which the crown itself drove this system is suggested particularly by the active use of approvers in the fight against treason and seditious words at the beginning of Henry IV's reign: in this case, there can be little doubt that appeals tended to reflect the concerns of the prevailing regime.[68]

In its search for an effective mechanism to counter the challenge of lawlessness, the fourteenth-century English state undertook a series of improvisations and innovations within the legal system. Some judicial initiatives were taken up, altered and developed; others were simply discarded. Historians have tended to focus on the judicial *structures* outlined in Chapters 2 and 3 without giving sufficient attention to the practical *applications* of the law – applications which, as this chapter has suggested, relied both on the evolution of new procedures to fit new needs and the willingness of individuals and communities to participate in the system. The desire to increase the numbers of people brought into the criminal courts necessitated not merely a change in the personnel of the bench but a series of more subtle alterations in procedure: the evidence provided by prototype grand juries and the inside knowledge divulged by detained criminals were but two of the ways in which the king's courts attempted to root out lawlessness and generate convictions.[69] The fact that increasing numbers of people had direct experience of the courts, principally through the prosecution of civil actions and minor trespasses, also contributed to a heightened awareness of the operation of the legal system – and, almost inevitably, of its shortcomings (see Chapter 6).

The Judicial Profession

The expansion of royal justice and the increased demand for legal remedies led to a corresponding need for the employment of those who could assist expertly in the complexities of litigation and consequently meet the growing 'consumer demand'. The services of professionals were required for the selection of writs to initiate proceedings, for making the plaintiff's 'count' (setting out the claim or grievance), for putting forward legal argument and presenting evidence to the court, and for general advice about how to proceed with litigation. The emergence of professional lawyers as a response to the shifting legal environment had a profound effect upon the nature of litigation and upon the direction of legal change itself.

The development of the legal profession has been charted in some detail both for the period up to the late thirteenth century and for that from the later fourteenth century onwards.[70] By Edward I's reign there were two particular types of legal representative: the attorney and the serjeant at law. The former was primarily the litigant's representative in court: he was responsible for securing the necessary writs and ensuring that the appropriate entries were made on the court roll. Each county had a recognised group of lawyers formally qualified to act as attorneys in the Westminster courts.[71] The serjeants, often engaged by attorneys, spoke on behalf of their client in court, having been briefed of the facts in conference beforehand. By the mid-fourteenth century, as we saw in Chapter 2, two key developments had taken place: serjeants at law were regularly appointed to judicial positions in the central courts, creating a fusion of the bar and the bench; and nascent institutions (the future inns of court) had emerged in London to provide for the accommodation and education of trainee lawyers.

The intervening years – the early fourteenth century – mark something of a transitional period, not only in terms of judicial agencies and administration, but also with regard to the legal profession. While there has been some examination of the role and ideology of various types of lawyer,[72] the focus of attention for this period has generally been on the central courts (because of the quality and quantity of the evidence provided by the year books) and the tracing of long-term trends within the profession. By contrast, the provincially based practitioners of the early fourteenth century have not, with a few notable exceptions, received much detailed investigation.[73] The present discussion aims to provide an indication of the scope of the activities of those who can be accorded the term 'lawyer' and to show how the proliferation of legal experts at various levels in the hierarchy of the courts and at different stages of professional development affected the evolution of justice in a wider context.

Legal Service

Men of law were available in every county, and fulfilled a wide range of functions. The professional attorney could be retained in the court of common pleas, but otherwise he was probably active in the county court, the seigneurial and possibly the hundred courts, and could be found at work in the courts of sizeable towns.[74] He was not restricted in his choice of patrons, nor was he necessarily tied to one individual or institution. Acting on behalf of the bishop of Coventry in 1307, John Hotoft gives the following description of his duties to a court inquiring of his activities:

> He was his [the bishop's] attorney for his pleas and for other business concerning the bishop that had to be prosecuted in the king's court ... and received money from him for supporting him in court ... and he is attorney and counsel for many other people in the realm in return for pensions and other emoluments they granted him and for money paid by them as is fit and proper in the prosecution and defence of their affairs and of all others who pay him.[75]

The employment of attorneys was given impetus not only by the increasingly complex nature of litigation, but also by changes in court practices. From 1318 the royal courts ceased to insist that defendants appear in person in cases brought under the assize of novel disseisin: such people were now allowed to appear by attorney.[76] Attorneys were increasingly employed in the central courts to enable landowners to prosecute disputes *in absentia* – thus, incidentally, providing the latter with the freedom to fight on another front at home.[77]

The major county offices such as sheriff, coroner, escheator and keeper of the peace also required a certain amount of legal knowledge and provided regular employment for county-based lawyers. Although the significance of his office was declining from the end of the thirteenth century, the sheriff was a financial, judicial and administrative agent upon whom much of the operation of central and local government depended. His judicial tasks included convening, presiding over and executing judgments of the county courts and the royal hundreds in his shire; as the recipient of royal writs, he was also responsible for executing summonses, distraints or attachments of defendants, and for implementing the subsequent penalties meted out by the king's justices.[78] Coroners heard confessions from approvers and abjurers of the realm, and held inquests concerning dead bodies. They kept a record of the pleas of the crown in the county court and were involved in appeals and the process of outlawry.[79] The escheator was mainly a fiscal officer appointed to investigate and safeguard royal feudal rights, but his post also required some expert knowledge of procedure: in particular, he held general inquests based on the articles of the escheator, which ranged widely over a series of administrative and legal issues.[80] Keepers of the peace were responsible for the pursuit and arrest of offenders; they held inquests, heard complaints of trespass, and took indictments for felonies. As justices, they were required to try cases brought before them at peace sessions. The same men who filled these regular posts in local government were also occasionally called upon to fulfil other judicial tasks as justices of assize, gaol delivery, and oyer and terminer. Clearly, the crown's jurisdictional and administrative expansion in the thirteenth and fourteenth centuries would not have been possible without the willingness of those with the legal skills and knowhow to participate in the many processes of local government.

It is hardly surprising to find, then, that those who began their careers working as attorneys not infrequently ended up being employed as royal judicial agents in the shires. John Heyford, one of the principal pleaders in the Warwickshire county court, acted as attorney in the court of common pleas 165 times between 1288 and 1306. After his retirement from this activity, he worked as a justice of gaol delivery in Warwickshire in 1312–15 and was a keeper of the county in 1332. Similarly, Robert Warwick, an attorney in the court of common pleas, where he appeared for a total of 168 clients between 1300 and 1304, was simultaneously undersheriff of Warwickshire and Leicestershire and later served as a gaol delivery justice.[81]

The provinces were not a domain inhabited solely by the county-based professional. Many who were destined to become, or were already, serjeants of the central courts practised in their 'home' territories, the areas of their birth and/or the regions where they possessed lands.[82] Robert Thorpe of Orton Waterville near Peterborough, who eventually became chief justice of common pleas in 1356, was steward of the abbot of Peterborough and a regular member of the assize and gaol delivery commissions for the Midland circuit, as well as being a keeper of the peace for Northamptonshire, before his appointment as serjeant at law in 1339 and king's serjeant in 1345.[83] Professional serjeants might also play a leading role in legal proceedings in the county court. Five or six members of this group were practising in the county courts of Warwickshire and Cambridgeshire in the early fourteenth century, and it is highly likely that this pattern was similar across the country.[84]

Both economic and legal development in the thirteenth and fourteenth centuries enhanced the importance of the provincial legal profession. The direct exploitation of manorial estates and the growing complexities of the common law encouraged ecclesiastical and lay landowners to appoint as their stewards men who had the necessary knowledge of legal formalities, tenures and pleas, and the ability to supervise domestic and agricultural affairs. In particular, the stewards of great ecclesiastical liberties had responsibilities comparable to those of the sheriff in terms of financial and judicial administration: under these circumstances, it is not surprising to find prominent lawyers such as John Shardlow, who became a serjeant at law in 1318, serving as steward of the abbey of Bury St Edmunds (1323–4).[85] Between the early years of Edward II and the later years of Edward III, there was a particularly significant change in the manner in which ecclesiastical institutions organised their legal representation: practitioners in the common law now usurped canon lawyers as the principal legal advisors of bishops, abbots and deans; and connections with the central courts were maintained not through the employment of attorneys on an ad hoc basis, but by permanently retaining serjeants at law to act as pleaders as and when need arose.[86]

Lay society also found it increasingly necessary to retain the services of lawyers. The growing practice from the mid-fourteenth century of making enfeoffments to use generated much legal manoeuvring and created a good deal of work for legal experts, both in formulating agreements and in undertaking the role of 'feoffee' or trustee.[87] The use of arbitration as an extra-judicial means of resolving disputes (a popular panacea for the rigidity of the common law, its expense and possible delays) was also shaped by the active involvement of lawyers, who often acted as arbitrators or architects of the settlement. Indeed, since it was recognised by disputing parties that, to be binding and lasting, an out-of-court resolution should be unchallengeable in the courts, it was obviously of particular importance that the resulting agreement should be professionally vetted.[88] Lawyers also became increasingly involved in commercial matters. From the later fourteenth century, when trading conditions were unfavourable, English merchants came to rely increasingly on legal devices to facilitate credit arrangements and thus keep their businesses afloat. The case of the grocer John Hall in 1396 reveals that a gift of goods and chattels (a deed usually employed for avoiding confiscation of property) could in turn be adapted to provide security for credit through the process known as 'bailment'.[89] (Bailment arises where one person is the owner of goods and another person has 'special property' or legal possession of them.) The services of a lawyer were crucial in such transactions, not only to ensure that the original owner retained his proper rights but also to protect his interests if a creditor subsequently tried to enforce the payment of a debt or loan involved in such a process.[90]

It is therefore evident that the legal profession as a whole became not only increasingly prominent, but also more varied in its experience, as the fourteenth century proceeded. To divide the lawyers into two groups – those who operated in the central courts and those who worked in the localities – would clearly be to oversimplify. Between these two poles there was an infinite variety of combinations: some practitioners were primarily employed in king's bench and common pleas, yet were engaged by networks of private clients in the provinces and frequently visited the counties on royal business; others were primarily county-based, but undertook work as attorneys in the central courts. The overlap between service in the provinces and at

Westminster is underlined by the fact that serjeants at law were often recipients of commissions of assize and gaol delivery and were frequently assigned to the circuit of counties where they had connections or estates. The inclusion of members of this group in the peace commissions as a regular convention after the 1340s is indicative not only of the widespread acceptance that expert lawyers were necessary to carry out the work of the commissions, but also of a deeper recognition of their relationship with local society.

The Fashioning of an Intellectual Domain

The possibility of exploiting the technicalities of the law not only led to the increasing need to employ those experienced in the language of the courts; it also fostered the growth of legal argument. Each writ corresponded to a particular form of action that could be invoked to provide remedy for a range of specific circumstances; each one had its own set of procedures to follow and distinct rules governing proof. Technical defects, factual errors and even simple mistakes in spelling or Latin grammar could all be exploited to challenge the validity of the writ. Defence lawyers could highlight discrepancies between the particulars of the writ and the plaintiff's oral statement of claim.[91] Special pleading between serjeants and justices even helped redefine certain areas of substantive law so as to make them fit more closely the circumstances of a changing society and thus (as in the case of the assize of novel disseisin) effectively remodelled many forms of action. Indeed, the elaborate courtroom discussions obvious in civil proceedings gave rise to many important developments in legal doctrine as lawyers endeavoured to achieve their clients' desired remedies.

Developments within the legal profession from the end of the thirteenth century therefore meant that law increasingly became an intellectual, as well as a procedural, process.[92] The result, not surprisingly, was the growth in the provision of legal education outlined in Chapter 2. Although we do not yet know enough about the organisation of legal education in the common law before the inns of court, or (in particular) for the vast majority of men of law not destined to become serjeants, there are certainly some tantalising hints of a quickening of activity from the time of Edward I. Some lecturers' texts and students' notes surviving from the late thirteenth and early fourteenth century indicate the availability of formal oral instruction, both in

London and elsewhere. Such education was provided not only at the standard suitable for a future serjeant but also at a more elementary level, as might befit a prospective attorney or legal adviser: the school of business operating in medieval Oxford, for example, provided a separate course in conveyancing. That there was increasing access to the system, or systems, of legal education and increasing transmission of that knowledge is suggested by the rapid growth during this period in the production of treatises relevant to the workings of the manorial as well as the royal courts and their inclusion in portable volumes also containing collections of statutes.

These developments in turn had a powerful influence on the way lawyers thought about the problems they encountered in interpreting and applying the law. The year books, which provided verbatim accounts of the pleadings on interesting cases in the central courts, were useful not only to students but also to more experienced practising lawyers. In particular, there seems to have been a growing awareness among the king's justices and the pleaders in the royal courts that they might refer to points of law argued in previous cases, and that this information could indeed be relevant, if not crucial, for the outcome of a case already in motion.[93] The desire for uniformity that underpinned this new interest in precedent and which found expression in the law reports from Edward I's reign onwards was further enhanced by the fact that some judges, such as William Herle (chief justice of common pleas, 1327–9, 1331–5), were known to have excellent memories and tried, as a matter of course, to cultivate consistency in their decisions. William Shareshull, a prominent figure in the courts under Edward III, was similarly known to support his arguments with references to specific cases. The longevity of tenure enjoyed by the justices of king's bench and common pleas obviously facilitated this strong sense of collective memory and respect for past practice. On the other hand, it should be pointed out that in the fourteenth century precedent was still merely a legal concept and an intellectual tendency, and not yet a procedural doctrine. Indeed, Shareshull himself felt strongly that 'precedent' should not override 'right'.[94]

Lawyers did not cease to have an effect on legal change simply because the royal courts were not directly involved. The cross-fertilisation of personnel observable between the central courts and the chancery and the presence of lawyers on the king's council (see Chapter 2) is particularly significant when considering the legal changes introduced through the provision of new chancery writs. As we have seen above, the actions of trespass on the case and assumpsit, which arguably pre-dated the Black Death but came into more general use from the 1350s, illustrate the capacity of the law to adapt to changing social and economic circumstances. Palmer argues that these writs were devised in the chancery in response to the pressures applied by suitors requiring new remedies at common law.[95] Without belittling the chancery's capacity for innovation, it is, however, unlikely that such significant changes would be effected without reference to current legal thought and direct input from royal lawyers – particularly since the office of the great seal was itself headed by common lawyers in the early 1340s and again in the 1370s. The chancery should be regarded not as an autonomous agency, but as part of an inter-related and co-operative system of judicial administration. We should thus recognise the likely influence of lawyers on a whole range of administrative and fiscal as well as merely judicial activities and thus acknowledge their significant contribution to the development of royal government at large.

Legislation

A considerable impetus for change, with consequences both for the administration of justice and for the role of the judicial profession as a whole, came through the new emphasis placed upon the statutory authority of parliament in the fourteenth century. As we have seen in Chapters 2 and 4, the fusion of its judicial and fiscal responsibilities during the first half of that century gave parliament a much greater prominence in the political life of the realm. While parliament continued to function as a court of appeal, as a tribunal for the resolution of difficult cases and as a venue for state trials, it was the grievances of the king's subjects articulated in the common petitions that came to be accorded an increasing amount of parliamentary time and attention. The adoption of the complaints and remedies outlined in the common petitions as a basis for the formulation of legislation in turn transformed the content and nature of the statutes. Under Edward I the term 'statute' had been understood to apply to a whole range of pronouncments issued on the authority of the king and his council. As early as 1318, however, it was declared that adjustments and alterations to the law of the land required full parliamentary deliberation; and by the 1350s there was formal acknowledgement that a parliamentary statute had the force to change the law. Such was the new acceptance of the legislative supremacy of parliament by the 1360s that it was possible for Chief Justice Thorpe to state that a statute, the highest form of lawmaking, was binding on everyone from the moment it was made, regardless of the need for proclamation.[96]

The process by which the crown responded to common petitions submitted in parliament therefore had three important consequences. In the first place, it created a rapidly expanding body of statutory legislation having binding authority throughout the realm and thus produced, in effect, a second tier of law to be enforced alongside the existing and evolving common law. Secondly, it altered the direction of legislative thinking and thus the purpose behind the formulation of statutes. Statutory legislation ceased to be merely judicial interpretations or declarations of the existing common law, as had been the case under Edward I. Now, it tended not just to provide confirmation of practices in existence but to bring many previously unregulated areas of human life and behaviour within the purview of government regulation. Modifications and additions to existing statutes were also used as a means of shaping administrative and procedural changes in the judicial system, as well as providing extra remedies and opening new possibilities for amending mischief in the common law.[97] Finally, there was a whole series of advantages for the legal profession. The legislative process itself required the input of those skilled in the law, whether in the formulation of petitions or in the preparation of statutes. The logistical challenge of enforcing new legislation also required the crown to consult with the experts in the judiciary and the courts. And the new body of written law created a further increase in litigation, thus generating yet more business for profit-minded lawyers.

Making and Presenting Parliamentary Petitions

Who composed the petitions presented in parliament during the fourteenth century? In the absence of direct evidence with which to answer such a question, one needs to consider the context in which petitions originated. Enough research has now been carried out on the *private* petitions submitted in the parliaments of this period to make it evident that provincial lawyers were crucial to the whole process: the composer of a petition not only needed to be able to write (usually in Anglo-Norman French), but also had to understand the appropriate formulae for such quasi-legal documents.[98] Since a number of early private petitions were expressed in the name of a shire or group of shires, and since these petitions were among some of the earliest to be recognised as of 'common' concern to the realm, it is particularly instructive to consider the role of the county court in the articulation of local grievances and the formulation of petitions. The variety of functions fulfilled by this court – judicial, administrative, political and social – made it a natural and regular point of contact between local landed society and provincial men of law. Furthermore, since it was in the county court that parliamentary representatives were selected for the shires, it is reasonable to suppose that it was in and around its monthly meetings that many of those who intended to send petitions to parliament sought out the legal services needed to set such a process in motion.[99]

The intimate connection between lawyers and petitioners is further suggested by the profile of those who were elected to serve in parliament as knights of the shire.[100] In the fourteenth century it was not uncommon for a career in public service to *begin*, rather than end, with election to parliament: so far as the county communities were concerned, the post of knight of the shire did not necessarily require either experience or status – particularly since the crown rarely tried to ensure that the shires returned 'real' knights. This makes it particularly difficult to discern what skills some of the more obscure members of parliament really did bring to their office. Nevertheless, by reading careers backwards, it becomes evident that at least a proportion of those elected to parliament in the earlier phases of their careers were indeed lawyers practising in the shires and/or the central courts. Robert Baynard, who was knight of the shire for Norfolk on various occasions between 1314 and 1326, was appointed a justice of the king's bench in 1327; Edmund Chelrey was returned five times as a member for Buckinghamshire (1339, 1341, 1344, 1346 and 1348) before his appointment as a serjeant at law in 1354; and Thomas Ingleby, who was created a serjeant at law in 1354 and appointed justice of king's bench in 1361, had earlier represented Yorkshire in 1348.[101] Furthermore, since there was nothing formally to prevent a serjeant at law from representing his native county in parliament, some quite prominent lawyers continued to sit as members of the commons. Robert Parving, for example, who became a serjeant at law in 1329, was knight of the shire for Cumberland in various parliaments from 1325 to 1331. Similarly, Thomas Moriz, who was styled *narrator* (pleader) in his will, was knight of the shire for Middlesex in 1358, 1360 and 1361; and William Lavenham, described as an 'apprentice of the bench' in 1343, may have been the member of parliament for Middlesex in 1348. Local legal professionals such as Ralph Bocking (knight of the shire for Suffolk, 1325–40 and 1343) and Constantine Mortimer (member for Norfolk, 1321–38) put in particularly long periods of unbroken service: they may be counted among the experienced members of the commons who brought a valuable sense of continuity and collective memory to parliamentary proceedings.[102]

In official terms, the tradition of electing lawyers working in the central courts to represent the counties in parliament came to an end in 1372, when a government ordinance directed that men of law pleading at Westminster were no longer eligible to serve as knights of the shire.[103] The intention, however, was not so much to discriminate against lawyers as to guard against abuses of the position of shire representative. It was felt that lawyers might be overly concerned with the interests of the private individuals whom they were already contracted to serve in court and would tend to forward the latter's interests (and their private petitions) in parliament at the expense of those of the whole community of the shire. (Interestingly, there was still nothing to prevent lawyers from being selected as representatives of the towns.) Analysis of the composition of parliaments during the 1380s and into the fifteenth century indicates that about 10 per cent of the commons were practising lawyers, with a greater proportion representing boroughs rather than shires. Under Henry V, this figure rose to 20 per cent or more, with a particularly significant increase in the number of lawyers returned as knights of the shire (possibly as a result of the involvement of the landed elite in the French war).[104] Whether these statistics provide some kind of base-line for the fourteenth century is, at present, unclear. In any case, they have to be taken very much as minimum proportions: the study from which they arise identifies only those men who were most obviously lawyers, draws a false distinction between 'professionals' and 'amateurs', and fails to recognise the degree of legal expertise within the gentry. Interestingly enough, the speakers of the commons during the late fourteenth and early fifteenth centuries were often lawyers. The first speaker, Sir Peter de la Mare, chosen at the Good Parliament of 1376, was steward of the earl of March; and Sir Thomas Hungerford, speaker in the parliament of 1377 was variously in the service of Queen Philippa, the Black Prince and the house of Lancaster.[105] Of particular relevance is Sir James Pickering, chief justice of Ireland in the late 1360s, who, despite the 1372 ordinance, was returned as a member for Westmorland for the four parliaments of 1377–82 and then for Yorkshire for the five parliaments of 1383–97 and acted as speaker in 1378 and 1383.[106]

Given that considerable numbers of lawyers were selected to represent shire and urban communities in parliament, it is reasonable to assume that, when the knights and burgesses began to formulate their own 'common' petitions in the 1320s and 1330s, the expert element within the parliamentary commons once again played a significant role in the process of defining and drafting the grievances forwarded in the name of the community of the realm. By identifying problems within the legal and administrative system, the common petitions provided the crown with a valuable measure of the practical applications of the law and the workings of the judiciary. And although (as we have seen in Chapter 4) the common petitions often tended simply to state the grievance, rather than propose a specific remedy, there were also issues, such as approvers' appeals, on which they included some very precise recommendations for reform – recommendations that once again help us to expose the legal experience and expertise of the knights and burgesses in parliament.[107]

It is no surprise, of course, that issues relating to law and order were among the most frequent preoccupations of the fourteenth-century common petitions. Too much emphasis has been placed, however, on the more 'political' aspects of this debate: historians have become preoccupied with the apparent hypocrisy of the knights and burgesses who championed right and justice in parliament but felt free to indulge in legal skulduggery, if not blatant criminality, as soon as they returned home.[108] To understand the motives of the parliamentary commons, we need to move away from those petitions that merely highlighted abuses of the system in a resigned and perhaps even disingenuous manner (for which, see Chapter 6), and to focus on those that actively questioned, criticised and confronted the system itself. The fact that shortcomings in judicial procedure were the subject of extended debates in successive parliaments strongly suggests that issues such as the efficient prosecution of notorious malefactors, or the safeguarding of the rights of the innocent, were espoused, and taken seriously, by the great majority of the king's subjects: certainly, the underlying thematic unity to some series of common petitions carries with it the implication that these and similar issues were sufficiently deep-rooted to survive successive political struggles and domestic upheavals.[109] Finally, the fact that this debate went beyond mere aspiration and took place within the context of specific procedural technicalities provides strong circumstantial evidence that the legal experts in the commons did indeed have a prominent part to play in articulating the agenda of fourteenth-century parliaments.

The Translation of Petitions into Statutes

The translation of petitions into legislation was a highly complex business. The process was undertaken in the council, the body of legal, administrative and political advisers that functioned (normally) in close consultation with the king. The legal impact of any new legislation needed to be considered before a statute could be promulgated; but the input of the justices of king's bench and common pleas, the king's serjeants and the barons of the exchequer was deemed of particular importance when a proposal touched upon the workings of the courts. The fact that most of the senior figures in the judiciary received personal summonses to parliament obviously strengthens the case for their influence upon its proceedings.[110] That said, it must also be admitted that much of the evidence linking the council with the legislative process is merely circumstantial. What follows is therefore not a general guide to the making of statute law in the fourteenth century but a more specific discussion of the role of the senior lawyers in the formulation and, in some cases, the subsequent enforcement of new legislation.

Enough has already been said in Chapter 2 to indicate that the justices of king's bench and common pleas, because they enjoyed a particular longevity of tenure, tended to be among the most experienced (and therefore, presumably, the more influential) of royal advisors in later medieval England. Under Edward I, when statute law did not arise directly or solely from deliberation in parliament and still represented a formalised version of the royal will, there is surely little doubt that the senior lawyers played a conspicuous role in the legislative process. Ralph Hengham, for instance, who was chief justice of king's bench from 1274 to 1289, is generally recognised as the architect and consolidator of Edward I's important law codes, such as the two great Statutes of Westminster (1275 and 1285).[111] Subsequently, during his time as chief justice of common pleas (1301–9), Hengham took issue with a pleader who attempted to offer an interpretation of one of the clauses of the 1285 statute: 'Do not gloss the statute; we understand it better than you do, for we made it.'[112] The statement, preserved and made famous through the year books, has been so often repeated that its force is now often lost: in fact, it provides us with direct and incontrovertible evidence of the creative contribution made by the senior judges to the legislation of Edward I.[113]

Under Edward III, the relationship between lawyers and legislation is rather more complex and ambiguous. The new procedural and political importance of the common petition, and the tendency of the crown to base the statutes on the communal grievances thus highlighted, has led some historians to view the legislation of the mid-fourteenth century as piecemeal and reactive, a 'series of repetitive and ill-digested statutes' that offer 'a marked contrast to the legislation of the first Edward'.[114] Enough additional research has been accomplished, however, to suggest that this perceived contrast is both oversimplified and exaggerated.[115] In particular, the careers and legislative contributions of Geoffrey Scrope (*c*.1280–1340) and William Shareshull (1289/90–1370) demonstrate the continued ability of senior figures within the judiciary to inform and direct the legislative process. Both men rose to the position of chief justice of king's bench, advocated distinct policies on the administration of justice, and were responsible for legislative flurries in the form of important and lasting statutes. It would be misleading to credit them with all the legal initiatives that emerged in their respective periods of ascendancy, but their vision and force of personality undoubtedly helped to devise, and implement, far-reaching legislative reforms in a period of rapid social, economic and political change.

Scrope regularly attended parliament after his appointment as a king's serjeant in 1315 and was high in the favour of Edward II's administration in 1322.[116] Surviving the upheavals of 1326–7, he became an influential member of Isabella and Mortimer's regime and remained a powerful force when Edward III himself took over the reins of government in 1330. Appointed a justice of common pleas in 1323, he was transferred to king's bench a year later, serving as chief justice from 1324 to 1338. Scrope's accelerated promotion has been attributed to a special aptitude for the business of government. He is now generally acknowledged to have been responsible for a good deal of the substance and wording of at least fifteen statutes promulgated during the productive legislative period lasting from 1327 until his death in 1340. His hand is particularly evident in the Statute of Northampton (1328), which consolidated and redefined many areas of criminal justice and its administration. Retaining his place on the council after his retirement from king's bench, Scrope was appointed to a special committee appointed to draft parliamentary legislation in 1340 (which also included the chief justice of common pleas, John Stonor, the chief baron of the exchequer, Robert Sadington, and Robert Parving, a newly appointed puisne justice of common pleas) and is likely to have made a significant contribution to the resulting statute, which revised a number of important aspects of legal process and administration.

Shareshull's influence upon government policy is evident at least from the 1330s.[117] His personal summons to the council and parliament began in September 1332, and his regular presence among the inner circle of advisors up to his brief fall from favour in 1340 may have enabled him to contribute his knowledge and experience to debates about legal administration in the later 1330s. Restored to favour in 1342, he was appointed a trier of private petitions from England in the parliament of 1343 and a trier of 'foreign' petitions (those from the king's subjects in Scotland, Ireland, Wales and lands outside the British Isles) in the following year. It is significant that the special committee of royal advisors appointed to provide answers to the common petitions of 1344 comprised the two chief justices, William Scot and John Stonor, and five other leading central court justices: Shareshull, Roger Hillary, Richard Willoughby, William Basset and Richard Kelshall. The statute of 1344 not only embodied the common petitions submitted to the parliament of that year, but established new judicial policy in the form of the quorum for determining felonies, created by 'afforcing' the peace commissions with men of law (see Chapter 3).

Shareshull may have had a hand in the Ordinance of Justices of 1346, and quite possibly played a part in formulating the Ordinance of Labourers of June 1349. It is more than likely that he devised the 'second ordinance', issued five months later, since it included the novel idea of subsidising taxpayers out of certain levies taken from those convicted under the labour legislation – a device that bore the trademark of one well versed in exploiting the profits of jurisdiction. It is surely no coincidence that, when Shareshull became chief justice of king's bench in 1350, the peace commissions included, for the first time, a quorum comprising the assize justices operating in their home counties, and gave powers to enforce the Ordinance of Labourers: these two innovations represent the merging together of important strands of legal thinking and judicial administration in which Shareshull had participated, if not played a leading part. Moreover, it was during Shareshull's eleven years as chief justice (1350–61) that some of the most significant statutes of the century were passed, implementing a range of ecclesiastical, economic and legal reforms that were, in their different ways, to have a profound effect upon contemporary society. The two major bouts of legislation, occurring in 1351–2 and 1361, will be discussed in more detail since there is convincing evidence that the legal experts on the king's council, including Shareshull and other senior judges, played an important role in drafting, if not indeed initiating, the key statutes of these years.

It is now reasonably well established that, although the statutes of the mid-fourteenth century increasingly addressed issues brought to the government's attention through common petitions, the legislative process itself was far from being dominated or controlled by the knights and burgesses and still left considerable room for manoeuvre by the crown and its legal advisors.[118] This is revealed particularly by the legislation of 1351–2. The two most important statutes of 1351 did not result from detailed common petitions outlining proposed forms of action. Indeed, there is some evidence that the lawyers on the council were already drawing up new legislation when this parliament opened, and thus effectively pre-empted the petitioning process.[119] The only petition connected with the new Statute of Labourers, for instance, simply recommended that the profits of the labour sessions be used to relieve the burden of a new direct tax granted in this assembly.[120] Similarly, the Statute of Provisors emerged from a common petition requesting remedial legislation on the issue of papal provisions (the practice of reserving to the pope certain forms of ecclesiastical patronage).[121] This had been a recurring grievance of the commons throughout the first half of the fourteenth century, and had recently been reinforced by the increasing concern and hostility of the bishops. Significantly, however, the solution offered by the statute of 1351 was angled to the king's advantage and, at least in the short term, enforced in his favour.[122] The implication is that these statutes were largely the work of the king's council; and since ecclesiastical patronage was challenged and enforced in the king's own courts, much of the technical input came, presumably, from the royal judges.

The parliament of 1352 is remembered chiefly for the promulgation of the Statute of Treasons (discussed in Chapters 2 and 4). Although the commons put in a long series of petitions whose specific grievances and recommendations were taken up in other legislation,[123] it is significant that the only mention of the issue of treason came in a petition requesting a definition (and an implied limitation) of the scope of this offence.[124] The resulting statute was therefore entirely the work of the council, and suggests considerable influence from the legal experts – not least because it was conditioned by, and to some extent reacted against, the more flexible and inclusive notions of treason that had been applied in the king's bench during the previous decade. It drew clear distinctions between treason and other acts of felony, and between high treason and petty treason. Shareshull was again probably a key contributor, though it also seems likely that he had assistance from his sole colleague in the court of king's bench, William Basset, and the chief justice of common pleas, John Stonor.[125] This exemplifies a point that may have been underplayed in this section: in the formulation of new statutes, there was undoubtedly discussion with and creative input from other men in senior judicial positions.

The parliament roll of 1361 has not survived, and it is therefore impossible to tell the precise content of the common petitions put forward on this occasion. The statute defining the nature and power of the justices of the peace does appear to have responded in a number of respects to ideas put forward by the commons since 1348, and may therefore have taken up and developed one or more of the petitions registered in this parliament.[126] Equally, however, the statute brought together in one enactment all the elements of previous policies pursued by Shareshull and his colleagues: the confirmation of determining powers for the justices of the peace; their jurisdiction over weights and measures; the application of more stringent laws against offending labourers; and sanctions against jurors who took bribes. In particular, the apparent desire to unify and rationalise the powers of the peace commissioners that had developed piecemeal over the previous quarter-century and more betrays the lawyer's preference and concern for the proper codification of statute law. It may even be that Shareshull's retirement from the king's bench later in 1361 was occasioned by this statute, representing as it did the ultimate fulfilment of the judicial policies that he had pursued in the course of his career in royal service.

Statutory legislation had its origins, then, in a number of sources and contexts. It arose out of the general grievances and particular problems articulated by the shire communities and channelled through common petitions in parliament. The need for definition and regulation arose from the growing complexity of society and the intrusion of the central government into areas hitherto unregulated by the state. Some legislation was designed to correct administrative anomalies. Equally, difficult cases in the royal courts could engender new statute law, replacing or complementing common law as appropriate. Indeed, statutory legislation could, on occasion, result from a single case, a private petition or a particular *cause célèbre*.[127] It has already been pointed out that the Spink case may have precipitated the 1352 legislation restricting the device whereby former villeins sought to prove their liberty in the royal courts. But there are a number of other significant examples of this phenomenon. A statute of 1351, which confirmed the legal rights of children of members of the peerage born outside the realm, named a series of individuals whose cases are likely to have provoked the legislation.[128] And the Statute of Rapes of 1382 arose directly from pressure applied for legal remedy by Sir Thomas West following the abduction of his daughter. In the latter case, moreover, there are signs of an over-hasty reaction: the statute was soon discovered to have failed in its intent, and was repealed in the subsequent parliament.[129]

In all of the various routes to the production of legislation, then, it is possible to argue that members of the legal profession played a distinctive role. In many instances, the original occasion or inspiration for legislation came from the provinces, sometimes articulated by county-based legal experts; but a proportion of men of law were also present in parliament as knights of the shire when the common petitions were discussed and formulated. Finally, the royal judges summoned in person to parliament and serving on the king's council applied their considerable judicial and administrative experience in the creative processes that generated the definitive form of royal statutes.

Statute law represented a powerful means of effecting legal change, and therefore has an important place in an 'evolutionary' interpretation of judicial development. It should not overshadow developments within the common law or minimise the effectiveness of non-statutory legal change. What makes statutory legislation particularly significant, however, is that the original reasons for the enactment of a piece of legislation, and its intended effects, were sometimes quite different from its actual impact and subsequent judicial interpretation.[130] The proclamation of a statute marked the end of one process (promulgation) and the beginning of another (enforcement); and the survival and utility of such legislation was determined at least in part by the degree to which the lawyers themselves, whether acting as attorneys, pleaders or judges, sought to interpret and apply the increasing body of law emanating from the king in parliament. The growth of statute law therefore contributed in turn to the intellectual development of the legal profession and provided one of the most conspicuous signs that the law was capable of generating change from within.

Conclusion

This chapter has demonstrated that there was a strong current of endogenously induced change directing or underpinning judicial evolution during the fourteenth century. This internal dynamic was powered by three key factors: 'consumer demand'; the growth of the judicial profession; and the advent of the statutory authority of parliament. Both private litigants and the crown fostered expansion in the range of remedies available and the adoption of procedural refinements designed to enhance the operation of existing mechanisms and extend public access to the courts.

The accessibility of royal justice was itself a feature of this internal momentum: the opportunity to initiate lawsuits represented an advantage which potential litigants sought to acquire and preserve by whatever means open to them. The stimulation of new growth areas within the law was in part the result of an appropriation by the king's courts of the litigation (particularly that involving negligence, consequential injury or breach of contract) which had previously been entertained mainly in the customary courts and for which new forms of writ were fashioned or adapted and made available in chancery. There was also an increase in the cases remediable before, and/or accepted by, the justices of the peace at their regular quarter sessions. Another important element underscoring the demand for justice was the comparative 'user-friendliness' of the legal system. This was achieved not only through procedural changes aimed at enhancing speed and effectiveness, but also through the growing practice of pursuing difficult litigation through professional attorneys and pleaders.

Demand for legal remedies produced an exponential rise in the number of legal practitioners and the consequent employment of men of law, both in the regions and at Westminster. The complexities of litigation and the need for expert knowledge and assistance in turn inspired legal thought and doctrine, fuelled legal education and helped to establish the practice of law as a profession that was indispensable to society – even if not always respected by it. Indeed, the services of lawyers became crucial for people engaged in many walks of life, be they landowners, ecclesiastics, merchants or villeins, and their influence was discernible across a whole range of business – administrative and fiscal as well as purely judicial. This influence was even more apparent in the formulation of private petitions, in the discussion of common grievances and legislation in the county court and parliament, in the preparation of statutes, and in the interpretation and application of statutory provisions in the courts. The increased regulation of daily life through a new body of written law itself generated much business for lawyers as clients sought clarification and advice, and brought the need for almanacs and statute books to provide precise references in court.

As we have emphasised throughout this book, it is not enough to judge judicial evolution in terms of a clear division (or implied tension) between exogenous and endogenous factors. Setting the above conclusions in conjunction with the preliminary findings of Chapter 4 enables us to provide a properly rounded assessment of the various influences at work upon the judicial system in the fourteenth century. This gives rise to three general points which may be outlined briefly before we finally proceed to an analysis of contemporary attitudes in Chapter 6.

The first conclusion concerns the impact of exogenous influences experienced as famine, plague, war and popular revolt. The natural disasters and political crises of the fourteenth century represent a series of external 'shocks' which inevitably had considerable impact upon the society that suffered and survived them. Yet it is arguable that historians have reacted more strongly to such dramatic events than did late medieval society itself. It is only comparatively recently that scholarship has begun to move away from a sensationalist attitude to the demographic and social history of this period and adopted a more cautious and balanced approach to the subject. In view of recent attempts to argue that war and plague did indeed represent the primary determinants in a 'transformation' of the judicial structure and legal culture of the late Middle Ages, the present study has argued the case not simply for 'evolutionary' change but also for the remarkable *resilience* of the system. Royal justice certainly adapted to new conditions and situations brought about by external influences, but was rarely thrown off course by them: arguably, indeed, its most striking feature was its capacity to *absorb* such shocks. This, in turn, made the whole process of judicial evolution much less regular and complete than has often been assumed: the second half of the fourteenth century, rather than witnessing a self-contained 'transformation' of the law, simply marked another stage in an on-going process of judicial experimentation – a process whose end-product, furthermore, was often a good deal less clear to contemporaries than it is to modern historians.

Secondly, the emergence of parliament as the primary political and legislative institution in the kingdom had a powerful influence upon the evolution of justice. By the later fourteenth century, parliament had developed two distinct roles with regard to the judicial system. Its emergent legislative authority had created a substantial and substantive body of statute law that appreciably widened the spectrum of offences and actions encompassed by the king's courts. The statutes, which were automatically binding throughout the realm, incorporated a broad range of remedial measures initiated and advanced variously by crown and community, and were intended to clarify, rationalise and supplement existing common law procedure. At the same time, however, parliament's role as the mouthpiece of the political community also gave it the opportunity to express the opinions of the king's subjects on the degree to which such legislation ought to be enforced and the perceived effectiveness of the resulting campaigns of enforcement. Although it retained (and even extended) some of the judicial authority it had itself enjoyed in the later thirteenth century, parliament's relationship with the law had therefore become primarily political, and its views on the judicial system increasingly represented a kind of litmus test of the general success or failure of the prevailing regime. The influence of such 'public opinion' upon judicial evolution was greater than ever before and made an enduring impression.

While the legislative and political authority of parliament was undoubtedly in part a product of the new political dynamics of the fourteenth-century 'war state', neither the opinions expressed by the commons nor the government policies thus influenced can in fact be said to have been profoundly altered by the natural and man-made disasters of the period. This point has special relevance to a discussion of justice, since there were certain widely held notions about the integrity and accessibility of the system that were not ultimately overturned by the supposed new cultural influences and political values emerging after the plague. This brings us to our final argument: that the judicial system existed in a symbiotic relationship with the society it served – a society, furthermore, that was defined in an inclusive manner. Precisely because access to royal justice had been offered to a wider range of people in the later thirteenth and early fourteenth centuries, so any attempts to restrict that access again in the aftermath of the Black Death proved both controversial and unworkable – even if it took organised resistance in the revolt of 1381 to make the point effectively. The notion that the judicial system conspired with the landed elite in a class war against the peasantry is the product of a historiography (in both the Marxist and the liberal traditions) that concentrates solely on one aspect of post-plague regulation – the labour laws – to the manifest neglect of the multiplicity of judicial remedies and procedures that had become, and remained, open to all the king's free (and even some of his unfree) subjects. To argue that royal justice was ultimately a consensual system reliant on high rates of participation by a wide variety of people acting as judges, jurors and litigants, is to offer a new emphasis on the essentially organic development and consequent continued viability of the state's response to the challenge of law-keeping in later medieval England.

6
CONCLUSION: ATTITUDES TO JUSTICE

This book argues that English royal justice evolved in the course of the fourteenth century to meet the changing needs of government and society. The resulting developments were shaped partly by the exogenous shocks of war, natural disaster and constitutional crisis, but also grew endogenously, from within, as the judicial system adapted to reflect longer-term changes in the society that it served. In Chapter 1, we repudiated the notion that evolution implies a process of advancement, and in subsequent chapters we have demonstrated how the primarily reactive nature of medieval law makes it unnecessary, as well as improbable, to say that the judicial system was any 'better' in 1390 than it had been in 1290. What we have not so far addressed is the question of why so many contemporaries seem to have thought that it had become 'worse' by the end of the fourteenth century. By way of conclusion to this study, the present chapter seeks to explore that issue by focusing on attitudes to justice. It begins with an analysis of the ways in which people spoke of, and complained about, the law in fourteenth-century England, and ends with a broader discussion of the nature, meaning and implications of these traditions of criticism.

Discourses on Justice

As we indicated in Chapter 4, the problems and limitations of -

quantitative analysis are, to some extent, resolved by adopting a qualitative approach to the evidence. This in turn significantly extends the range of that evidence by drawing us into a body of rhetorical material ranging from academic treatises through parliamentary petitions and statutes to literary texts. Legal historians have long acknowledged these sources, and used them in a number of ways: to provide amusing anecdotal evidence of medieval lawlessness; to illustrate collective concerns about the inadequacies of royal justice; and to argue that such social comment had a serious political (and even, in some cases, revolutionary) purpose. The present discussion attempts to re-examine this material, to assess its influence on the political culture of the fourteenth century and, more specifically, to determine what it may tell us about the supposed corruption and exclusivity of late medieval royal justice. For this purpose, we have chosen to organise the material according to its perceived function or intent and have identified four reasonably discrete categories of discourse: the didactic, which attempted to draw a moral or teach a lesson; the remedial, which sought or applied a resolution to a problem; the satirical, which made fun of the system; and the polemical, which aimed to challenge received opinions and offer real alternatives.[1] We shall treat each of these categories in turn before drawing some conclusions about political perceptions of royal justice in the fourteenth century.

Didactic Discourses

Didactic discourses on the theme of justice are found in a number of established medieval genres.[2] The most obvious are the formal treatises on government and law studied in the universities and (latterly) in the inns of court. More influential in framing the attitudes of the secular political elite, however, were the 'mirrors for princes' theoretically composed for, and often dedicated to, particular rulers. These were supplemented by historical, mythological and prophetic texts which aimed to present prototypes of good and bad kingship. The other important material relevant here comes from late medieval theological tracts and sermons – which, not surprisingly, often commented on contemporary social and political themes in working out their Christian moral.

Despite the diversity of the material, the basic message of the didactic discourses on law was remarkably unified. Justice was perceived to reside in the person of the king, whose primary function was to guarantee the rights of all his subjects, rich and poor alike, to supervise his judicial agents in order that they acted scrupulously, to temper the severity of the law through the prerogative of mercy, and to exercise discretion in reviewing established laws and making new ones. Such power, it was argued, must be exercised with due regard for the common good and not for the personal benefit of the ruler: indeed, to abuse the law for his own gain was the hallmark of the tyrant. This moral dimension also placed emphasis on the inner worth of the ruler: to govern the realm justly, a king must first learn how to control his passions and order his own mind. The abundance or lack of justice therefore became a measure of the king's own character and fitness to rule.

It is easy to dismiss these stock ideas: they were repeated so frequently between the twelfth and the fifteenth centuries that we may be tempted to consider them as tediously banal and increasingly irrelevant to the realities of government. This, however, is to forget their dignity as eternal truths and their consequent importance in the medieval conception of the constitution: the equation between the king and the law was immutable and non-negotiable. Furthermore, the models and lessons that percolated down from the academic and historical commentaries on kingship applied not just to kings but to their ministers and agents. Because they acted under royal commission, the justices were bound in theory to the same standards of integrity and honour as the king himself. This did much to spawn a parallel didactic literature specifically addressing the qualifications and qualities that made a good judge. By the end of the fourteenth century the mirrors for princes genre was being extended by the likes of John Gower (specifically in his Latin *Vox clamantis* and English *Confessio amantis*) and the anonymous author of the manuscript known as Digby 102 (c.1400) to present a whole series of role models to the governing classes in general.[3] The fact that certain members of the legal establishment were periodically accused of failing to live up to these high ideals is in itself testimony to the norms that had been inculcated in the ruling elite through such didactic discourses.

Remedial Discourses

'Remedial discourses' are here defined as those which sought, and applied, a judicial or legislative solution for the wrongs committed against the king's subjects. They are found in sources associated with the workings of the courts: the plaints and indictments registered before the king's justices; the private and common petitions heard before the council and in parliament; and the writs, judicial commissions and statutes promulgated by the crown in response to such requests. It is all too easy to take such material at its face value and use the often highly coloured comments on contemporary justice as evidence of the supposed deterioration in law and order during the later Middle Ages. It is not until we appreciate the form and purpose of these texts, however, that we can really begin to assess the reliability of their testimony.

The problem of interpretation emerges even with those documents that were ostensibly closest to 'real' events: the plaints, indictments and original writs that set out the plaintiff's grievances and request for justice. The courts were very exacting in their use of language, and accusations needed to conform to certain conventions if they were to be admitted and heard (see Chapter 5). Historians have long appreciated that the details of individual cases had therefore to be massaged to fit the requirements of legal process, and that some of the reality was often lost in the records of the courts.[4] We have already noticed in Chapter 2 how the crown's original notion that admissible trespasses had to have been committed *vi et armis* (by force and arms) created a whole fiction of violent crime in the late thirteenth and fourteenth centuries. Similarly, it was common form for plaints and indictments to apply adverbs – 'traitorously', 'feloniously' and so on – to descriptions of criminal action as a means of positioning the offence in relation to the common law.[5] The seriousness of the crime could also be enhanced by specific allegations: homicide was considered a heinous offence if it was perpetrated with malice aforethought, by ambush, or at dead of night.[6] The result was that many apparently colourful allegations of crime were actually little more than lists of standard formulae strung together to ensure that the crown took the action desired by the plaintiff. It is particularly important to recognise the imperfect nature of the truth contained in such accusations, since so many historians of crime have used the record of the plaintiff and the jury of presentment as if these were infallible accounts of real events. There was always the defendant's side of the story, even if it was never heard in court or recorded for the benefit of posterity.

A very similar point about bias emerges when we examine the debates on justice that took place in fourteenth-century parliaments.

Each side had its own role to play – the commons in articulating grievances, the crown in remedying them – and both sought to justify their position by reference to the current defects in the law. For the king, moreover, the remedial discourse offered particular advantages: by focusing on what had formerly been wrong with the system, he could present himself as a radical reformer who had guaranteed justice for his subjects. Edward I set the trend in this respect: the Statute of Winchester of 1285 opened with a general denunciation of the supposed increase in 'robberies, murders, burnings and thefts' and then went on to lay down new structures for the better preservation of the king's peace.[7] Over the following century these preambles became longer and more elaborate.[8] The purpose of such rhetoric was obviously political. It should be remembered that statutes, ordinances and other major policy decisions by the crown were proclaimed in the localities by the sheriffs and their agents. (They were also, incidentally, regularly cited in the preambles to letters patent appointing the justices of the peace).[9] Recent research has emphasised how thoroughly the task of proclamation was fulfilled and how important it was in disseminating information about central government to provincial society.[10] The crown was not blind to the public relations opportunities thus provided, and on some occasions clearly found it difficult to resist the temptation of playing to the gallery: Richard II's ordinance against livery of 1390 is a case in point. To take the preambles to royal legislation at their face value is therefore quite unnecessary: the device of exaggerating current evils in order to advertise future solutions is a political technique by no means confined to the Middle Ages.

There is a further dimension to the remedial discourse, however, which suggests that these and similar statutory promises had the effect of raising public consciousness and, in turn, of increasing expectations. There was a growing tendency in the fourteenth century for the king's subjects to cite the statutes back at the crown and put pressure on the government and the courts for more consistent enforcement.[11] The examples of this phenomenon are not confined to the members of the political elite and to collective grievances articulated by the peers, the parliamentary commons or the county communities.[12] They could also be made by private parties complaining of the crown's failure to abide by its own legislation on issues such as the empanelling of jurors, pardons, commissions of oyer and terminer, or the king's legally enforceable rights of ecclesiastical patronage.[13] Most striking of all, perhaps, is the evidence that defendants before the courts – or, rather, the lawyers representing them – were also capable of quoting the statutes at the judges in order to secure procedural advantage. A statute of 1352, for example, laid down that the king's justices could not proceed to exigend and outlawry in cases of felony until two writs of *capias* had been sent to the relevant sheriff and returned to the effect that the defendant could not be found. In reality, the number of such writs issued in any given process varied widely.[14] Nevertheless, this statute became a valuable means of challenging over-zealous judges, and in the following years several appeals were heard, and upheld, on the grounds that the king's courts had failed to observe the details of procedure laid down by this legislation.[15] The attitude in such cases was, of course, just as self-serving as that of the royal propaganda contained in the preambles to the statutes. The significance of such evidence therefore lies not in any crude measure it provides of the enforcement of statute law, but in what it reveals about the widespread reception of remedial discourses by the king's subjects in general, and by the emergent legal profession in particular.[16]

Satirical Discourses

Some of the most articulate expressions of concern for the workings of the legal system in the fourteenth century are found in the imaginative literature of the period. There has been a tendency in recent scholarship to draw this rather disparate body of material closer together and see it as part of a discernible trend, even a recognised genre, in the literary history of the later Middle Ages. Differences of language, for example, are no longer seen necessarily to represent different audiences (Latin for the clergy, French for the aristocracy, the vernacular for the lesser gentry, merchants and affluent peasants), but to indicate the relatively high degree of bi- and even tri-lingualism at many levels in this society. Nor is the inequality between numbers of extant manuscripts now taken as particularly significant: an early fourteenth-century poem surviving in a single manuscript may not have had a wide audience (indeed, it may never have been intended for circulation at all), but it can, in its way, tell us just as much about contemporary attitudes as can those widely disseminated texts written in the later part of the century, Langland's *Piers Plowman* and Chaucer's *Canterbury Tales*. Most significantly for our present purposes, there is a tendency to imbue much, if not all, of this literature with a serious purpose, as if its authors took a consciously political approach to their work and wished to promote a reformist or even revolutionary message. As a result, 'political songs' (as they were deceptively labelled in the nineteenth century) are now often dignified with collective titles such as 'poems of social protest' or 'the literature of social unrest'.[17]

To understand what these texts have to say about the royal judicial system, it is appropriate to draw something of a distinction between the literary material that merely aimed to satirise the law (discussed here) and that which sought more obviously to challenge it (discussed in the next section as 'polemical discourse'). On close inspection, a good deal of the extant literature of this period falls, in fact, into the first of these categories. The briefest review of the likely audience indicates why this was so. Most of the relevant manuscripts were owned by what one might call members of the establishment: monastic and secular clergy, nobles and gentry, professionals (including lawyers) and merchants. With the possible exception of some of the clergy, this was not an audience instinctively attuned to a radical political agenda. It was, however, perfectly capable of laughing at itself. Medieval satire was often meant as entertainment for the very social groups that it portrayed, rather than to expose their fallibilities to their superiors or inferiors.[18] Such a 'satire of the status quo' is nicely demonstrated by two of the important themes of the fourteenth century that were of immediate relevance to the debate on justice: venality and outlawry.

The theme of venality is, not surprisingly, almost as old as the law itself.[19] It first found its medieval expression in reference to the church, but from the twelfth century, and particularly from the early fourteenth, it was also applied to the workings of the royal courts in England. Some of the more ambitious of the venality satires – particularly the vernacular poems *The Simonie* and *Piers Plowman* – probably have a social message, if not a direct political purpose, and are discussed below. Much of the rest of the literature, however, is entirely predictable in what it says about the corruptibility of judges, lawyers and jurors, offers no suggestions as to how the system might be changed, and simply acknowledges that this, regrettably, is the way that things are in the world.

That is not to say that the satirical mood did not vary. Depending on the author and/or the intended audience, it could fluctuate from the mildly ironic to the wildly vituperative. The Latin poem *Beati qui esuriunt*, dating from the start of our period, is a bitter attack on the power of money in the courts; in common with *The Simonie* (the oldest version of which dates from the 1330s) and other texts on the subject, it extends its range beyond the judges to take in the corrupt activities of other royal agents in the shires, particularly the sheriffs and bailiffs of liberties who played such as important supporting role in the business of the courts.[20] Some of the vernacular literature of the second half of the fourteenth century, by contrast, is more measured in tone, no doubt reflecting its courtly or establishment audience. *Winner and Waster*, written in, or shortly after, the 1350s, presents the royal judges (and Sir William Shareshull in particular) in a seemingly straightforward manner as the vigorous upholders of the law. Its hints of criticism are altogether more subtle: the green device displayed on the lawyers' banner seems to be a reference to the summonses of the green wax, referred to in other fourteenth-century verse, by which the exchequer levied the profits of judicial sessions: the poet thus aims a subtle swipe at the profit-minded motives of royal justice.[21] Chaucer at first appears similarly guarded in his depiction of the Serjeant at Law in the prologue to the *Canterbury Tales*, emphasising as he does the professional expertise and dignified bearing of this member of the pilgrimage party. It is only when one looks behind this veneer that the satirical element becomes clearer: the lawyer emerges as a self-important, self-made man who has used the profits from his exorbitant fees to purchase landed property and seek out a place in the social elite.[22] Nevertheless, whether the mood is highly critical or relatively good-natured, these satirical discourses are united in their tacit acceptance of the status quo and their implication that the only practical way forward is to work with, rather than against, the system. That, of course, as we have suggested, says as much about the authors and audiences of such texts as it does about the true condition of royal justice.

The second relevant theme that emerges in the satirical literature of the fourteenth century is outlawry.[23] It is particularly significant because it opens up the possibility of a wider audience stretching beyond the elite and the professional classes and into the upper reaches of the peasantry. Two distinct but overlapping traditions appear to have been at work in the later Middle Ages. First, there were the outlaw romances, represented by the thirteenth-century tales of *Fulk Fitzwarin* and *Eustace the Monk* and the fourteenth-century *Tale of Gamelyn*: these conformed to the conventions of courtly literature and had their origins in the entertainments performed by minstrels in aristocratic households. Secondly, there were continuing or new oral traditions represented by the 'ballads' of Robin Hood. Although the earliest reference to 'rymes' of Robin Hood appears only in the B-text of *Piers Plowman* (*c.* 1377), it seems evident that oral ballads or tales of Robin Hood circulated reasonably widely throughout the fourteenth (if not indeed in the thirteenth) century, and there is a *prima facie* case for arguing that their audience was somewhat broader than that for the romance tradition. Even though the Robin Hood legends may have undergone some gentrification when they were committed to writing in the fifteenth century, it therefore remains remarkable that the two traditions should have demonstrated such similarity in their treatment of royal justice.

The outlaw was an aberration in medieval society: as one who had escaped the clutches of the king's judges, he represented the failure of the judicial system and a constant potential threat to public order. In theory, he was an outcast, without rights, who could be hunted down and killed with impunity. (In practice, it must be said, the penalties of outlawry were a good deal less severe.)[24] To turn the outlaw into a hero was therefore to turn society on its head – a familiar enough convention in medieval culture. In this inverted world, the outlaw himself became the source of justice, and dispensed it either in the king's court itself, where he overthrew the bench and presided in person over the trial of corrupt justices and sheriffs (as in the *Tale of Gamelyn*) or in the form of rough justice through what *Piers Plowman*, referring back to the criminal gangs of the 1320s and 1330s, called 'Folville's laws'.[25] The greenwood, the resort of the outlaw, therefore ceases to be an archaic world and takes on a utopian quality as a place of true or natural justice.

These ideas are nicely encapsulated in the so-called *Outlaw's song of trailbaston*, an Anglo-Norman French poem satirising the trailbaston inquiries of 1305.[26] The hero, who has fought in the king's wars, finds himself the victim of a malicious complaint brought before the justices by his servant, as a result of which he flees to the 'forest of Belregard'. Here he bemoans his fate and, recalling the bastons (sticks) that gave the commissions their nickname, fantasises about taking his vengeance on the justices.

> I will teach them the game of trailbaston
> And I will break their back and their rump,
> Their arms and their legs; it would be right;
> I will cut out their tongue and their mouth into the bargain.

Such direct criticism of a specific royal judicial initiative may read as a damning indictment of the structure of royal justice. But the outlaw literature cannot, in general terms, be read as a reformist agenda. The heroes are usually not criminals, but innocent victims of an iniquitous system: like the anonymous subject of the *Song of trailbaston*, both Gamelyn and (at least implicitly) Robin Hood take to the woods because they have no hope of demonstrating their innocence before a corrupt court. Their own subsequent 'criminal' campaigns of robbery and intimidation are not indiscriminate, but targeted: first against the wealthy clergy (it is striking that secular landlords are rarely singled out for such treatment); and secondly against corrupt officials of the crown (the packed court sent out to try Gamelyn, and the sheriff of Nottingham in the Robin Hood ballads). Finally, the stories are often resolved by royal intervention: the king is made aware of the wrongs that have been done to the outlaws, pardons them and, in the *Tale of Gamelyn*, goes on to promote them to the very highest levels of the judicial system. In fact, then, the outlaw literature tends to conclude with a resounding restoration of the status quo.

To the modern reader, the most difficult element to accommodate in this process of conciliation is probably the direct action taken by the outlaw bands to achieve their ends. It is now appreciated, however, that medieval society not only tolerated violence but actively endorsed its use as a means of enforcing societal obligations.[27] The puffed-up clergy and money-minded justices get no more than they deserve at the hands of the outlaws, and 'Folville's laws', far from confounding the judicial system, ultimately help to restore its authority. The final appeal to the king's grace in this literary tradition is particularly significant, since it legitimises the processes by which the reconciliation is effected and recognises the active role of the monarchy in guaranteeing right for all. What is most striking about the outlaw literature, then, is the absence of a serious political position: attempts to interpret the Robin Hood ballads as promoting a more radical agenda have faltered for lack of evidence.[28] From the point of view of the judicial system, indeed, the outlaw romances and ballads do little more than expand upon the existing theme of venality. Even though they offer some form of resolution, it is ultimately only an idealised and escapist one.[29]

Conclusion: Attitudes to Justice

Polemical Discourses

The polemical discourse upon justice is here defined as one that adopts a notably controversial stance and, in particular, has a reformist or revolutionary intent. Clearly, the boundaries between this category and those outlined above is blurred: didactic, remedial and satirical discourses can all contain elements of polemic. The difference is to do partly with genre and partly with audience. Remedial discourses were 'official' in the sense that they conformed to the requirements and traditions of governmental record; they were also 'public' in that they represented the business of the courts and the basis of communication between the crown and its subjects in the provinces. Polemical discourses, by contrast, were unofficial and unrestrained by the conventions of constitutional language (they are often, in fact, found in works of imaginative and satirical literature). Above all, they differ from satirical discourses in the sense that they provide a more far-reaching denunciation of contemporary evils (including the judicial system) and, in most cases, offer specific solutions to those ills.

The majority of such texts come from the later part of the fourteenth century. The central one is undoubtedly the Middle English alliterative poem *Piers Plowman*, originally composed in the 1360s (the so-called A-text), greatly enlarged in *c.* 1377 (the B-text) and further revised probably in the mid-1380s (the C-text). All three versions seem to have been the work of the same man, William Langland, a clerk in minor orders, originally from Shropshire, who lived in London for at least some of his career. Langland's is essentially the worm's-eye view: he was close enough to the centres of civic and royal government in the London Guildhall and Westminster Palace to be aware of the major political issues of the day, and he had some understanding of the technicalities of the law; but he had little comprehension of the dynamics of high politics and retained a rather naive belief in the power of the king to safeguard justice and good governance.[30] Not surprisingly, his treatment of such subjects is significantly different from many of the 'establishment' authors of satirical texts.

That difference is particularly apparent in his treatment of venality. Langland was reasonably well read in the literature of his day: it would seem, for example, that he had digested both *The Simonie* and *Winner and Waster*.[31] His own development of the theme of corruption is, however, altogether more ambitious than anything that had gone before. He exemplifies venality in the female character of Meed (the word means payment, reward or bribe), who is brought before the king in London. At first, she is successful in buying friends at court, especially among the judges and lawyers. Finally, however, she is overturned; the king decides to rule by the counsel of Reason and Conscience, and Meed is abandoned to her (unspecified) fate. Significantly, Langland excludes the corrupt men of law from the moral majority who comply with the king's new commitment to justice.[32] It is a mistake to interpret all episodes in *Piers Plowman* as mere parodies of contemporary events. But the possible parallels between Lady Meed and Edward III's mistress, Alice Perrers, are well charted, and suggest that this interlude had particular resonances for its fourteenth-century audience. Although the lawyers are not punished for their offences, their implicit refusal to join the ranks of the righteous may therefore have been read as a reference to those senior judges, such as William Thorpe and Henry Green, who had supposedly failed to live up to the standards of behaviour appropriate to their office (see Chapter 2).

This is not to say that Langland himself had an explicitly revolutionary message. Like *The Simonie*, *Piers Plowman* recognises that the quality of the judicial system rests on the king's commitment to good counsel. Furthermore, as is well known, Langland made certain alterations in the C-text specifically to counter any suggestion that his work had helped to incite insurrection during the Peasants' Revolt of 1381: his emphasis on obedience ultimately forced him to accept the binding force and legitimacy even of the labour laws.[33] This, however, is precisely where authorial intention and audience response may have deviated. For just as they appear to have appropriated certain of John Wyclif's radical theological ideas for their own political purpose, so also did the rebel captains of 1381 consciously or subconsciously demonstrate their familiarity with Langland's work and mobilise it particularly in their attack on corruption in high places.[34]

The chronicles of Henry Knighton and Thomas Walsingham preserve a series of enigmatic letters from the leaders of the 1381 rising which invoke both the name and some of the themes of *Piers Plowman*. For present purposes, the most significant of these letters is that of 'Jack Trueman':

> Jack Trueman would have you to know that falseness and guile have reigned too long, and that truth has been put under a lock, and falseness reigns in every flock. No man may come to truth, unless he sing *si dedero*. Speak, spend and speed, says John of Bamthon, and

therefore sin spreads like the wild flood, true love, that was good, is fled, and the clergy work us woe for gain.[35]

It is now established that this text drew on vernacular verses already circulating in later fourteenth-century England; it has also been argued that much of its additional vocabulary and metaphorical apparatus derived from Langland's Meed episode.[36] This in turn helps to give new relevance to some of its more obscure references. 'John of Bamthon' is presumably John Bampton, the putative leader of the judicial commission set up to investigate the levying of the poll tax in Essex, whose controversial sessions were recognised to have triggered the first outbreaks of disorder in 1381.[37] His motto, 'Speak, spend and speed', is itself a comment on venality: speech (complaint, or perhaps courtroom pleading) produces the desired outcome (speed) only when a payment is made (spend).[38] 'Truth', or justice, is available only *si dedero*, meaning literally 'if I will give' (that is, give a payment or bribe). This Latin tag is found in older Latin and Middle English satirical verses and in a wide range of literary texts of the late fourteenth and fifteenth centuries.[39] In the light of our discussion in Chapter 4 of the attacks on judges and lawyers during the revolt of 1381, it is reasonable to argue that Langland's treatment of venality satire within a poem that explicitly promoted the integrity of the common ploughman had indeed been taken as an agenda for direct political action by radical demagogues such as John Ball and Wat Tyler.

Langland's work is of additional interest in that it spawned a further series of polemical poems written in the late fourteenth and early fifteenth centuries (the so-called 'Piers Plowman Tradition').[40] The most radical of these, *Pierce the Ploughman's Crede*, is of interest for its theological position, and need not detain us here. Much more important from the perspective of justice are *Richard the Redeless*, written shortly after the deposition of Richard II, and *Mum and the Sothsegger*, probably composed towards the end of the first decade of the fifteenth century. These two poems survive in single (and incomplete) copies, so that, unlike *Piers Plowman*, they cannot be said to have enjoyed wide readership or direct political influence. They do, however, represent the maturing of a number of the traditions of political and social comment encountered above. *Richard the Redeless* is couched in the 'mirrors for princes' tradition, though its explicit radicalism makes it highly doubtful that it was intended for royal consumption. *Mum and the Sothsegger*, indeed, shows a keen awareness of the subversive potential of polemic, and seeks to defend its place in legitimate constitutional debate. This greater self-consciousness demonstrates the dynamic role that such discourses claimed to play in public affairs: 'In the absence of any strong institutionalised corrective, reforming poetry enters the political arena.'[41]

This new confidence is indeed apparent in the treatment of royal justice. The author of *Richard the Redeless* is particularly concerned with the contemporary debate on liveries and with Richard II's policy of retaining. He argues that badges should be distributed only to those worthy of them, including members of the judiciary: the justice who rejects the interference of meed in his efforts 'to try a truth between two sides' deserves to wear the 'sign' of royal favour.[42] These issues had keen political relevance in the years around 1399: they stand as a commentary on Richard's short-lived legislation on liveries, revived in substance by Henry IV in 1399, and on both kings' controversial policy of building up an independent royal affinity in the shires. They may also have something to say about changes in the system of rewarding royal judicial agents: the decision after 1388–90 to pay expenses to justices of the peace; the major increase in the annuities paid by the crown to the personnel of the central courts in 1389; and the subsequent withdrawal of the senior judges from the affinities of private lords. The focus of complaint is thus considerably more specific, and the historical context more precise, than in much other satirical and polemical discourse of the period.

The sustained criticism of judicial corruption found in both *Richard the Redeless* and *Mum and the Sothsegger* may, of course, imply nothing more than a general disillusionment at the apparent failure of all efforts to reform the system. But the picture of the impartial, incorruptible judge could also have represented more than an unattainable ideal. Although nothing direct is known of the authors, or the target audience, of these poems, both of them betray a relatively sophisticated knowledge of judicial procedure and political structures (more so, indeed, than is often found in *Piers Plowman*). They would therefore appear to represent a re-appropriation of Langland's polemic by the establishment. If that is so, then the sentiments they express, like those found in the C-text of *Piers Plowman* and Digby 102, were intended not to discredit the structures of government but, more particularly, to remind men of middling and high status that they had a public responsibility to assist in the task of upholding the law and maintaining good governance. Within a generation of the Peasants' Revolt, therefore, polemical discourses on justice appear once again to have become politically respectable. Some of the radicalism of 1381 was inevitably lost; but the agenda had also become more realistic, and the resulting form of the public debate more sophisticated. The political culture of justice had come of age.

Responses to Complaint

Having examined the principal traditions of criticism relating to the law in the fourteenth century, we shall now relate them more closely to their historical context and ask whether they signify a deeper dissatisfaction with the system of courts operated by the late medieval crown – and whether indeed that dissatisfaction was sufficiently deep-rooted and pervasive to challenge the very credibility of the legal profession and the judicial structure. The main issues underlying popular complaint may be neatly distilled into two essential charges: that the system was corrupt; and that it was socially exclusive and divisive. The remainder of this chapter addresses these issues, first by enumerating the existing interpretations presented by historians of late medieval law, and then by proposing a new and different reading of the evidence.

Medieval and modern commentators alike see corruption as having been endemic in the judicial system during the later Middle Ages: in an age when juries could be bribed to indict and convict innocent men, when pleaders could be persuaded to conspire in withholding incriminating evidence in order to secure acquittal, and when judges could rig proceedings for the benefit of powerful patrons, there could clearly be no absolute guarantee of impartial justice in the king's courts.[43] The idea that such judicial corruption actually *increased* in the fourteenth century relies chiefly on the contemporary equation between the growth of retaining and the apparent escalation of maintenance. In the last quarter of the century, as we saw in Chapter 4, this developed into a more specific debate on the distribution of liveries, the tangible signs of bastard feudalism, and of the abuses that were deemed to result from it. Moreover, it was also sometimes feared that the new agents of law enforcement in the shires, the justices of the peace, were less resistant than the staff of the central courts to the blandishments and intimidation that some of the more powerful members of provincial society undoubtedly used to confound their enemies and secure their interests at law: in other words, that the supposed devolution of justice into the hands of the gentry simply had the effect of delivering the provinces into the hands of unscrupulous magnates.[44] If these developments did indeed compromise the efficiency and integrity of the courts and thus undermine public confidence in the king's justice, they must stand as evidence of a failing judicial system.

The arguments concerning social exclusivity provide a potentially still more damaging indictment of that system. These are based on the two enduring historiographical traditions that we have already encountered at various points in this study. First, there is the structural thesis, proposed by Putnam and supported by, among many others, G. L. Harriss and Kaeuper, which argues that the emergence of the commissions of the peace allowed a relatively small group in society – those with proprietary interests in the rural and urban economies – to appropriate royal justice and use it for the pursuit of their own private and class interests.[45] Whereas the regional sessions of the eyre, the king's bench and the trailbastons in the later thirteenth and early fourteenth centuries had opened up new opportunities for the lower orders to participate in legal processes, the emergence of the commissions of the peace as the king's only regular judicial representatives in the shires supposedly closed the system down again and created what Steven Justice has called 'a local judiciary more concerned to oppress than redress'.[46] Secondly, there is the cultural argument, developed by R. H. Hilton, Rosamond Faith and others, and recently placed into a specifically judicial context by Palmer. This interpretation sees the labour legislation of 1349–51 as symptomatic of a broader desire to re-establish obedience and obligation after the social upheaval brought on by the Black Death. The new culture of responsibility and liability, although applied across the social spectrum, inevitably prioritised the economic interests and value system of the elite and thus tended to be applied with particular rigour against the third estate.[47] These two lines of approach – the structural and the cultural – intersect neatly in Harding's analysis of the Peasants' Revolt, outlined in Chapter 4, which sees the actions of the rebels as an outpouring of the resentment that had built up amongst the peasantry against the royal judicial system in the two generations before 1381.[48] In investigating the possibility that justice deteriorated during the fourteenth century, the most important question must therefore be the degree to which the system really did offer realistic access to the whole range of social groups which it theoretically encompassed.

The Accessibility of the Judicial System

The conventional argument about the increasing exclusivity of royal justice rests on a number of false assumptions and prejudices, not least with regard to the ability of the plaintiff of low status to proceed to law. The charge of social exclusivity can be countered by acknowledging the greater frequency of judicial sessions provided by the crown at the local level in the fourteenth century and the acceptance by the king's courts of a increasing range of litigation. Finally, the accusations of social prejudice can be challenged on the grounds that the range and diversity of people involved in bringing cases to court was not significantly diminished over the course of the century and that there is comparatively little evidence that the law itself was administered with a particular class bias.

It has been argued consistently in modern scholarship that the judicial machine of the later fourteenth century provided fewer opportunities for access to justice at the local level than had been the case a century earlier. This interpretation rests on the notion that the withdrawal of the eyre and the abandonment of the provincial sessions of king's bench put an end to the tradition of bringing cheap, accessible and immediate forms of royal justice into the localities. However, it needs to be stressed that, while the eyre and the king's bench undoubtedly did generate a great mass of litigation in the later thirteenth and early fourteenth centuries, the scale of that litigation is a measure not simply of the accessibility of royal justice but also of the very *irregularity* of such visitations. Chief Justice Scrope, speaking in 1329, believed that the eyre had been designed to visit each shire once every seven years (the reality had been a good deal more inconsistent);[49] the king's bench, as the Appendix indicates, made only erratic forays into the shires, and tended to make repeat visits only to a very small number of venues such as York and Lincoln. It is hardly surprising, therefore, that such rare appearances by the king's judges should have produced so much business, representing as it did the unusually wide range of powers enjoyed by the eyre, the acceptance of procedure upon bills by the king's bench, and the considerable backlog of litigation that was always pending in the shires. The contrast with the regular assize and peace sessions is obvious. Inevitably, there are some signs that the justices of assize sometimes failed to make their three visits a year to each shire, and that the justices of labourers and of the peace did not always fulfil their statutory duty to sit four times a year.[50]

But the evidence that becomes available after 1390 for the payment of daily expenses to the peace commissioners also demonstrates that in some areas the sessions were actually *more* frequent than the official norm.[51] The comparative regularity of sessions obviously enabled claims to be heard quickly. The empowering of the justices of assize to act at *nisi prius* and hear cases brought in the central courts while visiting the relevant shires, itself signified the practical advantages of a system of regular circuits and county sessions. Similarly, the continued willingness of the justices of the peace to receive bills of trespass in the second half of the fourteenth century meant that there was now a more regular forum in which peasant litigants might pursue this cheap and accessible means of justice. In terms of sheer judicial presence, then, it would be very difficult to sustain the argument that the king's subjects in the provinces had greater opportunities for access to royal justice in the age of the eyre than in the age of the quarter sessions.

Next, consideration should be given to the wide range of business entertained in the royal courts and the kaleidoscopic variety of remedies available to litigants. The crown's acceptance of trespass litigation from the mid-thirteenth century represented the beginning of a more general process of appropriating or attracting business away from the local courts. This was achieved in part through the various devices, invented from the twelfth century onwards, by which cases could be transferred out of the customary and into the royal courts. A tenant who was the defendant in land litigation or a dispute about feudal services in a local court could thus have the case removed to the king's court by opting to place himself on the grand assize (a type of grand jury for civil actions); and either or both parties in disputes involving land or services brought in the county court could have their cases accepted in a common law court by obtaining the writ *pone* (which ordered the sheriff to 'put' the defendant to response). The county court could also transfer cases of its own motion if they involved particularly complicated points of law.[52] More particularly in the fourteenth century, the jurisdiction of local courts was also diminished, and that of royal courts correspondingly increased, as a result of new statutory legislation and chancery practice. The Ordinance and Statute of Labourers embodied new notions of contract and employment negotiation which superseded older forms regulated by the local courts.[53] Furthermore, after the Black Death, writs of assumpsit and trespass on the case were available in chancery to remedy a range of breaches of duty (by way of negligence or breach of contract) that had earlier been handled by the local courts with only occasional forays into the court of common pleas. Royal justice in the fourteenth century therefore regulated or provided redress for considerably more areas of life – including areas of relevance to peasant society – than had been the case a hundred years before.

Finally, we should look at the nature of litigation itself: did the process of law enforcement represent a form of class conflict? As we have seen in Chapter 5, a whole range of people were involved in using the king's courts to seek redress, and even those of unfree status attempted (sometimes successfully) to secure recognition and access to royal justice. Was the considerable body of business brought by persons of lesser status nevertheless seen as marginal or controversial and therefore dispensable, particularly after the plague? Contrary to the argument that the parliamentary commons became more class-conscious and proprietorial in their outlook in the wake of the Black Death,[54] there is much to suggest that their general approach to justice remained remarkably unchanged: as in the 1340s, so after the plague, the commons continued to argue that the king's courts should be as accessible to the less prosperous (if not to the genuinely poor) as to the more affluent, and petitioned several times for a reduction in the costs of writs so as to guarantee full access to the judicial system.[55] Moreover, the fact that the people who presided as justices of labourers and of the peace were part of the elite does not mean that we should immediately call 'foul' and leap to the conclusion that they enforced the law solely in their own personal or class interests. As had already become the norm in a range of ad hoc judicial commissions, it was assumed and intended that the king's justices in the localities should represent the upper levels of county society and be selected from those who already bore the more general burden of government in the provinces: the inclusion of the gentry in the peace commissions was certainly not designed specifically for the purpose of oppressing the lower orders.

The peasantry, like their social superiors, got their cases into court through acknowledged processes: by writ, by bill, and by indictment. Whether or not a case was accepted by the jury of presentment and the judges depended on its own merits, not the status of the plaintiff or defendant. If this appears to idealise the integrity of medieval juries and judges, it should be remembered that cases involving persons of high status, which tended to generate most of the accusations of judicial corruption in the Middle Ages, were comparatively few: in the great majority of cases brought before the keepers and justices of the peace and the justices of gaol delivery, both plaintiffs and defendants were men and women of low rank.[56] Most of the business of the courts was therefore uncontentious to the political elite, and proceeded without interference. In the case of the labour laws, it is true that the employer (who was usually the plaintiff) was normally of higher social status than the employee (the defendant). Even here, however, as we remarked in Chapter 4, the idea of blatant class conflict being worked out through litigation tends to be undermined by the fact that a significant number of employers seeking redress through this mechanism were themselves of peasant status. The situation was obviously very different when either the alleged victim or the proposed defendant was of gentle or noble rank: here, corruption and intimidation were much more likely to be applied, with the result that, regardless of the rights and wrongs of the case, the wealthy party tended to come out best.[57] The problem was undoubtedly acute; but it should also be acknowledged that the system actually recognised the danger and aimed to contain it, in particular by making it necessary for the lawyers from the central courts to be present when judgments were given in the localities, or by transferring indictments involving men of high status and importance out of the peace sessions and into the king's bench.

Criticism of inaccessibility is perhaps justified in relation to one particular area of judicial administration, namely the opportunity to appeal against the misdoings of royal ministers in the localities. It was precisely to facilitate accusations against such persons that the thirteenth- and early fourteenth-century state had allowed first the eyre and then the itinerant king's bench to instigate cases on the basis of oral and written plaints; it was for much the same purpose that it had encouraged its subjects to present petitions to the king in parliament. The abandonment of visitations of the shires by the eyre (from the 1290s), by trailbaston commissions (from the 1340s) and by the king's bench (from the 1350s), coupled with the shift away from private to 'common' business in parliament from the 1330s, left those who felt themselves oppressed by the king's agents with few opportunities for redress. The Ordinance of Justices of 1346 recognised the problem by stating that the justices of assize were to have sufficient power to inquire into the misdeeds of sheriffs, escheators, bailiffs and jurors; but there is little evidence that this (or any other) section of the ordinance was ever observed.[58] And while those wishing to complain about the unjust actions of royal officials could still present bills at peace sessions, the bench usually refused to act in the manner of the old justices in eyre and accept the case immediately, preferring instead to have the accusations tested and approved by juries of presentment: this obviously allowed the office-holders against whom charges were being brought a valuable opportunity to rig the jury and prevent the suit from proceeding further. Otherwise, the only recourse was to take a civil action in the central courts, involving much time and expense in the purchase of writs and the employment of attorneys and pleaders. If there was a sense of alienation from the judicial system in the later fourteenth century, then, it may indeed have been caused by this issue: the attacks launched during the Peasants' Revolt of 1381 not only upon the justices of the peace but also on a whole range of local crown representatives – sheriffs, escheators, tax collectors, and so on – speak forcefully for the lower orders' sense that the new judicial system had effectively removed from them the lawful right to appeal against the oppressions of the king's own government.[59] The problem of how to guard against the abuses of officials in local government remained to be confronted by government and judiciary. On the other hand, the absence of an effective mechanism of complaint should not be taken as direct evidence of inefficiency – or, indeed, of corruption – in the judicial system itself.

The Responsibilities of Justices, Lawyers and Jurors

The judicial system's supposed capacity to guarantee impartial justice rested on the shoulders of those court officials – judges, lawyers and jurors – among whose various responsibilities it was to decide, interpret or uphold the law. As has been emphasised in Chapters 2, 3 and 5, judges and lawyers were themselves part of the social fabric, maintaining a stake in the landed elite (or aspiring thereto) and enjoying contact with other privileged groups at local and national levels. Juries, though they were drawn from a wider social background and included many men of peasant status, may also in general be said to have been staffed by those with aspirations to economic and political advancement.[60] The judicial system therefore existed within a complex network of personal, professional and political relationships. Indeed, the very operation and effectiveness of royal government was dependent upon the interaction of bureaucratic and judicial institutions with the web of patronage, clientage and friendship that has been indiscriminately characterised and demonised under the label of 'maintenance'.[61] As professionals, judges and lawyers were of course fully entitled to expect and demand rewards for their services. The concern over retaining that manifested itself in the later fourteenth century indicates on one level how the overt relationship between landowners and lawyers had come to be regarded as incompatible with the supposed impartiality of the law. On a deeper level it suggests just how difficult it was to eradicate or even substantially modify a relationship that was not simply pecuniary but one of the essential bonds of later medieval society. We have already made the point that the wholesale removal of the senior members of the judiciary or the indictment of their practices was largely a political phenomenon arising out of the events of 1289, 1340, 1381 and 1388. It should be noted, however, that there was no such reaction against the staff of the central courts in the fifteenth century – a contrast that has itself been seen as proof of a greater professional integrity on the part of the justices and serjeants at law operating in the courts of king's bench and common pleas.[62]

The question remains as to whether corruption was sufficiently widespread at all levels of royal justice in the fourteenth century that it threatened to undermine the whole system. Although such a charge cannot be answered in quantitative terms, it should be emphasised that the strength of the legal system lay in its ability to move with society and respond to those justifiable criticisms of its administration that cast its reputation in a poor light. This may be demonstrated in three ways: by showing how the judicial system was able to police itself; by highlighting the response of the judiciary to criticisms of its practices; and by illustrating how some allegations of corruption were in fact symptomatic of cultural changes occurring within the system as a whole. By acknowledging the positive potential of the new judicial structure of the fourteenth century, we are also able to put into sharper relief those specific issues that undoubtedly did undermine its effectiveness or credibility and consequently appear to justify the examples of public complaint.

From the late thirteenth century it is apparent that the crown and judiciary regarded the behaviour of certain members of the nascent legal profession as potentially disruptive to the smooth running of the courts and as having a negative impact on confidence in the legal system. Statutory regulation was initially confined to a vague and somewhat unspecific professional obligation contained in the First Statute of Westminster (1275), though this was more fully developed at least with regard to fees and retaining in the Ordinance of Justices (1346) and its restatement in 1384.[63] The 1275 statute created a duty on legal practitioners not to mislead the court or litigants and established harsh penalties for such malpractice: imprisonment for a year and a day, together with complete disbarment or permanent suspension from practising. In practice, enforcement was left to the judges who, through their presidency of the courts, elaborated on the statutory terms to provide norms of professional behaviour equating to an ethical standard. It appears that serjeants and professional attorneys alike were expected to conform to this code, and to observe it whether they operated in the customary or in the royal courts. The existence of such a code of conduct is confirmed by instances of professional misbehaviour coming to the attention of the justices either during a trial itself or as a result of subsequent complaints brought by disgruntled litigants.[64]

An analysis of such evidence demonstrates certain key precepts at work in the courts. A serjeant at law owed a primary duty of loyalty to his client. He was not allowed to leave the client's service before the conclusion of litigation unless informed that his services were no longer required or the client failed to pay his fee. There was also a continuing obligation to the client once the particular court case had ended: the serjeant could not be employed by his client's opponent without the former's permission, nor could he appear against his client in subsequent litigation. Secondly (in line with the legislation of 1275), he was under a duty not to deceive the court and was liable to be punished if he made an untrue statement in court or advised his client to sue more than once on the same matter. Thirdly, a serjeant's general conduct was subject to scrutiny, whether he was pleading for a client or undertaking his own private business. Wasting the court's time or persisting with an unconvincing argument were particularly frowned upon.

A professional attorney was similarly regulated in terms of his relationship with clients. It was expected that he would exercise due diligence in obtaining writs and ensure that there was the minimum of delay in pursuing the various stages of litigation. Like the serjeant, he was under a continuing obligation to his client and could be punished for deliberate fraud, negligence or incompetence. There were also obligations to a client's opponent (such as taking account of legitimate grounds for absence and not suing in default), to third parties, and to the court itself (such as following the correct procedures).

The fact that this code of professional ethics emerged out of, and may be reconstructed from, the breaches of good conduct exposed in court does, of course, provide direct evidence that abuse and malpractice continued to occur. The relative frequency of such cases cannot in itself be taken to indicate that relative levels of integrity and misconduct altered decisively. On the other hand, those cases do demonstrate that blatant deviation from the norms of good conduct was acknowledged and punished by the courts, and suggest that the judiciary regarded conformity to a code of ethics as a necessary corollary to professional status and to the 'special relationship' of lawyers with the courts. Allegations were often tried by juries of fellow-professionals, and the punishments reflected the seriousness with which each breach was viewed. If the conduct point arose during the trial itself, a warning or some form of judicial guidance might be given. In other instances men were fined (the money being split between the client and the crown) or spent brief periods in gaol. Others were punished by temporary suspension, by receiving the statutory period of imprisonment, or (in really serious cases, where perhaps a forged writ had been used or an entry on the plea roll falsified) by permanent suspension from practising in court. It can therefore be said with some assurance that there was a definite concern from inside the legal profession during the fourteenth century that the law should be upheld and its practices revered.

The judicial system also recognised both the possibility of abuse of its processes and the need to provide redress for complaints. The crown targeted 'conspirators', those who made false accusations in the courts, by devising a writ of conspiracy returnable in king's bench in 1293 and by incorporating the Ordinance of Conspirators of 1305 into the commissions of trailbaston of the same year.[65] 'Champerty' (the undertaking at one's own expense of another's suit in return for receiving a share of the subject in dispute) was highlighted in the Articles upon the Charters of 1300 and later in a statute of 1330, while 'ambidextry' (the taking of fees from both sides to a suit) was similarly addressed and included with conspiracy and champerty in the articles of inquiry of the general oyer and terminer commissions issued in the 1340s. Although the justices of the peace were given no formal jurisdiction over such cases (and indeed took a literal reading of their competence in 1336), it is clear that they were prepared to take a more expansive view of their powers later in the century and began to accept the cases of conspiracy that came before them.

These new notions of corruption produced interesting problems of definition and interpretation in the courts. Judges and counsel found it difficult to separate what might be regarded as legitimate alliances (for example, those of parentage or affinity) from those that were corrupt and illegal (especially relationships created by oath or agreement). The very reliance of the legal system on the swearing of oaths meant that it was difficult to exterminate the 'virus' (conspiracy) without mortally wounding the 'host' (the judicial structure). In fact, the comparative frequency of conspiracy cases during the fourteenth century reflects not so much a new distinction between acceptable and unacceptable forms of association as the willingness of the courts to use the offence as a generic term covering threats to the community, to political liberty, and to the workings of the state. The meaning of conspiracy therefore expanded beyond the simple obstruction of legal processes to encapsulate any form of sworn alliance or confederacy, whether it involved extortion in the customs system, the withdrawal of customary services by villein tenants, resistance to the labour laws, or the forcible eviction from office of the mayor of York in 1380. Since the definition of maintenance was also broadened to incorporate various types of concerted action, it is evident that the laws of conspiracy and maintenance came to cover acts of political subversion at all levels of society.

Under such circumstances, it is important to ask exactly what kinds of offences were perceived and what resolutions were being sought when cases of conspiracy and maintenance were brought before the courts. It is particularly significant in the present context that a proportion of such litigation was directed against lawyers and reflected contemporary perceptions (some of them very probably *mis*conceptions) about the role of such men in dispute settlement. The allegations of maintenance or champerty brought in the early trailbaston proceedings, for example, seem often to have been directed against persons who were in fact professional lawyers. In such cases, 'maintenance' was used to encompass some of the tasks usually performed by lawyers, often amounting to no more than professional assistance. Similarly, charges of champerty were brought simply because the lawyer had been paid after the court case or because land had been passed to him not as a reward but as a temporary tactic before being transferred on to others.[66] Not surprisingly, such allegations were vigorously denied. Appearing in king's bench in 1307 charged with conspiracy, John Hotoft, the bishop of Coventry's attorney, argued that his activities were legitimate and not tantamount to conspiracy so long as he observed his professional code of conduct.

He says that he who served his different lords in such duties [prosecution and defence] in the king's courts cannot be regarded as acting like a conspirator in giving aid and counsel to his employers, provided he did nothing to deceive the court.[67]

It seems, then, that the very explosion in litigation during the late thirteenth and early fourteenth century, and the increasing dependence on professional assistance that resulted, produced some kind of backlash on the part of contemporary society, which immediately became unduly suspicious of the motives of those growing fat on the profits of a new growth industry.

By the later fourteenth century this suspicion had developed into two forceful traditions of criticism. First, there was the belief advanced by churchmen that, because litigation represented the collapse of the normal obligations of Christian brotherhood, those who served the law must be guilty of stirring up animosity within society in the hope of personal gain: it was in this sense, for example, that John Wyclif appears to have launched his attack on the men of law who 'maintain falseness for winning'.[68] The notion that recourse to formal legal means of dispute settlement was morally reprehensible also found expression in the regulations of many of the religious guilds that flourished in the period after the Black Death, which specifically required the members of such fraternities to live in charity with each other and to settle their disputes *outside* the courts.[69] Secondly, there was also a new, secular tradition that assumed that the lawyers themselves must be responsible for the more unpopular and controversial forms of litigation being brought in the king's courts. Both the parliamentary commons' complaint against the 'counsellors, procurers, maintainers and abettors' who helped villeins to work out a 'malicious interpretation' of Domesday Book in 1377 and the rebels' verbal and physical attacks on 'questmongers' during the Peasants' Revolt of 1381 demonstrate the degree to which a number of social groups found it convenient, particularly at moments of crisis, to blame lawyers for the evils of the age and accuse them of corrupting the very system they served.[70] The disingenuousness – not to say hypocrisy – of this position is obvious.

While lawyers were convenient scapegoats for those attempting to explain corruption in the courts, the legal profession could obviously not bear the entire burden of blame. Much of the contemporary criticism focused on jurors – not least because it was upon the proper functioning of juries that the legal system rested. Although jurors were supposed to be honest and lawful and not close friends of the plaintiff or defendant, there is no clear indication that they conformed to the standards of impartiality expected of them: the textbooks are full of examples of the manner in which both presenting and trial juries were manipulated to the advantage of one or other party in the suit.[71] One particular problem on which contemporaries remarked was the refusal of juries of presentment to accept accusations made against those who were under the patronage and protection of powerful lords: from time to time in the later Middle Ages, particularly during periods of political uncertainty, it was claimed that individual magnates were able to establish an effective stranglehold on royal justice in the shires by blocking any attempt to indict their followers in the peace sessions.[72] Nevertheless, while subtle softeners and outright intimidation were undoubtedly sometimes a reality in the life of a juror, we must be cautious about assuming that such men regularly perjured themselves or automatically sold their voice to the highest bidder.[73] Certainly in criminal trials there was some element of jury nullification. In other words, the jury separated those whom they felt really deserved the death penalty from those for whom in their eyes such punishment was unwarranted.[74] If the acquittal rates are regarded as abnormally high, surely there is some scope for thinking that this was not simply a product of corruption but reflected the application of proper discretion and of humanitarian considerations?

There were, furthermore, certain checks within the system that allowed imbalances or inconsistencies on jury panels to be rectified by procedural means. Those persons who had been charged with crimes had the opportunity to challenge any of the trial jurors who were regarded as interested parties. Sometimes this procedure was used as a tactical device simply to impede the prosecution and delay the trial. Nevertheless, its availability – and the willingness of justices to allow such challenges – is indicative of a culture that generally refused to tolerate the possibility of corruption within the court.[75]

One particular issue relating to jurors that may seem to smack of bias and corruption is the possibility that men who had presented indictments were also chosen to serve on the trial jury. This was nothing new: in the 'golden age' of the eyre it had been commonplace for the personnel of juries of presentment and trial to overlap.[76] And while it remained a feature of the judicial system during the early fourteenth century, we need to be cautious of the view that it necessarily generated abuse. The reasons for the employment of the same people on both juries may often have been practical rather than conspiratorial. If the device was intended in some way to incriminate the defendant, it ought also to be remarked that not even a complete duplication of personnel necessarily guaranteed a conviction when the case was brought to trial: if anything, indeed, there was more of a tendency to convict when fewer than half of the original jury were present.[77] Although there is therefore no sure evidence that this practice made any difference to verdicts, public opinion was increasingly sensitive and hostile, and by the 1340s it was being argued in parliament that a man's indictors should not serve on his trial jury. This was eventually translated into legislation as part of the package of royal concessions awarded to the political community in 1352.[78] The existence of such a statute does not in itself, of course, mean that the practice was eradicated (the subject still awaits systematic investigation); but it does suggest that the crown was responsive to an alleged abuse of the system and had created another mechanism by which defendants could lodge additional challenges against the composition and bias of their trial juries.

In assessing the attitudes of fourteenth-century society to the system of justice operated by the king's courts, we should bear in mind that more people than ever before were turning to those courts for help or having dealings with them as defendants, witnesses and jurors. This did more than anything else to heighten awareness of the judicial system: direct experience of the agencies of the 'law state', like the face-to-face negotiation with the tax-gathering agents of the 'war state', represented the real points of contact between the late medieval crown and its subjects. It is unlikely that many of the lay people who participated in the courts really understood the full implications of what occurred there, let alone comprehended all the procedural technicalities – though it is worth pointing out that proceedings must have become a good deal more transparent after 1362, when the language of oral communication in the king's courts was changed from Anglo-Norman French to English.[79] While some of the authors of complaint literature undoubtedly had knowledge of legal affairs, much of the tradition of satire and criticism analysed earlier in this chapter was probably based on personal 'gut reaction', common cultural prejudice, and the simple desire to entertain at the expense of the legal establishment. Without the benefit of hindsight, contemporaries obviously could not see that changes in the judicial system occurred at different speeds and took effect in varying ways.

In the end, it was the perceived disparities between theory and practice that fuelled public dissatisfaction with the law. There is little indication that contemporaries perceived the system to be less corrupt in 1400 than a century earlier, and much circumstantial evidence to suggest that many did indeed feel it was in some ways 'worse'. However, these moral assumptions had developed within a culture that was at once more sensitive and more responsive to criticism. Consequently, there is much to support the notion, first proposed by McFarlane, that the perceived deterioration of justice in the later Middle Ages was less the product of a crisis of public order and much more a reflection of the higher standards of judicial integrity to which contemporary society aspired.[80] This study has deliberately underplayed the supposed invidious influence of 'bastard feudalism' on the judicial system, not simply because it has an unduly prominent place in the more anecdotal and sensationalist literature on law and order but also because the real context for a more extended debate on magnate affinities and aristocratic appropriation of the judicial system lies in the *fifteenth*, rather than the fourteenth, century. And by accentuating the positive moves towards self-regulation that emerged within the judicial structure from the reign of Edward I, the foregoing analysis has suggested that the judicial system was indeed capable of responding and adapting to changes in the standards and expectations set by contemporary society: an interpretation that also, of course, very much reinforces the underlying argument of this book concerning the importance of endogenous influence in the evolution of English justice.

Conclusion

The fourteenth century was an age of complaint. Whether in charges brought by plaintiffs before the courts, in common petitions registered in parliament, or in the satire and polemic of contemporary literature, the subjects of the English crown expressed their grievances with a clarity and vehemence that still today has the power to capture the imagination. It is easy to assume – and has frequently been argued – that people complained *more* than they had done in an earlier age, and did so because there was more to complain about. The assumption is not, of course, unreasonable. The growth of the state itself generated conflict in society: as the law state stretched out the long arm of justice into the provinces and the war state imposed more frequent burdens on the populace, the crown was bound to encounter resistance from an increasing number of its subjects, great and small.

It is equally possible, however, that the apparent upturn in the range and scale of complaint arose directly from the fact that the crown allowed those subjects more opportunity to express their discontent. By admitting charges of trespass brought by bill into the repertoire of the king's courts, and by specifically inviting petitioners to bring allegations of malpractice against royal ministers in parliament, the late thirteenth-century state created new channels of communication between the provinces and the centre and – perhaps rather to its surprise – was rapidly submerged under a torrent of new business. The emergence of the common petition in the fourteenth century created further opportunities for the political community to apply concerted pressure upon the crown for the resolution of contentious issues in government and law. Finally, the revival of the vernacular as a written language in the first half of the fourteenth century opened the way to a new, more vigorous and more widespread debate on such issues in polite and popular literature. These new opportunities for the articulation of grievances, coupled with the more systematic preservation of records and the higher survival rate of literary manuscripts after the late thirteenth century, means that the sudden change to a 'complaint culture' during the fourteenth century may be more apparent than real.

Furthermore, even if we accept that there *was* more to complain about during the fourteenth century, it does not necessarily follow that this demonstrates the failure of the judicial system. This chapter has suggested that only a small proportion of the criticism levelled against royal justice in the fourteenth century was intended seriously to undermine the system, and that most of it aimed either simply to satirise an inevitably imperfect institution or actively to promote reform from within. The fact that most of the social groups represented in the discourses outlined above were actually reconciled to the great expansion of royal justice and chose to work with, rather than kick against, that system is testimony to the remarkably inclusive nature of the law in late medieval England.

So long as the judicial, political and literary evidence is skewed towards the attitudes of the elite, the peasantry's experience of, and responses to, the evolution of justice inevitably remain obscure. Naturally enough, when those attitudes surface, they tend to emphasise the negative: the iniquities of a judicial system based as much on the purchasing capacity of the parties as on the relative merits of their cases, and the sense of alienation from a structure designed to prevent the lower orders from achieving the affluence they merited after the plague. Such cries of helplessness should not, however, blind us to the fact that the English peasantry were much more fully engaged with the king's courts than were their contemporaries in most other parts of later medieval Europe, and that they could be the beneficiaries, just as much as the victims, of that system. The repressive nature of some of the legislation enacted in parliament and the litigation conducted in the royal courts after the Black Death is not to be underestimated, and provides an important background to the revolt of 1381. But the argument that the third estate was alienated from the king's courts does less than credit to the increasing scope of royal justice, its greater accessibility at the local level, and the established litigious tendencies of at least some sections of peasant society.

Although the nature and scale of certain kinds of business therefore altered markedly, the judicial system as a whole seems to have remained available to a remarkably wide spectrum of society throughout the fourteenth century. Furthermore, the judiciary itself became more representative of the society it served. The employment of provincial landholders and lawyers as justices of the peace opened up a second recruitment stream running parallel with the promotion systems for senior judges in the central courts. This process has too often been seen as a means by which provincial elites hijacked royal justice for their own purposes: too little attention has been paid to the fact that the variety of political and social influences represented on the bench often cancelled each other out, and that the peace commissions, by harnessing the administrative expertise and local knowledge of the gentry and men of law for the task of maintaining law and order, offered the new magistracy a valuable opportunity to prove its integrity and worth.[81] The result was a remarkably integrated system that linked the centre to the provinces and for the first time established a permanent judicial presence by the crown in the localities.

To return, finally, to the literary evidence is to encounter this newly integrated system in subtle but clearly recognisable form. Above all it is exemplified in the relationship between the Serjeant at Law and the Franklin in the Prologue to Chaucer's *Canterbury Tales*.[82] It is no accident that these two pilgrims are presented as travelling companions: they symbolise the twin faces of the judicial system as it had developed by the late fourteenth century. The Serjeant at Law, steeped in the jargon of his profession, is the representative of the central courts, a member of that select band of pleaders who acted for the king in civil actions and toured the shires during the vacations between law terms to hold assizes ('He often had been justice of assize / By letters patent and in full commission'). The Franklin, by contrast, is the country gentleman whose position in local society has won him a place on the peace commission and the *de facto* presidency of the bench ('At sessions there was he lord and sire'). Chaucer therefore makes explicit reference to the two regular judicial tribunals available in the shires – the assizes and the quarter sessions – and thus, though this time implicitly, to the obvious points of professional and social contact between the two men: just as the Franklin may have been present at the assize sessions as plaintiff or defendant, so the Serjeant at Law, as a member of the quorum on the peace commission, would be a regular attender at the quarter sessions.

Nor, significantly, is there any suggestion of criticism in Chaucer's treatment of this relationship: the Serjeant at Law may be ridiculed for his self-importance, but there is no hint of any underhand collaboration between him and the Franklin. This contrasts significantly with the representative of the ecclesiastical courts, the Summoner, whose homosexual liaison with the Pardoner is used to impute a sinister, corrupt and self-serving system. There are all sorts of reasons why Chaucer chose to present the representatives of royal justice in a favourable light.[83] But his silent – even, perhaps, unwitting – testimony still stands: the balance between central supervision and local initiative that is so often forgotten in the historiography of judicial devolution is thus encapsulated by one of the most accomplished literary figures of the late fourteenth century.

A few years later, the author of *Richard the Redeless*, writing in a very different context, was similarly able to identify the fact that permanent judicial bodies were now to be found not just at Westminster but also in the shires. His ideal justices are those who, living on their own incomes (in other words, not succumbing to corruption) and eschewing lordship and maintenance, are able to dispense the law to poor plaintiffs and keep their 'countries' (that is, counties) 'in quiet and in rest'.[84] For all the administrative and political challenges they created, the network of assize and goal delivery circuits and the permanent, county-based commissions of the peace represented the most effective mechanism that the English crown had yet devised to ensure that tranquillity. And it was the state's continued commitment to social stability and public order that was to preserve the achievements of the fourteenth century and retain these essential agencies of law enforcement for the rest of the Middle Ages and beyond.

Appendix: The Sessions and Itineraries of the Court of King's Bench and Parliament, 1290–1399

Year	Law terms				Parliaments	
	Hilary	*Easter*	*Trinity*	*Michaelmas*		
1290	Westminster	Westminster	Westminster	Bakewell Boultham Clipston Lincoln	after 13 Jan: 23 Apr: 26 Oct:	Westminster Westminster Clipston
1291	Westminster	Heatherslaw	Newcastle upon Tyne	Bristol Gloucester Hereford Worcester	7 Jan:	Ashridge
1292	Westminster	Cattishall Norwich Lincoln	Berwick-on-Tweed	Penrith Berwick-on-Tweed Roxburgh	7 Jan: 2 June: 13 Oct:	Westminster Berwick-on-Tweed Berwick-on-Tweed
1293	Nottingham	?	Westminster	Oxford	29 Mar: 13 Oct: after 25 Dec:	London/Canterbury Westminster London
1294	Sandwich	Westminster	Kingston upon Thames	?		

Appendix

Year	Law terms				Parliaments	
	Hilary	Easter	Trinity	Michaelmas		
1295	Chester	Chester	?	?	1 Aug:	Westminster
					27 Nov:	Westminster
1296	?	?	Nottingham	Stamford	3 Nov:	Bury St Edmunds
			Sandiacre	Cattishall		
1297	Cambridge	?	Westminster	Westminster	24 Feb:	Salisbury
					8 July:	Westminster
					30 Sept/6 Oct:	London
1298	Westminster	Lincoln	York	York	30 Mar:	Westminster
1299	York	York	York	Westminster	8 Mar:	London
					3 May:	Westminster/Stepney
					18 Oct:	London
1300	?	York	?	York	6 Mar:	London
1301	Lincoln	Worcester	York	York	20 Jan:	Lincoln
1302	York	Canterbury	Westminster	Westminster	1 July:	Westminster
			Canterbury		14 Oct:	Westminster
			Rochester			
1303	Westminster	York	York	York		
1304	York	York	York	York		

Year	Law terms				Parliaments
	Hilary	Easter	Trinity	Michaelmas	
1305	Westminster	Westminster	Westminster	Westminster	28 Feb: Westminster 15 Sept: Westminster
1306	Westminster	Westminster	Westminster	Westminster	30 May: Westminster
1307	Westminster	Westminster	Westminster	Westminster Northampton	20 Jan: Carlisle 13 Oct: Northampton
1308	Westminster	Westminster	Westminster	Westminster	3 Mar: Westminster 28 Apr: Westminster 20 Oct: Westminster
1309	Westminster	Westminster	Westminster	Westminster	27 Apr: Westminster 27 July: Stamford
1310	Westminster	Westminster	Westminster	Westminster	8 Feb: Westminster
1311	Newcastle upon Tyne	Westminster	Westminster	Westminster	8 Aug: London 5 Nov: Westminster
1312	Westminster	Westminster	Westminster	Westminster	20 Aug: Westminster
1313	Westminster	Westminster	Westminster	Westminster	18 Mar: Westminster 8 July: Westminster 23 Sept: Westminster
1314	Westminster	Westminster	Westminster	Westminster	9 Sept: York
1315	Westminster	Westminster	Westminster	Westminster	20 Jan: Westminster

Appendix

Year	Law terms				Parliaments	
	Hilary	Easter	Trinity	Michaelmas		
1316	Lincoln	Westminster	Westminster	Westminster	27 Jan:	Lincoln
1317	Westminster	Westminster	Westminster	Westminster		
1318	Westminster	Westminster	Westminster	York	20 Oct:	York
1319	York	York	York	York	6 May:	York
1320	York	Westminster	Westminster	Westminster	20 Jan:	York
					6 Oct:	Westminster
1321	Westminster	Westminster	Westminster	Westminster	15 July:	Westminster
1322	Shrewsbury Gloucester	York	York	York	2 May:	York
					14 Nov:	York
1323	Lincoln	London Lincoln York	York	York, Wigan Nottingham Derby Tutbury		
1324	Worcester Hereford Gloucester Westminster	Westminster	Westminster	Westminster	23 Feb:	Westminster
					20 Oct:	Westminster

Year	Law terms				Parliaments	
	Hilary	Easter	Trinity	Michaelmas		
1325	Westminster	Westminster Guildford Winchester Southampton	Westminster	Westminster	25 June: 18 Nov:	Westminster Westminster
1326	Norwich	Warwick	Westminster	Westminster		
1327	Westminster	York	York	York	7 Jan:	Westminster
1328	York	Northampton	York	Westminster	7 Feb: 24 Apr: 16 Oct:	York Northampton Salisbury
1329	Bedford St Albans Maidenhead Westminster	Westminster Canterbury	Westminster	Westminster	9 Feb:	Westminster
1330	Westminster	Banbury	Banbury Oxford	Westminster	11 Mar: 26 Nov:	Winchester Westminster
1331	Westminster	Westminster	Lincoln	Westminster	30 Sept:	Westminster
1332	Westminster	Westminster	Westminster	York Stamford	16 Mar: 9 Sept: 4 Dec:	Westminster Westminster York
1333	York	York	York	York Lincoln	20 Jan:	York

Appendix

Year	Law terms				Parliaments	
	Hilary	Easter	Trinity	Michaelmas		
1334	Lincoln	Warwick	Wigan Lancaster	York	21 Feb: 19 Sept:	York Westminster
1335	York	York	York	York	26 May:	York
1336	Lincoln	Lincoln	Northampton Nottingham	Nottingham Blyth Lincoln York	11 Mar:	Westminster
1337	York	York Tickhill Blyth	Stamford Stamford Bridge Bradcroft	Canterbury	3 Mar:	Westminster
1338	Canterbury Westminster	Colchester	Colchester	Cambridge Westminster Lambeth St Albans	3 Feb:	Westminster
1339	Westminster	Westminster	Norwich Beccles Dunwich Colchester Westminster	Westminster	3 Feb: 13 Oct:	Westminster Westminster
1340	Westminster	Westminster	Westminster	Westminster Aylesbury Northampton York	20 Jan: 29 Mar: 12 July:	Westminster Westminster Westminster

200   The Evolution of English Jusice

Year	Law terms				Parliaments	
	Hilary	Easter	Trinity	Michaelmas		
1341	Westminster	Westminster	Westminster	Westminster Colchester Lynn	23 Apr:	Westminster
1342	Lynn Norwich	Norwich	Westminster	Westminster		
1343	Westminster	Westminster	Westminster	York	28 Apr:	Westminster
1344	York	Westminster	Westminster	Westminster Ipswich	7 June:	Westminster
1345	Ipswich	Westminster	Westminster	Westminster		
1346	Norwich Bury St Edmunds	Westminster	Westminster	Westminster	11 Sept:	Westminster
1347	Westminster	Westminster	Westminster	Westminster		
1348	Westminster	Westminster	Westminster	York	14 Jan: 31 Mar:	Westminster Westminster
1349	York	Lincoln	[closed]	Westminster		
1350	Westminster	Westminster	Westminster	Westminster		
1351	Westminster	Westminster	Aylesbury	Westminster Chelmsford	9 Feb:	Westminster

Appendix

Year	Law terms				Parliaments	
	Hilary	Easter	Trinity	Michaelmas		
1352	Westminster Chelmsford Bury St Edmunds	Bedford	Warwick Coventry	Norwich Ipswich Bury St Edmunds	13 Jan:	Westminster
1353	Westminster	Norwich	Westminster	Westminster Kingston upon Thames		
1354	Westminster	Westminster	Westminster	Westminster	28 Apr:	Westminster
1355	Westminster Ipswich	Westminster	Westminster	Westminster	23 Nov:	Westminster
1356	Westminster Stratford Langthorn	Westminster	Westminster	Westminster		
1357	Westminster	Westminster	Westminster Wycombe	Wycombe Dunstable St Albans Barnet Westminster	17 Apr:	Westminster
1358	Westminster	Wells	Sherborne Westminster	Westminster Deptford	5 Feb:	Westminster
1359	Westminster	Westminster	Westminster	Westminster		
1360	Westminster	Westminster	Westminster	Westminster	15 May:	Westminster

Year	Law terms				Parliaments	
	Hilary	Easter	Trinity	Michaelmas		
1361	Westminster	Westminster	[closed]	Westminster	24 Jan:	Westminster
1362	Westminster	Westminster	York	York	13 Oct:	Westminster
1363	Westminster	Westminster	Gloucester Bristol Newport Worcester	Westminster	6 Oct:	Westminster
1364	Westminster	Norwich	Norwich Bury St Edmunds	Colchester Bury St Edmunds		
1365	Westminster	Westminster	Westminster	Westminster Colchester	20 Jan:	Westminster
1366	Westminster	Westminster	Westminster	Westminster	4 May:	Westminster
1367	Westminster	Westminster	Westminster	Westminster		
1368	Gloucester	Westminster	[closed]	Westminster	1 May:	Westminster
1369	Westminster	Westminster	Westminster	Westminster	6 Apr:	Westminster
1370	Westminster Stratford	Westminster	Westminster	Westminster		
1371	Westminster	Westminster	Winchester Westminster	Westminster	24 Feb:	Westminster

Appendix

Year	Law terms				Parliaments	
	Hilary	*Easter*	*Trinity*	*Michaelmas*		
1372	Westminster	Westminster	Westminster	Westminster Southwark	3 Nov:	Westminster
1373	Westminster	Westminster	Westminster	Westminster	21 Nov:	Westminster
1374	Westminster	Westminster	Westminster	Westminster		
1375	Westminster	Westminster	Westminster	Lincoln		
1376	Westminster	Westminster	Westminster	Westminster	28 Apr:	Westminster
1377	Westminster	Westminster	Winchester	Westminster	27 Jan: 13 Oct:	Westminster Westminster
1378	Westminster	Westminster	Westminster	Gloucester Westminster	20 Oct:	Gloucester
1379	Westminster	Westminster	Westminster	Westminster Chelmsford Bury St Edmunds Thetford	24 Apr:	Westminster
1380	Westminster	Westminster	Westminster	Westminster Northampton	16 Jan: 5 Nov:	Westminster Northampton
1381	Westminster	Westminster	[closed]	Deptford Westminster	3 Nov:	Westminster

Year	Law terms				Parliaments	
	Hilary	Easter	Trinity	Michaelmas		
1382	Westminster	Westminster	Westminster	Westminster	7 May: 6 Oct:	Westminster Westminster
1383	Westminster	Westminster	Westminster	Cambridge Westminster	23 Feb: 26 Oct:	Westminster Westminster
1384	Westminster Newenton	Salisbury	Westminster	Westminster	29 Apr: 12 Nov:	Salisbury Westminster
1385	Westminster	Westminster	Westminster	Westminster	20 Oct:	Westminster
1386	Westminster	Westminster	Westminster	Westminster	1 Oct:	Westminster
1387	Westminster	Westminster	Coventry	Gloucester Reading		
1388	Westminster	Westminster	Westminster	Westminster	3 Feb: 9 Sept:	Westminster Cambridge
1389	Westminster	Westminster	Westminster	Westminster Brentwood Wycombe		
1390	Westminster Southwark	Westminster	Westminster	Westminster	17 Jan: 12 Nov:	Westminster Westminster
1391	Westminster	Westminster	Westminster	Westminster	3 Nov:	Westminster
1392	Westminster	Westminster	Nottingham	York Nottingham		

1393	Winchester	York	Derby	Westminster	20 Jan:	Winchester
1394	Westminster	Westminster	Westminster	Westminster	27 Jan:	Westminster
1395	Westminster	Westminster	Westminster	Westminster	27 Jan:	Westminster
1396	Nottingham	Lincoln	Westminster	Westminster		
1397	Westminster	Westminster	Westminster	Westminster Coventry	22 Jan: 17 Sept:	Westminster Westminster
1398	Worcester	Reading Grandpont Oxford	Gloucester Westminster	Westminster	27 Jan:	Shrewsbury
1399	Westminster	Westminster	Westminster	Westminster	6 Oct:	Westminster

Sources: G. O. Sayles (ed.), *Select Cases in the Court of King's Bench*, SS 55, 57, 58, 74, 76, 82, 88 (London, 1936–71): vol. 4, pp. xcviii–cv; vol. 6, pp. xlvi–l; vol. 7, pp. liii–lviii. A. J. Prescott, Judicial Records of the Rising of 1381', University of London PhD thesis (1984). E. B. Fryde, D. E. Greenway, S. Porter and I. Roy (eds), *Handbook of British Chronology*, 3rd edn (Cambridge: Cambridge University Press, 1996), pp. 548–66.

NOTES

Notes to Chapter 1: Introduction

1. D. M. Stenton, *English Justice between the Norman Conquest and the Great Charter* (London: George Allen & Unwin, 1965), p. 22.
2. Putnam, 'Transformation'; Palmer, *English Law*.
3. A. Ayton, *Knights and Warhorses: Military Service and the English Aristocracy under Edward III* (Woodbridge: Boydell Press, 1994), pp. 9–25; M. Prestwich, *Armies and Warfare in the Middle Ages: The English Experience* (New Haven, CT and London: Yale University Press, 1996), pp. 334–46; W. M. Ormrod, 'The West European Monarchies in the Later Middle Ages', in R. Bonney (ed.), *Economic Systems and State Finance* (Oxford: Clarendon Press, 1995), pp. 123–60.
4. J.-P. Genet, 'L'état moderne: un modèle opératoire?', in J.-P. Genet (ed.), *L'état moderne: genèse* (Paris: Centre National de la Recherche Scientifique, 1990), pp. 261–81.
5. R. W. Kaeuper, *War, Justice and Public Order: England and France in the Later Middle Ages* (Oxford: Clarendon Press, 1988).
6. Putnam, 'Transformation', pp. 41–8; Putnam, *Enforcement*; B. H. Putnam, 'Shire Officials: Keepers of the Peace and Justices of the Peace', in *EGW*, vol. 3, pp. 185–217.
7. Palmer, *English Law*, *passim*.
8. For a useful survey, see R. R. Richards, 'Evolution', in E. Fox Keller and E. A. Lloyd (eds), *Keywords in Evolutionary Theory* (Cambridge, MA: Harvard University Press, 1992), pp. 95–105.
9. S. J. Gould, *The Panda's Thumb: More Reflections in Natural History* (New York and London: Norton, 1980), pp. 179–85 (quotation at p. 184).
10. S. J. Gould, *Ever Since Darwin: Reflections in Natural History* (London: Burnett Books, 1978), pp. 21–45 (quotation at p. 36).
11. For a vigorous statement of this position, see A. Harding, *The Law Courts of Medieval England* (London: George Allen & Unwin, 1973), pp. 92–8; for recent critical reviews of such older notions, see G. L. Harriss, 'Political Society and the Growth of Government in Late Medieval England', *P&P*,

138 (1993), pp. 46–56; W. M. Ormrod, *Political Life in Medieval England, 1300–1450* (Basingstoke: Macmillan, 1995), pp. 109–29. The terminology of privatisation is used by E. Powell, 'Law and Justice', in R. Horrox (ed.), *Fifteenth-Century Attitudes: Perceptions of Society in Late Medieval England* (Cambridge: Cambridge University Press, 1994), p. 38.
12. K. B. McFarlane, *The Nobility of Later Medieval England* (Oxford: Clarendon Press, 1973), pp. 115–18; G. L. Harriss, 'Introduction', in K. B. McFarlane, *England in the Fifteenth Century* (London: Hambledon Press, 1981), pp. xix–xxiii; Powell, *Criminal Justice*, pp. 19–20.
13. As such it rejects the notions of progress outlined by F. L. Utley, 'Editor's Introduction', in F. L. Utley (ed.), *The Forward Movement of the Fourteenth Century* (Columbus, OH: Ohio State University Press, 1961), pp. 3–8, and deployed in a legal context by D. W. Sutherland, *The Assize of Novel Disseisin* (Oxford: Clarendon Press, 1973), p. 168.
14. See the application of Gould's work in H. Spruyt, *The Sovereign State and Its Competitors: An Analysis of Systems Change* (Princeton, NJ: Princeton University Press, 1994), pp. 16–20, 22–9.
15. See R. M. Smith, 'Demographic Developments in Rural England, 1300–48: A Survey', in B. M. S. Campbell (ed.), *Before the Black Death: Studies in the 'Crisis' of the Early Fourteenth Century* (Manchester: Manchester University Press, 1991), pp. 25–77.
16. P. J. P. Goldberg, 'Introduction', in W. M. Ormrod and P. G. Lindley (eds), *The Black Death in England* (Stamford: Paul Watkins, 1996), p. 13.
17. Palmer, *English Law*, *passim*.
18. Putnam, 'Transformation', pp. 19–48; Putnam (ed.), *Proceedings*, pp. xxxvi–xlviii.
19. For a useful survey, see A. L. Brown, *The Governance of Late Medieval England, 1272–1461* (London: Edward Arnold, 1989), pp. 100–40.
20. D. W. Sutherland, *Quo Warranto Proceedings in the Reign of Edward I* (Oxford: Clarendon Press, 1963).
21. H. M. Cam, *Liberties and Communities in Medieval England* (London: Merlin Press, 1963), pp. 183–204; Putnam, *Enforcement*, pp. 138–43.
22. J. H. Baker, *An Introduction to English Legal History*, 3rd edn (London: Butterworths, 1990), pp. 26–7.
23. For the consequent continued vulnerability of copyhold (the late medieval version of villein tenure) upon the will of the lord, see E. B. Fryde, *Peasants and Landlords in Later Medieval England c. 1380–c. 1525* (Stroud: Alan Sutton, 1996), pp. 227–41.
24. J. C. Holt, *Magna Carta*, 2nd edn (Cambridge: Cambridge University Press, 1992), pp. 290, 325, 456–7.
25. Putnam (ed.), *Proceedings*, pp. xxxvi–xxxvii.
26. C. Carpenter, *Locality and Polity: A Study of Warwickshire Landed Society, 1401–1499* (Cambridge: Cambridge University Press, 1992), pp. 340–1; M. L. Bush, *The English Aristocracy* (Manchester: Manchester University Press, 1984), p. 198.
27. See the interesting perspective of Baker, *Introduction*, pp. 28–31.
28. For recent comments, see M. R. Somers, 'Citizenship and the Place of the Public Sphere: Law, Community, and Political Culture in the Transition to

Democracy', *American Sociological Review*, 58 (1993), pp. 587–620; J. A. Sharpe, 'The Law, Law Enforcement, State Formation and National Integration in Late Medieval and Early Modern England', in X. Rousseau and R. Levy (eds), *Le pénal dans tous ses états: Justice, états et sociétés en Europe (XIIe–XXe siècles)*, Publications des Facultés universitaires Saint-Louis, 74 (Brussels, 1997), pp. 65–80.

Notes to Chapter 2: Royal Justice at the Centre

1. T. F. Tout, *Collected Papers* (Manchester: Manchester University Press, 1932–4), vol. 3, pp. 223–75.
2. For what follows, see J. H. Baker, *An Introduction to English Legal History*, 3rd edn (London: Butterworths, 1990), pp. 20–4, 44–59.
3. J. C. Holt, *Magna Carta*, 2nd edn (Cambridge: Cambridge University Press, 1992), pp. 323–4, 454–5.
4. M. T. Clanchy, 'Magna Carta and the Common Pleas', in H. Mayr-Harting and R. I. Moore (eds), *Studies in Medieval History Presented to R. H. C. Davis* (London: Hambledon Press, 1985), pp. 219–32.
5. *SCCKB*, vol. 2, pp. lxxiii, lxxvi–lxxvii; D. M. Broome, 'Exchequer Migrations to York in the Thirteenth and Fourteenth Centuries', in A. G. Little and F. M. Powicke (eds), *Essays in Medieval History Presented to T. F. Tout* (Manchester: Manchester University Press, 1925), pp. 291–300.
6. Palmer, *English Law*, pp. 3–4, n. 10; W. M. Ormrod, 'The Politics of Pestilence: Government in England after the Black Death', in W. M. Ormrod and P. G. Lindley (eds), *The Black Death in England* (Stamford: Paul Watkins, 1996), pp. 150–1; W. M. Ormrod, 'The Peasants' Revolt and the Government of England', *JBS*, 29 (1990), p. 8. For the comparable record of king's bench, see the Appendix. Note that king's bench did not follow common pleas and adjourn in Trinity 1377.
7. C. M. Barron, 'The Quarrel of Richard II with London 1392–7', in F. R. H. Du Boulay and C. M. Barron (eds), *The Reign of Richard II* (London: Athlone Press, 1971), pp. 173–201; P. Lindley, 'Westminster Kings and the Medieval Palace of Westminster', *Kunstchronik*, 49 (1996), pp. 236–43.
8. B. Wilkinson, *The Chancery under Edward III* (Manchester: Manchester University Press, 1929), p. 60; J. C. Davies, 'Common Law Writs and Returns, Richard I to Richard II', *BIHR*, 26 (1953), pp. 140–1. For what follows, see Baker, *Introduction*, pp. 63–110.
9. B. Wilkinson, 'The Seals of the Two Benches under Edward III', *EHR*, 42 (1927), pp. 397–401; M. Blatcher, *The Court of King's Bench, 1450–1550* (London: Athlone Press, 1978), pp. 16–17.
10. E. Powell, 'Jury Trial and Gaol Delivery in the Late Middle Ages: The Midland Circuit, 1400–1429', in J. S. Cockburn and T. A. Green (eds), *Twelve Good Men and True: The Criminal Jury in England, 1200–1800* (Princeton, NJ: Princeton University Press, 1988), pp. 78–116.
11. M. Hastings, *The Court of Common Pleas in Fifteenth Century England* (New York: Columbia University Press, 1947), pp. 269–70; C. R. Cheney (ed.),

Handbook of Dates for Students of English History, Royal Historical Society Guides and Handbooks 4 (London, 1978), pp. 65–7.
12. For what follows, see Baker, *Introduction*, pp. 63–83; Hastings, *Common Pleas*, pp. 158–84; Palmer, *English Law*, pp. 139–293.
13. 28 Edw. I c. 5 (*SR*, vol. 1, p. 139). For what follows, see *SCCKB*, vols 1–7; M. Blatcher, 'The Working of the Court of King's Bench in the Fifteenth Century', University of London PhD thesis (1936); Blatcher, *King's Bench*.
14. *SCCKB*, vol. 2, pp. lxiii–lxv; vol. 3, pp. lxxxiii–lxxxviii; vol. 4, pp. xxxviii–xlvi, xcvi–cv; C. Given-Wilson, *The Royal Household and the King's Affinity: Service, Politics and Finance in England, 1360–1413* (New Haven, CT and London: Yale University Press, 1986), pp. 48–53.
15. *SCCKB*, vol. 4, p. cvi.
16. Powell, *Criminal Justice*, pp. 47–64.
17. *SCCKB*, vol. 2, pp. xxxv–xxxvii.
18. Putnam (ed.), *Proceedings*, pp. lxiii–lxiv.
19. For what follows see A. Harding, 'Plaints and Bills in the History of English Law', in D. Jenkins (ed.), *Legal History Studies 1972* (Cardiff: University of Wales, 1975), pp. 65–86.
20. *SCCKB*, vol. 4, pp. lxxi–lxxii.
21. W. M. Ormrod, 'York and the Crown under the First Three Edwards', in S. Rees Jones (ed.), *The Government of Medieval York. Essays in Commemoration of the 1396 Royal Charter*, Borthwick Studies in History 3 (York, 1997), pp. 14–33.
22. The phrase is that of Putnam, *Shareshull*, p. 80; it is employed, most recently, by Powell, *Criminal Justice*, p. 55 and *passim*. For criticism of Putnam's work, see *SCCKB*, vol. 6, pp. ix–xii.
23. For the itinerary after 1399, see *SCCKB*, vol. 7, pp. lviii–lxi; Powell, *Criminal Justice*, pp. 173–94.
24. Putnam (ed.), *Proceedings*, p. lxiv; Blatcher, *King's Bench*, p. 47.
25. Hastings, *Common Pleas*, p. 16.
26. For what follows, see: J. F. Baldwin, *The King's Council in England during the Middle Ages* (Oxford: Clarendon Press, 1913); I. S. Leadam and J. F. Baldwin (eds), *Select Cases before the King's Council, 1243–1482*, SS 35 (London, 1918); A. L. Brown, *The Governance of Late Medieval England, 1272–1461* (London: Edward Arnold, 1989), pp. 30–42; W. M. Ormrod, *The Reign of Edward III: Crown and Political Society in England, 1327–1377* (New Haven, CT and London: Yale University Press, 1990), pp. 74–7.
27. G. D. Squibb, *The High Court of Chivalry* (Oxford: Clarendon Press, 1959), pp. 1–28.
28. M. Keen, 'The Jurisdiction and Origins of the Constable's Court', in J. Gillingham and J. C. Holt (eds), *War and Government in the Middle Ages: Essays in Honour of J. O. Prestwich* (Woodbridge: Boydell Press, 1984), pp. 159–69.
29. R. G. Marsden (ed.), *Select Cases in the Court of Admiralty I*, SS 6 (London, 1894), pp. xiv–xvi.
30. M. Hemmant (ed.), *Select Cases in the Exchequer Chamber*, SS 51 (London, 1933), pp. xii–xx.
31. For example: *CPR 1345–8*, pp. 136–8; C 256/1/1, no. 1d.

32. See the case of William Rouceby and John Avenal, the opening stages of which are printed in Leadam and Baldwin (eds), *Select Cases before the King's Council*, pp. 37–41. Rouceby was brought before the council in 1354 and placed in the custody of Phillip Whitton. Later that year, Whitton claimed to have handed Rouceby over to Avenal, but the latter disclaimed any knowledge of this (C 256/6/1, no. 10). Avenal was himself placed in the Tower of London in 1355 (*CCR 1354–60*, p. 135) and his lands were seized (SC 8/246/12295, datable in C 81/1334/23), but this did nothing to solve the problem of Rouceby's whereabouts.
33. For what follows, see W. M. Ormrod, 'The Origins of the *Sub pena* Writ', *Historical Research*, 61 (1988), pp. 11–20; W. M. Ormrod, 'Government by Commission: The Continual Council of 1386 and English Royal Administration', *Peritia*, 10 (1996), pp. 309–11.
34. For what follows, see T. S. Haskett, 'The Medieval English Court of Chancery', *Law and History Review*, 14 (1996), pp. 245–313.
35. Wilkinson, *Chancery*, pp. 94–7.
36. Ormrod, 'Origins of the *Sub pena* Writ', pp. 12–13.
37. Baldwin, *King's Council*, p. 249.
38. Palmer, *English Law*, p. 111, and the sources cited there.
39. J. L. Barton, 'The Medieval Use', *LQR*, 81 (1965), pp. 562–77; Palmer, *English Law*, pp. 127–30.
40. The quotation comes from the coronation oath: Brown, *Governance*, p. 13.
41. G. L. Harriss, *King, Parliament and Public Finance in Medieval England to 1369* (Oxford: Clarendon Press, 1975).
42. These two categories are suggested by G. L. Harriss, 'The Formation of Parliament, 1272–1377', in R. G. Davies and J. H. Denton (eds), *The English Parliament in the Middle Ages* (Manchester: Manchester University Press, 1981), p. 35.
43. T. F. T. Plucknett, 'Parliament', *EGW*, vol. 1, pp. 110–11.
44. H. G. Richardson and G. O. Sayles (eds), *Fleta II*, SS 72 (London, 1955), p. 109; B. Wilkinson, *The Constitutional History of England, 1216–1399* (London: Longmans, Green, 1948–58), vol. 3, p. 170.
45. 5 Edw. II c. 29 (*SR*, vol. 1, p. 165).
46. J. G. Edwards, '"Justice" in Early English Parliaments', in E. B. Fryde and E. Miller (eds), *Historical Studies of the English Parliament* (Cambridge: Cambridge University Press, 1970), vol. 1, pp. 279–97.
47. For what follows, see T. F. T. Plucknett, *Studies in English Legal History* (London: Hambledon Press, 1983), chapters VI, VIII–X; J. G. Bellamy, *The Law of Treason in England in the Later Middle Ages* (Cambridge: Cambridge University Press, 1970).
48. J. R. Maddicott, 'Parliament and the Constituencies, 1272–1377', in Davies and Denton (eds), *English Parliament*, pp. 64–6; N. M. Fryde, 'Edward III's Removal of his Ministers and Judges, 1340–1', *BIHR*, 48 (1975), pp. 149–61. The Ordinances of 1311 specifically endorsed this as a function of parliament: 5 Edw. II c. 29 (*SR*, vol. 1, p. 165).
49. 15 Edw. III st. 1 c. 2 (*SR*, vol. 1, p. 295), adapted in Wilkinson, *Constitutional History*, vol. 2, p. 201.
50. G. Lambrick, 'The Impeachment of the Abbot of Abingdon in 1368', *EHR*,

82 (1967), pp. 250–76. See also J. G. Bellamy, 'Appeal and Impeachment in the Good Parliament', *BIHR*, 41 (1966), pp. 35–46.
51. G. Holmes, *The Good Parliament* (Oxford: Clarendon Press, 1975), esp. pp. 2, 100–58.
52. J. S. Roskell, *The Impeachment of Michael de la Pole Earl of Suffolk in 1386* (Manchester: Manchester University Press, 1984).
53. Bellamy, *Law of Treason*, p. 211.
54. *SCCKB*, vol. 1, pp. cxxix–cxli; vol. 4, pp. lxxxvii–xcv; vol. 6, pp. li–cvii; vol. 7, pp. xxviii–xli; D. M. Broome, 'The Exchequer in the Reign of Edward III. A Preliminary Investigation', University of Manchester PhD thesis (1922), p. 71.
55. Wilkinson, *Chancery*, p. 65.
56. *SCCKB*, vol. 1, p. lxiii; vol. 4, p. xix; Broome, 'Exchequer', p. 70; R. L. Storey, 'Gentlemen-bureaucrats', in C. H. Clough (ed.), *Profession, Vocation, and Culture in Later Medieval England* (Liverpool: Liverpool University Press, 1982), pp. 97–9.
57. For what follows, see P. Brand, *The Making of the Common Law* (London: Hambledon Press, 1992), pp. 57–75; P. Brand, *The Origins of the English Legal Profession* (Oxford: Blackwell, 1992), pp. 106–19.
58. W. M. Ormrod, 'Accountability and Collegiality: The English Royal Secretariat in the Mid-Fourteenth Century', in K. Fianu and D. J. Guth (eds), *Ecrit et pouvoir dans les chancelleries médiévales: espace français, espace anglais* (Louvain-la-Neuve: Fédération Internationale des Institute d'Etudes Médiévales, 1997), pp. 55–86.
59. Tout, *Collected Papers*, vol. 2, pp. 143–71.
60. D. Higgins, 'Justices and Parliament in the Early Fourteenth Century', *Parliamentary History*, 12 (1993), p. 11.
61. J. R. L. Highfield, 'The Early Colleges', in J. I. Catto (ed.), *The History of the University of Oxford I: The Early Schools* (Oxford: Clarendon Press, 1984), pp. 236–8; D. R. Leader, *A History of the University of Cambridge I: The University to 1546* (Cambridge: Cambridge University Press, 1988), pp. 78–80.
62. A. B. Emden, *A Biographical Register of the University of Oxford to 1500* (Oxford, 1957–9), vol. 2, pp. 1007, 1370, 1392, 1864; G. P. Cuttino, *English Diplomatic Administration 1259–1339*, 2nd edn (Oxford: Clarendon Press, 1971), pp. 143–4; P. Chaplais, *Essays in Medieval Diplomacy and Administration* (London: Hambledon Press, 1981), chapter XXII.
63. H. Coing, 'English Equity and the *Denunciatio evangelica*', *LQR*, 70 (1955), pp. 223–41; M. Bielby, 'The Profits of Expertise: The Rise of the Civil Lawyers and Chancery Equity', in M. Hicks (ed.), *Profit, Piety and the Professions in Later Medieval England* (Gloucester: Alan Sutton, 1990), pp. 72–90. The family link between Thoresby and Waltham is emphasised by Ormrod, 'Origins of the *Sub pena* Writ', pp. 12, 18–19.
64. C. T. Allmand, 'The Civil Lawyers', in Clough (ed.), *Profession, Vocation, and Culture*, p. 156.
65. *SCCKB*, vol. 5, pp. xlvi–xlvii.
66. J. H. Baker, *The Order of Serjeants at Law*, SS Supplementary Series 5 (London, 1984), *passim*, summarising extensive biographical data from *SCCKB*, vols 3–6.

67. Biographical material taken from T. F. Tout, *Chapters in the Administrative History of Mediaeval England* (Manchester: Manchester University Press, 1920–33); Emden, *Biographical Register of the University of Oxford*; J. R. L. Highfield, 'The English Hierarchy in the Reign of Edward III', *TRHS*, 5th series, 6 (1956), pp. 115–38.
68. Tout, *Chapters*, vol. 3, pp. 124, 266; Fryde, 'Edward III's Removal of his Ministers and Judges', pp. 159–61; W. M. Ormrod, 'An Experiment in Taxation: The English Parish Subsidy of 1371', *Speculum*, 63 (1988), pp. 59–60; W. M. Ormrod, *Political Life in Medieval England, 1300–1450* (Basingstoke: Macmillan, 1995), pp. 29–30.
69. W. M. Ormrod, 'Edward III's Government of England, *c.* 1346–1356', University of Oxford DPhil thesis (1984), pp. 52–5.
70. Palmer, *English Law*, pp. 104–32.
71. K. B. McFarlane, *The Nobility of Later Medieval England* (Oxford: Clarendon Press, 1973), p. 22. For further discussion, see C. Given-Wilson, *The English Nobility in the Late Middle Ages* (London and New York: Routledge & Kegan Paul, 1987), p. 157; B. P. Vale, 'The Scropes of Bolton and of Masham, *c.* 1300–*c.* 1450', University of York DPhil thesis (1988).
72. Figures based on biographical detail in Tout, *Chapters*, vol. 6; and *SCCKB*, vols 1–6. The calculations discount the interregna between chancellorships, when the great seal was held by temporary custodians.
73. J. Alexander and P. Binski (eds), *Age of Chivalry: Art in Plantagenet England, 1200–1400* (London: Royal Academy of Arts, 1987), p. 227.
74. *SCCKB*, vol. 4, pp. xxii–xxv; Higgins, 'Justices and Parliament', p. 15.
75. *SCCKB*, vol. 6, pp. xxi–xxii; vol. 7, p. xv.
76. *SCCKB*, vol. 4, p. xxii; E. W. Ives, *The Common Lawyers of Pre-Reformation England* (Cambridge: Cambridge University Press, 1983), pp. 322–3.
77. Baker, *Serjeants at Law*, pp. 34–8.
78. B. Vale, 'The Profits of the Law and the "Rise" of the Scropes: Henry Scrope (d. 1336) and Geoffrey Scrope (d. 1340), Chief Justices to Edward II and Edward III', in Hicks (ed.), *Profit, Piety and the Professions*, p. 99.
79. For what follows, see J. R. Maddicott, *Law and Lordship: Royal Justices as Retainers in Thirteenth- and Fourteenth-Century England*, P&P Supplement 4 (Cambridge, 1978).
80. Maddicott, *Law and Lordship*, pp. 35–6.
81. Brand, *Common Law*, pp. 103–33.
82. Fryde, 'Edward III's Removal of his Ministers and Judges', p. 157.
83. 20 Edw. III (*SR*, vol. 1, pp. 303–6).
84. T. F. Tout and H. Johnstone (eds), *State Trials of the Reign of Edward the First, 1289–1293*, Camden Society, 3rd series, 9 (London, 1906), p. 39. There is confusion in the secondary literature over the amount of the fine: see *SCCKB*, vol. 1, p. liv, n. 1; Brand, *Common Law*, p. 105.
85. L. O. Pike (ed.), *Year Books of Edward III: 14, 15 Edward III*, RS 31 (London, 1889), p. 258. The original record of the case is JUST 1/258, mm. 3–3d.
86. *SCCKB*, vol. 1, p. lxviii and n. 3; vol. 6, p. xvii.
87. *RP*, vol. 2, p. 219; M. V. Clarke, *Fourteenth Century Studies* (Oxford: Clarendon Press, 1937), p. 51; Maddicott, *Law and Lordship*, p. 66.

88. Maddicott, *Law and Lordship*, pp. 69–81.
89. V. J. Scattergood, *Politics and Poetry in the Fifteenth Century* (London: Blandford Press, 1971), pp. 319–25.
90. Powell, *Criminal Justice*, pp. 40–2, 107–14.

Notes to Chapter 3: Royal Justice in the Provinces

1. W. L. Warren, *Henry II* (London: Methuen, 1973), pp. 281–4, 286; W. T. Reedy, 'The Origins of the General Eyre', *Speculum*, 41 (1966), pp. 717–23. Localised eyres had been common since the beginning of the twelfth century.
2. H. M. Cam, *Studies in the Hundred Rolls*, Oxford Studies in Social and Legal History 6 (Oxford, 1921), pp.10–29.
3. C. A. F. Meekings (ed.), *Crown Pleas of the Wiltshire Eyre, 1249*, Wiltshire Record Society 16 (Devizes, 1960), pp. 37–69.
4. Cam, *Studies in the Hundred Rolls*, pp. 22–41; D. W. Sutherland, *Quo Warranto Proceedings in the Reign of Edward I* (Cambridge: Cambridge University Press, 1963), pp. 19–20, 25–6.
5. A. Harding, 'Plaints and Bills in the History of English Law', in D. Jenkins (ed.), *Legal History Studies 1972* (Cardiff: University of Wales, 1975), p. 65.
6. A. Harding (ed.), *Roll of the Shropshire Eyre of 1256*, SS 96 (London, 1980), pp. xvi–xvii; Sutherland, *Quo Warranto*, pp. 23–4; Harding, 'Plaints and Bills', pp. 65–70.
7. Sutherland, *Quo Warranto*, pp. 27–9.
8. D. Crook, 'The Later Eyres', *EHR*, 97 (1982), pp. 241–3, 248; Sutherland, *Quo Warranto*, pp. 29–30, 180–3. Between 1290 and 1294 such pleas were referred to king's bench and continued there.
9. D. Crook, *Records of the General Eyre*, Public Record Office Handbooks 20 (London, 1982), pp. 144–5, 170–1; Sutherland, *Quo Warranto*, p. 29.
10. A. Harding, 'Early Trailbaston Proceedings from the Lincoln Roll of 1305', in R. F. Hunnisett and J. B. Post (eds), *Medieval Legal Records Edited in Memory of C. A. F. Meekings* (London: HMSO, 1978), p. 149.
11. Crook, 'Later Eyres', pp. 245, 248–9.
12. D. W. Sutherland (ed.), *The Eyre of Northamptonshire, 1329–1330*, SS 97–8 (London, 1983), vol. 1, p. xviii; A. Harding, *The Law Courts of Medieval England* (London: George Allen & Unwin, 1973), p. 91; Crook, 'Later Eyres', p. 262.
13. Crook, 'Later Eyres', p. 265; W. N. Bryant, 'The Financial Dealings of Edward III with the County Communities, 1330–60', *EHR*, 83 (1968), pp. 763–4.
14. Sutherland (ed.), *Eyre of Northamptonshire*, vol. 1, pp. xxii, xxvii.
15. J. G. Bellamy, *Crime and Public Order in England in the Later Middle Ages* (London: Routledge & Kegan Paul, 1973), p. 2.
16. Crook, 'Later Eyres', pp. 243–6.
17. Crook, 'Later Eyres', pp. 245–6.
18. Warren, *Henry II*, pp. 336–50.

19. M. M. Taylor, 'Justices of Assize', in *EGW*, vol. 3, pp. 225–8.
20. *CCR 1272–9*, p. 52. Initially there were six county groupings, but this was reorganised and reduced to four in 1274: *CCR 1272–9*, p. 135.
21. An adjustment to the circuits occurred in 1285, for example, following the second Statute of Westminster: *CCR 1279–88*, p. 365.
22. 21 Edw. I (*SR*, vol. 1, p. 112).
23. C 66/112, m. 22d; *CCR 1288–96*, p. 394; Musson, *Public Order*, p. 95.
24. R. B. Pugh, *Imprisonment in Medieval England* (Cambridge: Cambridge University Press, 1968), pp. 280–1.
25. 27 Edw. I c. 3 (*SR*, vol. 1, pp. 129–30).
26. Some entries give no name, just 'justice of assize' and the particular county: see C 66/119, m. 28d (Yorkshire), m. 24d (Nottinghamshire).
27. C 66/121, m. 14d (1301); C 66/122, m. 16d (1302).
28. For example: C 66/141, m. 19d (Cumberland, Westmorland); C 66/147, m. 4d (Lancashire, Westmorland, Cumberland); C 66/148, m. 18d (Lancashire).
29. *CCR 1307–13*, pp. 336–7: seven circuits were named; six resembled those of 1328, while the seventh consisted of three pairs of counties which 'floated' between established circuits in the early years of Edward III.
30. 2 Edw. III c. 2 (*SR*, vol. 1, p. 258).
31. 4 Edw. III c. 2 (*SR*, vol. 1, pp. 261–2).
32. C 66/169, m. 6d (19 May 1328); C 66/174, m. 17d (19 December 1330).
33. 18 Edw. III st. 2 c. 2 (*SR*, vol. 1, pp. 300–1).
34. Powell, 'Administration', pp. 51–6.
35. Cam, *Studies in the Hundred Rolls*, pp. 53–7, 73–9; for what follows, see R. W. Kaeuper, 'Law and Order in Fourteenth-Century England: The Evidence of Special Commissions of Oyer and Terminer', *Speculum*, 54 (1979), pp. 734–84.
36. B. Wilkinson, 'The Authorisation of Chancery Writs under Edward III', *Bulletin of the John Rylands Library*, 8 (1924), pp. 117–18.
37. R. B. Pugh (ed.), *Calendar of London Trailbaston Trials under Commissions of 1305 and 1306* (London: HMSO, 1975), pp. 1–4.
38. Harding, 'Early Trailbaston Proceedings', pp. 144–5.
39. For example: C 66/126, m. 14d (18 August 1305, home circuit).
40. *RP*, vol. 1, p. 178; Cambridge University Library Dd. 7. 6, f. 61 (articles of trailbaston); Harding, 'Early Trailbaston Proceedings', pp. 144–5.
41. 33 Edw. I (*RP*, vol. 1, p. 183; *SR*, vol. 1, p. 145); A. Harding, 'The Origins of the Crime of Conspiracy', *TRHS*, 5th series, 33 (1983), p. 97.
42. Cam, *Studies in the Hundred Rolls*, p. 77; B. W. McLane (ed.), *The 1341 Royal Inquest in Lincolnshire*, Lincoln Record Society 78 (Lincoln, 1988).
43. Pugh (ed.), *London Trailbaston Trials*, pp. 37–8.
44. *RP*, vol. 2, pp. 133–4, 148; Putnam, *Shareshull*, pp. 64–7; G. L. Harriss, *King, Parliament and Public Finance in Medieval England to 1369* (Oxford: Clarendon Press, 1975), pp. 405–10.
45. Kaeuper, 'Law and Order', p. 741; *CPR 1377–99*, *passim*.
46. For example: *CPR 1385–9*, pp. 546, 547; *CPR 1388–92*, pp. 135, 142, 272, 349, 440–1; *CPR 1391–6*, pp. 84, 232, 354, 433–4, 520, 588–9; *CPR 1396–9*, p. 226.

47. Palmer, *English Law*, pp. 11–16, 23–4; W. M. Ormrod, *The Reign of Edward III: Crown and Political Society in England, 1327–1377* (New Haven, CT and London, 1990), pp. 62–7.
48. A. Harding, 'The Origins and Early History of the Keeper of the Peace', *TRHS*, 5th series, 10 (1960), pp. 85, 96–7.
49. 13 Edw. I (Statute of Winchester) (*SR*, vol. 1, pp. 96–8); Harding, 'Origins', pp. 99–100.
50. M. Powicke, *Military Obligation in Medieval England* (Oxford: Clarendon Press, 1962), pp. 64, 119–20; H. Summerson, 'The Enforcement of the Statute of Winchester, 1285–1327', *Journal of Legal History*, 13 (1992), pp. 232–50.
51. Taylor, 'Justices of Assize', pp. 220–1.
52. 28 Edw. I (Articles upon the Charters) cc. 1, 17 (*SR*, vol. 1, pp. 136–7, 140); *CPR 1292–1301*, pp. 515–17.
53. As exemplified in records from 1308 and 1320: JUST 1/262, printed in Cam, *Liberties and Communities*, pp. 167–72; JUST 1/640, printed in M. Gollancz (ed.), *Rolls of Northamptonshire Sessions of the Peace*, Northamptonshire Record Society 11 (Northampton, 1940).
54. For example: C 66/150, m. 31d (Gloucester), m. 30d (Old Sarum), m. 23d (Chichester), m. 18d (Canterbury), m. 16d (Worcester); B. H. Putnam (ed.), *Kent Keepers of the Peace, 1316–1317*, Records of the Kent Archaeological Society 13 (Canterbury, 1933).
55. *CPR 1313–17*, pp. 128–30 (18 June 1314), 225–6 (10 July 1314); *CPR 1324–7*, pp. 292–3, 352 (8 June 1326); B. H. Putnam, 'Records of the Keepers of the Peace and their Supervisors, 1307–1327', *EHR*, 45 (1930), pp. 435–44.
56. *RP*, vol. 1, p. 371; JUST 1/1016, mm. 9, 9d (Wiltshire).
57. *CPR 1327–30*, pp. 429–31.
58. 4 Edw. III c. 2 (*SR*, vol. 1, pp. 261–2).
59. *CPR 1330–4*, pp. 136–7, 285–8, 292–7; *CPR 1334–8*, pp. 208–10, 367–71; *CPR 1338–40*, pp. 135–40; Putnam, 'Transformation', pp. 27–34.
60. 2 Edw. III cc. 3, 6 (*SR*, vol. 1, pp. 258–9); Cam, *Liberties and Communities*, p. 156.
61. 18 Edw. III st. 2 c. 2 (*SR*, vol. 1, p. 301); Putnam, 'Transformation', p. 42.
62. *CPR 1350–4*, pp. 85–91; 25 Edw. III st. 2 c. 5 (*SR*, vol. 1, p. 312).
63. 34 Edw. III c. 1 (*SR*, vol. 1, pp. 364–5).
64. 25 Edw. III st. 2 c. 7 (*SR*, vol. 1, p. 313); 36 Edw. III c. 12 (*SR*, vol. 1, p. 374).
65. Powell, 'Administration', pp. 53–7.
66. 13 Edw. I (Statute of Winchester) c. 6 (*SR*, vol. 1, pp. 97–8); Powicke, *Military Obligation*, p. 120.
67. *CPR 1321–4*, pp. 42–3.
68. *CPR 1334–8*, pp. 137–9, 208–10.
69. A. J. Verduyn, 'The Selection and Appointment of Justices of the Peace in 1338', *Historical Research*, 68 (1995), pp. 6–8; Musson, *Public Order*, pp. 70–4.
70. *CPR 1343–5*, p. 576; *CPR 1345–8*, p. 301.
71. Putnam (ed.), *Proceedings*, p. xxviii.
72. Verduyn, 'Attitude', pp. 137–8.

73. F. Palgrave (ed.), *Parliamentary Writs and Writs of Military Summons* (London: Record Commission, 1827–34), vol. 2(ii), Appendix, pp. 8–9, 11–12.
74. *CPR 1345–8*, p. 183.
75. 23 Edw. III (*SR*, vol. 1, pp. 307–9); Putnam, 'Transformation', p. 43; Putnam, *Enforcement*, pp. 9–15.
76. R. Sillem (ed.), *Some Sessions of the Peace in Lincolnshire, 1360–75*, Lincoln Record Society 30 (Lincoln, 1937), pp. xlv–xlvii; B. H. Putnam (ed.), *Yorkshire Sessions of the Peace, 1361–64*, Yorkshire Archaeological Society Record Series 100 (Wakefield, 1939), p. xiv; 34 Edw. III cc. 9–11 (*SR*, vol. 1, pp. 366–7); 36 Edw. III cc. 12, 14 (*SR*, vol. 1, pp. 374, 375).
77. 42 Edw. III c. 6 (*SR*, vol. 1, p. 388).
78. 34 Edw. III c. 5 (*SR*, vol. 1, p. 365).
79. *CPR 1301–7*, pp. 354–5.
80. *SCCKB*, vol. 4, pp. xix, lix–lxv; vol. 6, pp. ix–xii; G. H. Tupling (ed.), *South Lancashire in the Reign of Edward II*, Chetham Society 3rd series, 1 (Manchester, 1949).
81. Powell, *Criminal Justice*, pp. 14, 63.
82. Putnam, 'Transformation', pp. 29–30.
83. Putnam (ed.), *Proceedings*, p. cxviii, cited by Verduyn, 'Attitude', pp. 199–200.
84. *RP*, vol. 2, pp. 148 (12), 174 (70).
85. Verduyn, 'Attitude', pp. 136–41.
86. 34 Edw. III c. 1 (*SR*, vol. 1, p. 364).
87. R. Virgoe, 'The Crown and Local Government: East Anglia under Richard II', in F. R. H. Du Boulay and C. M. Barron (eds), *The Reign of Richard II: Essays in Honour of May McKisack* (London: Athlone Press, 1971), pp. 223, 232–3.
88. 12 Ric. II c. 10 (*SR*, vol. 2, p. 58); R. L. Storey, 'Liveries and Commissions of the Peace, 1388–90', in Du Boulay and Barron (eds), *Reign of Richard II*, pp. 137–9; N. Saul, *Knights and Esquires: The Gloucestershire Gentry in the Fourteenth Century* (Oxford: Clarendon Press, 1981), pp. 133–4.
89. Verduyn, 'Attitude', p. 118.
90. Verduyn, 'Attitude', p. 284, n. 42.
91. Virgoe, 'Local Government', pp. 233–5; Saul, *Knights and Esquires*, pp. 134–5.
92. Powell, 'Administration', pp. 55–6; S. Payling, *Political Society in Lancastrian England: The Greater Gentry of Nottinghamshire* (Oxford: Clarendon Press, 1991), pp. 177–80.
93. J. H. Baker, *The Order of Serjeants at Law*, SS Supplementary Series 5 (London, 1984).
94. 12 Edw. II c. 4 (*SR*, vol. 1, p. 178).
95. See, for example, the cases of Henry Scrope, John Doncaster, William Herle, Geoffrey Scrope and Walter Friskeney: Baker, *Serjeants at Law*, *passim*.
96. 2 Edw. III c. 2 (*SR*, vol. 1, p. 258).
97. C 66/169, mm. 6d, 2d.
98. 4 Edw. III c. 2 (*SR*, vol. 1, p. 261).
99. Pugh, *Imprisonment*, pp. 282–3.

100. Taylor, 'Justices of Assize', p. 232.
101. For example: Travers (C 66/173, m. 49d; C 66/174, m. 31d); Middleton (C 66/174, m. 17d; C 66/175, m. 37d).
102. 14 Edw. III st. 1 c. 16 (*SR*, vol. 1, p. 287); Baker, *Serjeants at Law*, p. 36.
103. Musson, *Public Order*, pp. 95–8, 102–16.
104. E. L. G. Stones, 'Sir Geoffrey le Scrope (*c*. 1280 to 1340), Chief Justice of the King's Bench', *EHR*, 69 (1954), pp. 12–15; Putnam, *Shareshull*, pp. 1–11.
105. J. L. Grassi, 'Royal Clerks from the Archdiocese of York in the Fourteenth Century', *Northern History*, 5 (1970), p. 33; Ormrod, *Edward III*, p. 72 and n. 9; Musson, *Public Order*, pp. 116–17.
106. *RP*, vol. 2, p. 334 (75); 8 Ric. II c. 2 (*SR*, vol. 2, p. 36); Powell, 'Administration', p. 59; Verduyn, 'Attitude', p. 179.
107. 13 Edw. I (Statute of Westminster II) c. 29 (*SR*, vol. 1, p. 85); Harding, 'Origins', p. 103.
108. Kaeuper, 'Law and Order', p. 753.
109. W. S. Thomson (ed.), *A Lincolnshire Assize Roll for 1298*, Lincoln Record Society 36 (Hereford, 1944), p. xiv.
110. Musson, *Public Order*, pp. 54, 57–60.
111. *CPR 1338–40*, pp. 141–2.
112. Powell, 'Administration', p. 51.
113. For example: JUST 3/145, mm. 2d, 3, 3d, 5, 5d, 6, 7, 11d, 12, 12d, 14d, 15d, 16.
114. *CPR 1361–4*, pp. 63–6.
115. Powell, 'Administration', pp. 52–4; JUST 3/142, mm. 8–11d, 13.
116. Powell, 'Administration', pp. 54–6.
117. Summerson, 'Enforcement of the Statute of Winchester', pp. 238–9.
118. Putnam (ed.), *Proceedings*, p. xliii; Palmer, *English Law*, pp. 23–4.
119. Kaeuper, 'Law and Order', p. 753.
120. 27 Edw. I c. 3 (*SR*, vol. 1, pp. 129–30).
121. JUST 1/417.
122. C 66/171, m. 5d; C 66/172, m. 9d; C 66/173, m. 36d; C 66/176, m. 7d.
123. Musson, *Public Order*, pp. 112, 114–15.
124. JUST 3/109, *passim* (Kent); JUST 3/112, mm. 3d, 4, 7 (Surrey).
125. JUST 3/109, m. 7d (Northamptonshire); JUST 3/55/3, m. 3d (Nottinghamshire); JUST 3/74/3, m. 1 (Yorkshire).
126. *CPR 1313–17*, pp. 128–30.
127. Twenty of those men were previously keepers of the peace under the 13 April commissions as well.
128. Putnam (ed.), *Kent Keepers*, p. xxi.
129. For example: JUST 3/53/1, mm. 10d, 12, 13, 15d (Northamptonshire).
130. *CPR 1324–7*, pp. 285–6; see also the 1325 peace commission, *CPR 1324–7*, pp. 228–9.
131. John Whitfield (Oxfordshire), Henry Pentelowe (Berkshire), Philip Aylesbury (Buckinghamshire), Richard Baskerville (Herefordshire).
132. For what follows, see Musson, *Public Order*, pp. 60–4.
133. Putnam, 'Transformation', p. 30; see also Cam, *Liberties and Communities*, p. 157.

134. *CPR 1338–40*, pp. 135–40.
135. Verduyn, 'Selection', pp. 10, 13–25.
136. *RP*, vol. 2, pp. 160, 161.
137. JUST 3/145, mm. 3, 3d.
138. Powell, 'Administration', p. 53.
139. Putnam (ed.), *Proceedings*, p. 291.
140. *RP*, vol. 3, pp. 83–5.
141. J. B. Post, 'The Peace Commissions of 1382', *EHR*, 91 (1976), pp. 98–101.
142. Powell, 'Administration', pp. 55–6.
143. S. Walker, 'Yorkshire Justices of the Peace, 1389–1413', *EHR*, 108 (1993), pp. 281–311.
144. R. Horrox, *Richard III: A Study of Service* (Cambridge: Cambridge University Press, 1989), pp. 1–26.
145. For example: C. Carpenter, *Locality and Polity: A Study of Warwickshire Landed Society, 1401–1499* (Cambridge: Cambridge University Press, 1992), pp. 267–72; E. Acheson, *A Gentry Community: Leicestershire in the Fifteenth Century, c. 1422–c. 1485* (Cambridge: Cambridge University Press, 1992), pp. 129–32.
146. Saul, *Knights and Esquires*, pp. 128–35.
147. Musson, *Public Order*, pp. 25, 93, 159–61.
148. Musson, *Public Order*, pp. 229–32.
149. Verduyn, 'Selection', pp. 6–8.
150. *CPR 1338–40*, p. 134.
151. Putnam, 'Transformation', p. 38; Verduyn, 'Selection', pp. 11–12.
152. Musson, *Public Order*, pp. 72–3.
153. Verduyn, 'Selection', p. 11.
154. *RP*, vol. 2, p. 201 (6); Verduyn, 'Attitude', pp. 102–3 and p. 272, n. 163.
155. Verduyn, 'Attitude', pp. 116–18.
156. *RP*, vol. 2, p. 238; Ormrod, *Edward III*, p. 112.
157. Storey, 'Liveries', pp. 131–52.
158. S. Walker, *The Lancastrian Affinity, 1361–1399* (Oxford: Clarendon Press, 1990), pp. 244–6. For evidence of Thomas Beauchamp, earl of Warwick, receiving indictments in Worcestershire in the late 1370s, see JUST 3/166, mm. 7–8d, 10d, 12d.
159. Walker, *Lancastrian Affinity*, pp. 212–13; Putnam (ed.), *Proceedings*, pp. lxxii, 275–89; Sillem (ed.), *Some Sessions of the Peace in Lincolnshire, 1360–75*, pp. lxxviii, 212–17.

Notes to Chapter 4:
External Influences on the Evolution of Justice

1. J. B. Post, 'Some Limitations of the Medieval Peace Rolls', *Journal of the Society of Archivists*, 4 no. 8 (1973), pp. 633–9.
2. And see also, for example, J. G. Bellamy, *Crime and Public Order in the Later Middle Ages* (London: Routledge & Kegan Paul, 1973), pp. 32–5; D. J. Guth, 'Enforcing Late-Medieval Law: Patterns in Litigation during Henry VII's Reign', in J. H. Baker (ed.), *Legal Records and the Historian*, Royal Historical

Society Studies in History 7 (London, 1978), pp. 80–96, esp. pp. 82–3.
3. E. Powell, 'Social Research and the Use of Medieval Criminal Records', *Michigan Law Review*, 79 (1980–1), pp. 967–78.
4. C. Carpenter, 'Law, Justice and Landowners in Late Medieval England', *Law and History Review*, 1 (1983), pp. 205–37, esp. pp. 225–9.
5. Bellamy, *Crime*, pp. 10–11; J. R. Maddicott, *Law and Lordship: Royal Justices as Retainers in Thirteenth- and Fourteenth-Century England*, P&P Supplement 4 (London, 1978), p. 44.
6. A. Herbert, 'Herefordshire: Some Aspects of Society and Public Order', in R. A. Griffiths (ed.), *Patronage, the Crown and the Provinces in Later Medieval England* (Gloucester: Alan Sutton, 1981), pp. 103–22; E. G. Kimball (ed.), *The Shropshire Peace Roll, 1400–1414* (Shrewsbury: Shropshire County Council, 1959), p. 40.
7. C. McNamee, *The Wars of the Bruces: Scotland, England and Ireland, 1306–1328* (East Linton: Tuckwell, 1997), pp. 72–122.
8. *SCCKB*, vol. 4, pp. 78–9; M. Prestwich, 'Gilbert de Middleton and the Attack on the Cardinals, 1317', in T. Reuter (ed.), *Warriors and Churchmen in the High Middle Ages: Essays Presented to Karl Leyser* (London: Hambledon Press, 1992), pp. 179–94; N. Fryde, *The Tyranny and Fall of Edward II, 1321–1326* (Cambridge: Cambridge University Press, 1979), pp. 156–9.
9. R. L. Storey, 'The North of England', in S. B. Chrimes, C. D. Ross and R. A. Griffiths (eds), *Fifteenth-Century England, 1399–1509* (Manchester: Manchester University Press, 1972), pp. 131–2; H. Summerson, 'Responses to War: Carlisle and the West March in the Later Fourteenth Century', in A. Goodman and A. Tuck (eds), *War and Border Societies in the Middle Ages* (London: Routledge, 1992), p. 166.
10. N. Denholm-Young (ed.), *Vita Edwardi Secundi* (London: Thomas Nelson and Sons, 1957), pp. 135–6; *CPR 1324–7*, p. 65. For similar complaints in the 1370s, see *RP*, vol. 2, pp. 352, 354.
11. E. Searle and R. Burghart, 'The Defense of England and the Peasants' Revolt', *Viator*, 3 (1972), pp. 365–88.
12. W. S. Thomson (ed.), *A Lincolnshire Assize Roll for 1298*, Lincoln Record Society 36 (Hereford, 1944), pp. xxxii–xxxiii, xci–cii, cxxvii–cxxvii; B. W. McLane (ed.), *The 1341 Royal Inquest in Lincolnshire*, Lincoln Record Society 78 (Lincoln, 1988), pp. xxv–xxix; J. R. Maddicott, 'The English Peasantry and the Demands of the Crown, 1294–1341', in T. H. Aston (ed.), *Landlords, Peasants and Politics in Medieval England* (Cambridge: Cambridge University Press, 1987), pp. 285–359.
13. Maddicott, *Law and Lordship*, pp. 40–8. For specific complaints about the failure of justice during royal absences from the realm, see SC 8/158/7891 (1331); SC 8/208/10360 (undatable); SC 8/209/10430 (1340).
14. N. D. Hurnard, *The King's Pardon for Homicide before 1307* (Oxford: Clarendon Press, 1969), pp. 311–26.
15. 5 Edw. II c. 28; 2 Edw. III c. 2; 4 Edw. III c. 13; 10 Edw III st. 1 cc. 2, 3; 14 Edw III st. 1 c. 15 (*SR*, vol. 1, pp. 164, 257–8, 264–5, 275, 286); T. F. T. Plucknett, 'Parliament', in *EGW*, vol. 1, pp. 119–20.
16. H. J. Hewitt, *The Organization of War under Edward III* (Manchester: Manchester University Press, 1966), pp. 29–30; W. M. Ormrod, *The Reign*

of Edward III: Crown and Political Society in England, 1327–1377 (New Haven, CT and London: Yale University Press, 1990), pp. 54–5; S. L. Waugh, *England in Reign of Edward III* (Cambridge: Cambridge University Press, 1991), p. 159; J. Aberth, *Criminal Churchmen in the Age of Edward III: The Case of Bishop Thomas de Lisle* (University Park, PA: Pennsylvania State University Press, 1996), p. 194.

17. B. A. Hanawalt, *Crime and Conflict in English Communities, 1300–1348* (Cambridge, MA: Harvard University Press, 1979), pp. 234–6.
18. A. Harding, 'Early Trailbaston Proceedings from the Lincoln Roll of 1305', in R. F. Hunnisett and J. B. Post (eds), *Medieval Legal Records Edited in Memory of C. A. F. Meekings* (London: HMSO, 1978), pp. 146–7.
19. E. L. G. Stones, 'The Folvilles of Ashby-Folville, Leicestershire, and their Associates in Crime, 1326–1347', *TRHS*, 5th series, 7 (1957), pp. 117–36; J. G. Bellamy, 'The Coterel Gang: an Anatomy of Fourteenth-Century Criminals', *EHR*, 79 (1964), pp. 698–717.
20. M. Jones and S. Walker (eds), 'Private Indentures for Life Service in Peace and War 1278–1476', *Camden Miscellany XXXII*, Camden Society 5th series, 3 (London, 1994), pp. 1–190. Jones and Walker stress the influence of military recruitment on the development of life retaining at pp. 15–16.
21. Ormrod, *Edward III*, pp. 111–13.
22. G. L. Harriss, 'Political Society and the Growth of Government in Late Medieval England', *P&P*, 138 (1993), p. 32.
23. D. Crook, *Records of the General Eyre*, Public Record Office Handbooks 20 (London, 1982), p. 171.
24. M. Prestwich, *War, Politics and Finance under Edward I* (London: Faber & Faber, 1972), p. 237; M. Prestwich, *Armies and Warfare in the Middle Ages* (New Haven, CT and London: Yale University Press, 1996), p. 109.
25. E. B. Fryde, 'Parliament and the French War, 1336–40', in E. B. Fryde and E. Miller (eds), *Historical Studies of the English Parliament* (Cambridge: Cambridge University Press, 1970), vol. 1, pp. 253–4; G. L. Harriss, *King, Parliament and Public Finance in Medieval England to 1369* (Oxford: Clarendon Press, 1975), pp. 244–5.
26. J. M. W. Bean, *The Decline of English Feudalism* (Manchester: Manchester University Press, 1968), pp. 66–79, 104–48.
27. Putnam, *Enforcement*, pp. 23–4, 138–43, 31*–2*; W. M. Ormrod, 'Edward III's Government of England, c. 1346–1356', University of Oxford DPhil thesis (1984), pp. 210–11; Verduyn, 'Attitude', p. 138.
28. W. M. Ormrod, 'The Politics of Pestilence: Government in England after the Black Death', in W. M. Ormrod and P. G. Lindley (eds), *The Black Death in England* (Stamford: Paul Watkins, 1996), p. 157 and n. 29.
29. The following deliberately excludes discussion of pardons from visitations by the eyre or oyer and terminer commissions, as well as general pardons from the penalties of the eyre (granted in 1340, 1357, 1362 and 1380); the latter type in particular tended to have more of a fiscal than a judicial significance. See J. R. Maddicott, 'Magna Carta and the Local Community', *P&P*, 102 (1984), pp. 25–65; W. N. Bryant, 'The Financial Dealings of Edward III with the County Communities, 1330–60', *EHR*, 83 (1968), pp. 760–71; Harriss, *Public Finance*, pp. 399–410.

30. 50 Edw. III c. 3 (*SR*, vol. 1, pp. 396–7), confirmed in Richard II's first parliament as 1 Ric. II c. 10 (*SR*, vol. 2, p. 4); *RP*, vol. 3, 103. For the general pardon of 1382, which is a special case, see the discussion of the Peasants' Revolt later in this chapter.
31. R. L. Storey, 'Index to Pardon Rolls', unpublished typescript in Public Record Office.
32. 21 Ric. II c. 15 (*SR*, vol. 2, p. 106); *RP*, vol. 3, p. 139. R. L. Storey, *The End of the House of Lancaster*, new edn (Gloucester: Alan Sutton, 1986), p. 212, and Powell, *Criminal Justice*, p. 84, n. 88, quote the price of a general pardon as 16s. 4d., but this excludes the additional 2s. payable to the chancellor: see H. C. Maxwell Lyte, *Historical Notes on the Use of the Great Seal of England* (London: HMSO, 1926), p. 332.
33. Powell, *Criminal Justice*, pp. 229–46.
34. A. Harding, 'The Origins and Early History of the Keeper of the Peace', *TRHS*, 5th series, 10 (1960), pp. 100–2.
35. M. Prestwich, 'England and Scotland during the Wars of Independence', in M. Jones and M. Vale (eds), *England and her Neighbours, 1066–1453* (London: Hambledon Press, 1989), pp. 188–97; C. J. Neville, 'Keeping the Peace on the Northern Marches in the Later Middle Ages', *EHR*, 109 (1994), pp. 1–25.
36. Harding, 'Origins', pp. 92, 99–100; Musson, *Public Order*, p. 16.
37. Musson, *Public Order*, pp. 11–82, *passim*; *CCR 1302-7*, pp. 396–7; *CPR 1307-13*, p. 588; 20 Edw. III (*SR*, vol. 1, pp. 303–6); Maddicott, *Law and Lordship*, p. 44.
38. H. M. Cam, *The Hundred and the Hundred Rolls* (London: Methuen, 1930), pp. 34–46; P. Brand, *The Making of the Common Law* (London: Hambledon Press, 1992), pp. 103–33.
39. Thomson (ed.), *Lincolnshire Assize Roll*, pp. ix–xiv, lii–lxxxviii; Prestwich, *War, Politics and Finance*, p. 289; Musson, *Public Order*, p. 36; N. Fryde, 'Edward III's Removal of his Ministers and Judges, 1340-1', *BIHR*, 48 (1975), pp. 148–61; W. R. Jones, '*Rex et ministri*: English Local Government and the Crisis of 1341', *JBS*, 13, no. 1 (1973), pp. 1–20; W. R. Jones, 'Keeping the Peace: English Society, Local Government, and the Commissions of 1341–44', *American Journal of Legal History*, 18 (1974), pp. 307–20; Verduyn, 'Attitude', pp. 86–7.
40. 34 Edw. III c. 1 (*SR*, vol. 1, p. 364), adapted in *EHD*, vol. 4, p. 541.
41. J. R. Maddicott, *Thomas of Lancaster* (Oxford: Oxford University Press, 1970), pp. 113–14; *CCR 1330-3*, p. 610; *CCR 1337-9*, p. 134; Putnam, 'Transformation', pp. 32–3; Verduyn, 'Attitude', pp. 43–4, 57 (which identifies other influences at work in 1337); Musson, *Public Order*, pp. 65–70.
42. Bellamy, *Crime*, pp. 5–6; Waugh, *Edward III*, pp. 153–69; Aberth, *Criminal Churchmen*, pp. 61–93.
43. 3 Edw. II c. 2 (*SR*, vol. 1, p. 158), adapted in *EHD*, vol. 3, p. 527; M. Prestwich, *English Politics in the Thirteenth Century* (Basingstoke: Macmillan, 1990), pp. 129–45.
44. G. L. Harriss, 'The Formation of Parliament, 1272–1377', in R. G. Davies and J. H. Denton (eds), *The English Parliament in the Middle Ages*

(Manchester: Manchester University Press, 1981), pp. 29–60; A. Harding, *England in the Thirteenth Century* (Cambridge: Cambridge University Press, 1993), pp. 217–19.
45. Putnam, 'Transformation', pp. 19–48; B. H. Putnam, 'Shire Officials: Keepers of the Peace and Justices of the Peace', in *EGW*, vol. 3, pp. 185–217; Putnam (ed.), *Proceedings*, pp. xxxviii–xliii.
46. Putnam's ideas on the politics of law-keeping in the early fourteenth century are self-consciously repeated by A. Harding, *The Law Courts of Medieval England* (London: George Allen & Unwin, 1973), pp. 94–5; Bellamy, *Crime*, p. 95; J. R. Lander, *The Limitations of English Monarchy in the Later Middle Ages* (Toronto: University of Toronto Press, 1989), p. 30; Palmer, *English Law*, p. 23.
47. The following two paragraphs draw on the data summarised in tabular form in Musson, *Public Order*, pp. 16–17, 52–3, and Ormrod, *Edward III*, p. 208.
48. Harriss, *Public Finance*, pp. 408–9; G. L. Harriss, 'Theory and Practice in Royal Taxation: Some Observations', *EHR*, 97 (1982), p. 813 and n. 4.
49. Ormrod, *Edward III*, pp. 79–80; A. L. Brown, 'Parliament, c. 1377–1422', in Davies and Denton (eds), *English Parliament*, p. 132.
50. Verduyn, 'Attitude', pp. 17, 38, 42, 48, 55, 75.
51. A. J. Verduyn, 'The Selection and Appointment of Justices of the Peace in 1338', *Historical Research*, 68 (1995), pp. 1–25.
52. Harriss, *Public Finance*, pp. 405–6.
53. *RP*, vol. 2, pp. 174, 201. Verduyn, 'Attitude', pp. 102–3 and p. 272, n. 163 (which provides important textual corrections to the printed edition of the parliament rolls).
54. Verduyn, 'Attitude', pp. 103, 116, 118, 138–9.
55. 25 Edw. III st. 2 c. 7; 36 Edw. III c. 12 (*SR*, vol. 1, pp. 313, 374).
56. 12 Ric. II c. 9 (*SR*, vol. 2, p. 59); Putnam (ed.), *Proceedings*, pp. lxxxix–xc.
57. Putnam, 'Transformation', pp. 43–4.
58. Harriss, *Public Finance*, pp. 354–5.
59. H. E. Hallam, 'Prices and Wages', in H. E. Hallam (ed.), *The Agrarian History of England and Wales II* (Cambridge: Cambridge University Press, 1988), pp. 787–91; I. Kershaw, 'The Great Famine and Agrarian Crisis in England 1315–1322', in R. H. Hilton (ed.), *Peasants, Knights and Heretics* (Cambridge: Cambridge University Press, 1976), p. 131; Z. Razi, *Life, Marriage and Death in a Medieval Parish: Economy, Society and Demography in Halesowen, 1270–1400* (Cambridge: Cambridge University Press, 1980), pp. 27–45.
60. A. R. H. Baker, 'Evidence in the *Nonarum inquisitiones* of Contracting Arable Lands in England during the Early Fourteenth Century', *Economic History Review*, 2nd series, 19 (1966), pp. 518–32; Maddicott, 'English Peasantry', pp. 346–8.
61. M. C. Prestwich, 'The Crown and the Currency: The Circulation of Money in Late Thirteenth and Early Fourteenth Century England', *Numismatic Chronicle*, 142 (1982), pp. 51–65; N. J. Mayhew, 'Money and Prices in England from Henry II to Edward III', *Agricultural History Review*, 35 (1987), pp. 121–32.

62. Hanawalt, *Crime and Conflict*, pp. 238–60; B. H. Putnam (ed.), *Kent Keepers of the Peace, 1316–1317*, Records of the Kent Archaeological Society 13 (Canterbury, 1933), discussed by Kershaw, 'Agrarian Crisis', pp. 94–5.
63. J. F. Willard, *Parliamentary Taxes on Personal Property, 1290 to 1334* (Cambridge, MA: Medieval Academy of America, 1934), pp. 170–4; R. H. Hilton, *Class Conflict and the Crisis of Feudalism*, rev. edn (London: Verso, 1990), pp. 59–60; Verduyn, 'Attitude', pp. 51–4.
64. Maddicott, 'English Peasantry', pp. 348–51.
65. E. Miller, 'The Economic Policies of Governments: France and England', in M. M. Postan, E. E. Rich and E. Miller (eds), *The Cambridge Economic History of Europe III: Economic Organization and Policies in the Middle Ages* (Cambridge: Cambridge University Press, 1963), pp. 281–339.
66. R. H. Britnell, '*Forstall*, Forestalling and the Statute of Forestallers', *EHR*, 102 (1987), pp. 89–102, esp. pp. 95, 100–1. For the proceedings of one of the 1308 commissions (for Essex), see H. M. Cam, *Liberties and Communities in Medieval England* (London: Merlin Press, 1963), pp. 165, 170–2.
67. *RP*, vol. 1, p. 295.
68. T. Rymer (ed.), *Foedera, conventiones, literae et cujuscunque generis acta publica* (London: Record Commission, 1816–30), vol. 2, pt 1, p. 286.
69. R. H. Britnell, *The Commercialisation of English Society, 1000–1500* (Cambridge: Cambridge University Press, 1993), pp. 173–5.
70. J. C. Holt, *Magna Carta*, 2nd edn (Cambridge: Cambridge University Press, 1992), pp. 34–5, 460–1; Britnell, *Commercialisation*, pp. 90–1.
71. *CFR 1319–27*, pp. 314–16, citing *CCR 1313–18*, p. 455; *CPR 1313–17*, pp. 688–9.
72. Maddicott, 'English Peasantry', pp. 308–18, 338–43; W. M. Ormrod, 'Agenda for Legislation, 1322–c. 1340', *EHR*, 105 (1990), p. 23.
73. 14 Edw. III st. 1 c. 12 (*SR*, vol. 1, p. 283); *CPR 1340–3*, pp. 310, 363, 441, 446, 580–1, 587; *CPR 1343–5*, pp. 72, 282–3.
74. *RP*, vol. 2, pp. 149, 150; R. R. Sharpe (ed.), *Calendar of Letter Books of the City of London* (London: Corporation of London, 1899–1912), *Letter Book F*, p. 107; Ormrod, 'Edward III's Government', p. 204.
75. E 368/121, m. 17; *CPR 1348–50*, p. 533.
76. Putnam, *Shareshull*, pp. 72–3; Ormrod, 'Edward III's Government', pp. 205–9; *CPR 1354–8*, pp. 396–7.
77. Putnam, *Enforcement*, pp. 25*–27*; Putnam (ed.), *Proceedings*, p. xxiii; Putnam, *Shareshull*, p. 58.
78. J. Bolton, '"The World Upside Down": Plague as an Agent of Economic and Social Change', in Ormrod and Lindley (eds), *Black Death*, pp. 26, 28.
79. R. Horrox (ed.), *The Black Death* (Manchester: Manchester University Press, 1994), pp. 237–9.
80. 23 Edw. III (*SR*, vol. 1, pp. 307–8); Horrox (ed.), *Black Death*, pp. 287–9.
81. 25 Edw. III st. 2 cc. 1–7 (*SR*, vol. 1, pp. 311–13); Horrox (ed.), *Black Death*, pp. 312–16.
82. 34 Edw. III cc. 9–10 (*SR*, vol. 1, pp. 366–7). There is no evidence that the justices ordered brandings: B. H. Putnam (ed.), *Yorkshire Sessions of the Peace, 1361–1364*, Yorkshire Archaeological Society Record Series 100 (Wakefield, 1939), p. xxxvii.

83. 2 Ric. II st. 1 c. 8 (*SR*, vol. 2, p. 11).
84. 12 Ric. II cc. 3–9 (*SR*, vol. 2, pp. 56–8).
85. B. H. Putnam, 'Maximum Wage-laws for Priests after the Black Death', *American Historical Review*, 21 (1915–16), pp. 12–32.
86. J. H. Tillotson, 'Peasant Unrest in the England of Richard II: Some Evidence from Royal Records', *Historical Studies*, 16 (1974–5), pp. 1–16.
87. R. H. Hilton, 'Resistance to Taxation and to other State Impositions in Medieval England', in J.-P. Genet and M. le Mené (eds), *Genèse de l'état moderne: Prélèvement et redistribution* (Paris: Centre National de la Recherche Scientifique, 1987), pp. 172–3.
88. 37 Edw. III cc. 3–15 (*SR*, vol. 1, pp. 378–83).
89. See esp. the Statute of Cambridge of 1388: 12 Ric. II cc. 6–8 (*SR*, vol. 2, pp. 57–8).
90. 38 Edw. III st. 1 c. 2 (*SR*, vol. 1, p. 383).
91. W. M. Ormrod, 'The English Government and the Black Death of 1348–49', in W. M. Ormrod (ed.), *England in the Fourteenth Century: Proceedings of the 1985 Harlaxton Symposium* (Woodbridge: Boydell Press, 1986), p. 179.
92. Ormrod, 'Politics of Pestilence', p. 157.
93. S. A. C. Penn and C. Dyer, 'Wages and Earnings in Late Medieval England: Evidence from the Enforcement of the Labour Laws', *Economic History Review*, 2nd series, 43 (1990), pp. 356, 358, 359.
94. 13 Ric. II st. 1 c. 8 (*SR*, vol. 2, p. 63); Putnam (ed.), *Proceedings*, pp. cviii–cix; L. R. Poos, 'The Social Context of Statute of Labourers Enforcement', *Law and History Review*, 1 (1983), p. 30.
95. For what follows, see E. Clark, 'Medieval Labor Law and English Local Courts', *American Journal of Legal History*, 27 (1983), pp. 330–53; Poos, 'Social Context', pp. 27–52; Penn and Dyer, 'Wages and Earnings', pp. 356–76.
96. *RP*, vol. 2, p. 296, discussed by M. M. Postan, *The Medieval Economy and Society* (Harmondsworth: Penguin, 1975), p. 170. See also Hilton, *Class Conflict*, p. 63; J. A. Tuck, 'Nobles, Commons and the Great Revolt of 1381', in R. H. Hilton and T. H. Aston (eds), *The English Rising of 1381* (Cambridge: Cambridge University Press, 1984), pp. 194–212.
97. Putnam, 'Transformation', pp. 41–8; Palmer, *English Law*, *passim*. See also M. J. Hettinger, 'Defining the Servant: Legal and Extra-legal Terms of Employment in Fifteenth-Century England', in A. J. Frantzen and D. Moffat (eds), *The Work of Work: Servitude, Slavery and Labor in Medieval England* (Glasgow: Cruithne Press, 1994), pp. 206–28.
98. Hilton, *Class Conflict*, pp. 49–65; R. Faith, 'The "Great Rumour" of 1377 and Peasant Ideology', in Hilton and Aston (eds), *English Rising*, pp. 43–73.
99. *RP*, vol. 3, pp. 83–5; *CPR 1377–81*, pp. 512–15; R. Sillem, 'Commissions of the Peace, 1380–1485', *BIHR*, 10 (1932–3), pp. 98–100; Powell, 'Administration', p. 54.
100. R. B. Dobson (ed.), *The Peasants' Revolt of 1381*, 2nd edn (London: Macmillan, 1983), pp. 25–211; R. H. Hilton, *Bond Men Made Free: Medieval Peasant Movements and the English Rising of 1381* (London: Methuen, 1977),

pp. 220–30; H. M. Hansen, 'The Peasants' Revolt of 1381 and the Chronicles', *Journal of Medieval History*, 6 (1980), pp. 393–415.
101. *CFR 1377–83*, pp. 248–50; Dobson (ed.), *Peasants' Revolt*, pp. 119–22.
102. Ormrod, 'Politics of Pestilence', p. 166, n. 57.
103. Putnam, *Shareshull*, pp. 59–78; Bryant, 'Financial Dealings', pp. 760–71; Harriss, *Public Finance*, pp. 401–10; P. H. W. Booth, 'Taxation and Public Order: Cheshire in 1353', *Northern History*, 12 (1976), pp. 16–31; Ormrod, 'Edward III's Government', pp. 210–20.
104. A. Harding, 'The Revolt against the Justices', in Hilton and Aston (eds), *English Rising*, pp. 165–6, 174.
105. Harding, 'Revolt against the Justices', pp. 165–93.
106. C. Dyer, 'The Social and Economic Background to the Rural Revolt of 1381', in Hilton and Aston (eds), *English Rising*, p. 17; N. Brooks, 'The Organization and Achievements of the Peasants of Kent and Essex in 1381', in H. Mayr-Harting and R. I. Moore (eds), *Studies in Medieval History Presented to R. H. C. Davis* (London: Hambledon Press, 1985), pp. 247–70, *passim*; Ormrod, 'Politics of Pestilence', p. 166 and n. 58.
107. W. M. Ormrod, 'The Peasants' Revolt and the Government of England', *JBS*, 29 (1990), pp. 11–14.
108. Maddicott, *Law and Lordship*, pp. 63–4.
109. Dobson (ed.), *Peasants' Revolt*, p. 365, and see also p. 160.
110. Ormrod, 'Peasants' Revolt', pp. 2–10; *SCCKB*, vol. 7, p. xxii.
111. B. Harvey, 'Draft Letters Patent of Manumission and Pardon for the Men of Somerset in 1381', *EHR*, 80 (1965), pp. 89–90.
112. A. J. Prescott, 'Judicial Records of the Rising of 1381', University of London PhD thesis (1984), pp. 30–87; Ormrod, 'Peasants' Revolt', pp. 20–2.
113. L. C. Hector and B. F. Harvey (eds), *The Westminster Chronicle, 1381–1394* (Oxford: Clarendon Press, 1982), p. 16; G. H. Martin (ed.), *Knighton's Chronicle, 1337–1394* (Oxford: Clarendon Press, 1995), p. 241 (both cited by Prescott, 'Judicial Records', p. 24). See also Dobson (ed.), *Peasants' Revolt*, pp. 306–16; E. M. Thompson (ed.), *Chronicon Angliae*, RS 64 (London, 1874), pp. 322–4; *SCCKB*, vol. 7, p. x.
114. *CCR 1381–5*, pp. 7–8.
115. M. McKisack, *The Fourteenth Century* (Oxford: Clarendon Press, 1959), p. 419. See also Prescott, 'Judicial Records', pp. 194–252.
116. *RP*, vol. 3, p. 103; Dobson (ed.), *Peasants' Revolt*, pp. 331–3. Only the amnesty for lords was enrolled as a statute: 5 Ric. II st. 1 c. 5 (*SR*, vol. 2, p. 20).
117. *RP*, vol. 3, p. 139; 6 Ric. II st. 1 c. 13 (*SR*, vol. 2, pp. 29–30).
118. Tuck, 'Nobles, Commons and the Great Revolt', p. 210.
119. *CCR 1381–5*, p. 104; *CPR 1381–5*, pp. 84–6.
120. Sillem, 'Commissions', pp. 94–5; *CPR 1381–5*, pp. 251–5.
121. Powell, 'Administration', pp. 54–5; E. G. Kimball, 'Commissions of the Peace for Urban Jurisdictions in England, 1327–1485', *Proceedings of the American Philosophical Society*, 121 (1977), p. 463; A. Verduyn, 'The Revocation of Urban Peace Commissions in 1381: The Lincoln Petition', *Historical Research*, 65 (1992), pp. 108–11.
122. J. B. Post, 'The Peace Commissions of 1382', *EHR*, 91 (1976), pp. 98–101.
123. Maddicott, *Law and Lordship*, pp. 64–6.

124. Kimball, 'Commissions', p. 465; Powell, 'Administration', pp. 55–6.
125. Putnam (ed.), *Proceedings*, pp. xlviii–liv; Powell, *Criminal Justice*, pp. 141–67; Storey, *End of the House of Lancaster*, pp. 61–8.
126. 25 Edw. III st. 5 c. 2 (*SR*, vol. 1, p. 320).
127. M. V. Clarke, *Fourteenth Century Studies* (Oxford: Clarendon Press, 1937), pp. 130–1.
128. J. Conway Davies, 'The Despenser War in Glamorgan', *TRHS*, 3rd series, 9 (1915), pp. 21–64; S. L. Waugh, 'The Profits of Violence: The Minor Gentry in the Rebellion of 1321–1322 in Gloucestershire and Herefordshire', *Speculum*, 52 (1977), pp. 843–69; G. H. Tupling (ed.), *South Lancashire in the Reign of Edward II*, Chetham Society 3rd series, 1 (Manchester, 1949), esp. pp. xxi–xii, lii; Musson, *Public Order*, p. 42.
129. Ormrod, *Edward III*, p. 177.
130. Ormrod, 'Agenda', p. 20.
131. S. B. Chrimes and A. L. Brown (eds), *Select Documents of English Constitutional History, 1307–1485* (London: Adam & Charles Black, 1961), pp. 37–8.
132. Ormrod, 'Agenda', p. 21 and n. 2; N. Fryde, 'A Medieval Robber Baron: Sir John Molyns of Stoke Poges, Buckinghamshire', in Hunnisett and Post (eds), *Medieval Legal Records*, pp. 198–221; N. Saul, *Knights and Esquires: The Gloucestershire Gentry in the Fourteenth Century* (Oxford: Clarendon Press, 1981), pp. 266–7.
133. J. S. Aberth, 'Crime and Justice under Edward III: The Case of Thomas de Lisle', *EHR*, 107 (1992), pp. 283–301.
134. Musson, *Public Order*, pp. 42–3; *SCCKB*, iv, p. xli.
135. *CPR 1324–7*, pp. 285–6, 292–3, 352–3; Musson, *Public Order*, pp. 44–5.
136. Putnam, 'Transformation', pp. 24–30; Putnam, 'Shire Officials', pp. 187–93; Putnam (ed.), *Proceedings*, pp. xxxviii–xxxix.
137. Musson, *Public Order*, p. 58 and n. 54.
138. E. L. G. Stones, 'Sir Geoffrey le Scrope (*c*. 1280 to 1340), Chief Justice of the King's Bench', *EHR*, 69 (1954), pp. 1–17.
139. S. B. Chrimes, 'Richard II's Questions to the Judges, 1397', *LQR*, 72 (1956), pp. 365–90.
140. Chrimes, 'Richard II's Questions to the Judges', p. 383; J. G. Bellamy, *The Law of Treason in England in the Later Middle Ages* (Cambridge: Cambridge University Press, 1970), p. 112.
141. Bellamy, *Law of Treason*, p. 113.
142. McKisack, *Fourteenth Century*, pp. 480–3.
143. C. M. Barron, 'The Tyranny of Richard II', *BIHR*, 41 (1968), pp. 10–14.
144. For what follows, see C. D. Ross, 'Forfeiture for Treason in the Reign of Richard II', *EHR*, 71 (1956), pp. 560–75.
145. C. Given-Wilson (ed.), *Chronicles of the Revolution, 1397–1400* (Manchester: Manchester University Press, 1993), pp. 177–8, 180–1 (articles 16, 26, 27).
146. Sillem, 'Commissions', p. 84; Powell, 'Administration', p. 54; J. G. Bellamy, *Bastard Feudalism and the Law* (Portland, OR: Areopagitica Press, 1989), p. 19.
147. For the wider implications of this strategy, see C. Given-Wilson, *The Royal Household and the King's Affinity: Service, Politics and Finance in England,*

1360–1413 (New Haven, CT and London: Yale University Press, 1986), pp. 212–26; N. Saul, *Richard II* (New Haven, CT and London: Yale University Press, 1997), pp. 261–9.
148. *CPR 1388–92*, pp. 135–7; R. L. Storey, 'Liveries and Commissions of the Peace 1388–90', in F. R. H. Du Boulay and C. M. Barron (eds), *The Reign of Richard II: Essays in Honour of May McKisack* (London: Athlone Press, 1971), pp. 137–8.
149. *EHD*, vol. 4, p. 1116; Storey, 'Liveries', p. 131; J. M. W. Bean, *From Lord to Patron: Lordship in Late Medieval England* (Manchester: Manchester University Press, 1989), pp. 203–4.
150. Storey, 'Liveries', pp. 131–52.
151. J. A. Tuck, 'The Cambridge Parliament 1388', *EHR*, 74 (1969), pp. 225–43.
152. Powell, 'Administration', pp. 55–6.
153. Storey, 'Liveries', p. 151.
154. See, in another context, W. M. Ormrod, 'State-building and State Finance in the Reign of Edward I', in W. M. Ormrod (ed.), *England in the Thirteenth Century: Proceedings of the 1989 Harlaxton Symposium* (Stamford: Paul Watkins, 1991), pp. 15–35.
155. Britnell, *Commercialisation*, pp. 90–1.
156. Harriss, 'Formation of Parliament', p. 51 and n. 53.
157. Ormrod, *Edward III*, p. 176; S. Rees Jones, 'York's Civic Administration, 1354–1464', in S. Rees Jones (ed.), *The Government of Medieval York: Essays in Commemoration of the 1396 Charter*, Borthwick Studies in History 3 (York, 1997), pp. 115–27.

Notes to Chapter 5:
Internal Influences on the Evolution of Justice

1. See the critique of legal historiography by Palmer, *English Law*, pp. 147–51.
2. J. G. Bellamy, *Crime and Public Order in England in the Later Middle Ages* (London: Routledge & Kegan Paul, 1973), p. 29 and n. 64; N. Saul, *Scenes from Provincial Life: Knightly Families in Sussex, 1280–1400* (Oxford: Clarendon Press, 1986), pp. 76–7.
3. D. W. Sutherland, *The Assize of Novel Disseisin* (Oxford: Clarendon Press, 1973), p. 2.
4. A. Harding, 'Plaints and Bills in the History of English Law', in D. Jenkins (ed.), *Legal History Studies 1972* (Cardiff: University of Wales, 1975), p. 75.
5. E. Clark, 'Medieval Labor Law and English Local Courts', *American Journal of Legal History*, 27 (1983), p. 334.
6. Sutherland, *Novel Disseisin*, pp. 173–5.
7. Powell, *Criminal Justice*, pp. 87, 93; Saul, *Provincial Life*, p. 84; R. C. Palmer, *The Whilton Dispute, 1264–1380: A Socio-legal Study of Dispute Settlement in Medieval England* (Princeton, NJ: Princeton University Press, 1984), p. 4.
8. A. Harding, *The Law Courts of Medieval England* (London: George Allen & Unwin, 1973), p. 77; F. W. Maitland, *Collected Papers* (Cambridge, 1911), vol. 2, pp. 110–73; E. De Haas and G. D. G. Hall (eds), *Early Registers of Writs*, SS 87 (London, 1970), p. cxxii.

9. Palmer, *English Law*, pp. 158–9.
10. W. M. Ormrod, 'Edward III's Government of England, *c*. 1346–1356', University of Oxford DPhil thesis (1984), p. 190; Palmer, *English Law*, p. 3, n. 10; N. Saul, 'Conflict and Consensus in English Local Society', in J. Taylor and W. Childs (eds), *Politics and Crisis in Fourteenth-Century England* (Gloucester: Alan Sutton, 1990), p. 42; M. Hastings, *The Court of Common Pleas in the Fifteenth Century* (New York: Columbia University Press, 1947), pp. 43, 157.
11. Palmer, *Whilton Dispute*, p. 5.
12. *SCCKB*, vol. 5, pp. xcviii, ci; vol. 6, pp. xlvi–xlvii.
13. *SCCKB*, vol. 4, pp. lxvii–lxxvi; Ormrod, 'Edward III's Government', pp. 189–93.
14. M. Clanchy, 'Law and Love in the Middle Ages', in J. Bossy (ed.), *Disputes and Settlements* (Cambridge: Cambridge University Press, 1983), pp. 60–6; E. Powell, 'Arbitration and the Law in England in the Later Middle Ages', *TRHS*, 5th series, 33 (1983), pp. 94–103; Powell, *Criminal Justice*, p. 93.
15. R. W. Kaeuper, 'Law and Order in Fourteenth-Century England: The Evidence of Special Commissions of Oyer and Terminer', *Speculum*, 54 (1979), pp. 734–84 (quotation at p. 748).
16. 34 Edw. III c. 1 (*SR*, vol. 1, p. 365).
17. *CPR 1377–99, passim*.
18. Putnam (ed.), *Proceedings*, pp. lxiii–lxiv.
19. M. D. Legge and W. Holdsworth (eds), *Year Book 10 Edward II*, SS 52, 54 (London, 1934–5), vol. 1, p. 8.
20. Sutherland, *Novel Disseisin*, pp. 2–3, 5, 126–7.
21. F. Pollock and F. W. Maitland, *The History of English Law before the Time of Edward I*, 2nd edn (Cambridge: Cambridge University Press, 1968), vol. 2, pp. 50. 51, 81; W. M. Ormrod, 'Agenda for Legislation, 1322– *c*.1340', *EHR*, 105 (1990), p. 25.
22. Sutherland, *Novel Disseisin*, pp. 133–44.
23. Sutherland, *Novel Disseisin*, pp. 144–53.
24. 5 Ric. II st. 1 c. 7 (*SR*, vol. 2, p. 20).
25. Sutherland, *Novel Disseisin*, pp. 169–80.
26. W. M. Ormrod, 'The Origins of the *Sub pena* Writ', *Historical Research*, 61 (1988), p. 14 and n. 22.
27. T. F. T. Plucknett, *Legislation of Edward I* (Oxford: Clarendon Press, 1949), pp. 138–43 and p. 143, n. 1.
28. J. I. Kermode, 'Medieval Indebtedness: The Regions *versus* London', in N. Rogers (ed.), *England in the Fifteenth Century: Proceedings of the 1992 Harlaxton Symposium* (Stamford: Paul Watkins, 1994), pp. 72–88.
29. Palmer, *English Law*, pp. 139–293.
30. Palmer, *English Law*, pp. 149–51; A. K. Kiralfy, *The Action on the Case* (London: Sweet & Maxwell, 1951), pp. 231–5.
31. Palmer, *English Law*, pp. 159–60, 163–6, 171–9, 182–4, 211–13, 219–26; Kiralfy, *Action on the Case*, pp. 35–44, 54–7, 137–43.
32. Palmer, *English Law*, p. 140.
33. Palmer, *Whilton Dispute*, pp. 8–9.
34. Kaeuper, 'Law and Order', pp. 747–53.

35. *CPR 1377–99, passim*.
36. For what follows, see B. W. McLane, 'Changes in the Court of King's Bench, 1291–1340: The Preliminary View from Lincolnshire', in W. M. Ormrod (ed.), *England in the Fourteenth Century: Proceedings of the 1985 Harlaxton Symposium* (Woodbridge: Boydell Press, 1986), pp. 152–60, esp. pp. 158–9. Since McLane did not distinguish a separate class of townspeople, it is not altogether clear how accurately his label of 'villagers' represents the social base producing the mass of litigation included under that category.
37. P. Tucker, 'London's Courts of Law in the Fifteenth Century: The Litigant's Perspective', in C. W. Brooks and M. Lobban (eds), *Communities and Courts in Britain, 1150–1900* (London: Hambledon Press, 1997), p. 33 and p. 34, n. 26. An ordinance of 1356 set the limit for fees payable to pleaders and attorneys in the sheriffs' court (city of London) at this rate (which may or may not have been higher at an earlier date).
38. Putnam (ed.), *Proceedings*, p. xxvi, followed, among others, by Harding, *Law Courts*, p. 77 and p. 85, n. 22.
39. M. M. Taylor (ed.), *Some Sessions of the Peace in Cambridgeshire in the Fourteenth Century, 1340, 1380–3*, Cambridge Antiquarian Society Publications 55 (Cambridge, 1942), p. lvii.
40. Putnam (ed.), *Proceedings*, pp. c–cii, cv–cvi.
41. For an impressionistic approach, see Bellamy, *Crime*, pp. 121–61, *passim*.
42. Saul, *Provincial Life*, p. 80.
43. Kaeuper, 'Law and Order', p. 751; Sutherland, *Novel Disseisin*, p. 2; Clark, 'Medieval Labor Law', pp. 446–8.
44. P. R. Hyams, *Kings, Lords and Peasants in Medieval England* (Oxford: Clarendon Press, 1980), pp. 153–5; W. S. Thomson (ed.), *A Lincolnshire Assize Roll for 1298*, Lincoln Record Society 36 (Hereford, 1944), p. 74, n. 323.
45. In fact, and for obvious reasons, it was a standard claim made by defendants in the assize that the plaintiff was unfree: Sutherland, *Novel Disseisin*, pp. 12, 14, 70–2.
46. Kaeuper, 'Law and Order', p. 752, n. 75. For the villeins of Ogbourne, see also R. H. Hilton, *Class Conflict and the Crisis of Feudalism*, 2nd edn (London: Verso, 1990), pp. 59–60.
47. J. S. Aberth, 'A Medieval Norwich Feud: The Bitter Dispute between Richard Spynk and Thomas de Lisle, Bishop of Ely', *Norfolk Archaeology*, 82 (1992), pp. 294–304; J. S. Aberth, *Criminal Churchmen in the Age of Edward III: The Case of Thomas de Lisle* (University Park, PA: Pennsylvania State University Press, 1996), pp. 95–115.
48. *RP*, vol. 2, p. 242; 25 Edw. III st. 5 c. 18 (*SR*, vol. 1, p. 323).
49. P. R. Hyams, 'The Action of Naifty in the Early Common Law', *LQR*, 90 (1974), p. 331, n. 31.
50. M. K. McIntosh, 'The Privileged Villeins of the English Ancient Demesne', *Viator*, 7 (1976), pp. 295–328; R. Faith, 'The "Great Rumour" of 1377 and Peasant Ideology', in Hilton and Aston (eds), *English Rising of 1381*, pp. 43–52; E. M. Hallam, *Domesday Book through Nine Centuries* (London: Thames and Hudson, 1986), pp. 99–105; W. M. Ormrod, *The Reign of*

Edward III: Crown and Political Society in England, 1327–1377 (New Haven, CT and London, 1990), pp. 146–7.
51. Powell, *Criminal Justice*, p. 65.
52. B. Hamilton, *The Medieval Inquisition* (London: Edward Arnold, 1981); R. M. Fraher, 'Conviction According to Conscience: The Medieval Jurists' Debate Concerning Judicial Discretion and the Law of Proof', *Law and History Review*, 7 (1989), pp. 23–88; M. Schüssler, 'German Crime in the Late Middle Ages: A Statistical Analysis of the Nuremberg Outlawry Books, 1285–1500', *Criminal Justice History*, 13 (1992), pp. 1–60.
53. D. Crook, 'Triers and the Origin of the Grand Jury', *Journal of Legal History*, 12 (1991), pp. 103–16.
54. A. Musson, 'Twelve Good Men and True? The Character of Early Fourteenth-Century Juries', *Law and History Review*, 15 (1997), pp. 123–6.
55. JUST 1/477/2; JUST 1/470.
56. E. L. G. Stones, 'The Folvilles of Ashby-Folville, Leicestershire, and their Associates in Crime, 1326–1347', *TRHS*, 5th series, 7 (1957), pp. 119–20; Musson, *Public Order*, pp. 265–8.
57. C. Hamil, 'The King's Approvers', *Speculum*, 11 (1936), pp. 238–58.
58. H. Röhrkasten, 'Some Problems of the Evidence of Fourteenth-Century Approvers', *Journal of Legal History*, 5 (1984), pp. 14–22.
59. H. Summerson, 'The Criminal Underworld of Medieval England', *Journal of Legal History*, 17 (1996), pp. 204–8.
60. J. B. Post, 'The Evidential Value of Approvers' Appeals: The Case of William Rose, 1389', *Law and History Review*, 3 (1985), pp. 91–100.
61. JUST 3/48, m. 20d.
62. A. J. Musson, 'Turning King's Evidence: The Prosecution of Crime in Late Medieval England' (forthcoming).
63. Röhrkasten, 'Problems of the Evidence', p. 17.
64. JUST 3/49/1, m. 26.
65. Musson, *Public Order*, pp. 213, 245.
66. Musson, *Public Order*, pp. 213–14, 244.
67. Röhrkasten, 'Problems of the Evidence', pp. 14–15.
68. Powell, *Criminal Justice*, p. 73.
69. There was always a discrepancy between the number of people appealed or indicted, the number actually located and brought to court, and the number convicted – though this, of course, does not necessarily reflect ineffectiveness in the system. For some statistics, see B. W. McLane, 'The Royal Courts and the Problem of Disorder in Lincolnshire, 1290–1341', University of Rochester PhD thesis (1979), pp. 105–6.
70. P. Brand, *The Origins of the English Legal Profession* (Oxford: Blackwell, 1992); R. C. Palmer, 'The Origins of the English Legal Profession', *Law and History Review*, 5 (1987), pp. 31–50; N. Ramsay, 'The English Legal Profession c. 1340–1450', University of Cambridge PhD thesis (1985).
71. N. Ramsay, 'What was the Legal Profession?', in M. Hicks (ed.), *Profit, Piety and the Professions in Later Medieval England* (Gloucester: Alan Sutton, 1990), p. 67.
72. D. J. M. Higgins, 'Judges in Government and Society in the Reign of Edward II', University of Oxford DPhil Thesis (1986); N. Ramsay,

'Retained Legal Counsel, *c.* 1275–*c.* 1475', *TRHS*, 5th series, 35 (1985), pp. 95–112.
73. R. C. Palmer, 'County Year Book Reports: The Professional Lawyer in the Medieval County Court', *EHR*, 91 (1976), pp. 776–801.
74. Brand, *Origins*, pp. 73–5, 84–5.
75. *SCCKB*, vol. 2, p. cxxxv.
76. 12 Edw. II c. 1 (*SR*, vol. 1, p. 177); Sutherland, *Novel Disseisin*, pp. 44–5.
77. McLane, 'Changes in the Court of King's Bench', p. 160.
78. W. A. Morris, 'The Sheriff', in *EGW*, vol. 2, p. 108; R. C. Palmer, *The County Courts of Medieval England, 1150–1350* (Princeton, NJ: Princeton University Press, 1982), p. 28.
79. R. F. Hunnisett, *The Medieval Coroner* (Cambridge: Cambridge University Press, 1961), pp. 55–7, 75–86.
80. S. L. Waugh, 'The Origins and Early Development of the Articles of the Escheator', in P. R. Coss and S. D. Lloyd (eds), *Thirteenth-Century England V: Proceedings of the Newcastle upon Tyne Conference 1993* (Woodbridge: Boydell Press, 1995), pp. 89–113.
81. Palmer, *County Courts*, pp. 89, 97; Musson, *Public Order*, p. 161, n. 138.
82. Higgins, 'Judges in Government and Society', pp. 223–4.
83. *SCCKB*, vol. 6, p. lxx; J. H. Baker, *The Order of Serjeants at Law*, SS Supplementary Series 5 (London, 1984), p. 156; Musson, *Public Order*, p. 158.
84. Brand, *Origins*, p. 83.
85. H. M. Cam, 'Shire Officials: Coroners, Constables and Bailiffs', in *EGW*, vol. 3, p. 149; Baker, *Serjeants at Law*, p. 154; J. R. Maddicott, *Law and Lordship: Royal Justices as Retainers in Thirteenth- and Fourteenth-Century England*, P&P Supplement 4 (Cambridge, 1978), pp. 10–11, 30.
86. Ramsay, 'Retained Legal Counsel', pp. 95, 100–2, 108.
87. Sutherland, *Novel Disseisin*, p. 188; Ramsay, 'What was the Legal Profession?', p. 65.
88. E. Powell, 'Arbitration', pp. 49–67; Powell, *Criminal Justice*, pp. 97–106.
89. P. Nightingale, 'Monetary Contraction and Mercantile Credit in Later Medieval England', *Economic History Review*, 2nd series, 43 (1990), pp. 573–4.
90. J. I. Kermode, 'Money and Credit in the Fifteenth Century: Some Lessons from Yorkshire', *Business History Review*, 65 (1989), pp. 484–9.
91. P. Brand, *The Making of the Common Law* (London: Hambledon Press, 1992), pp. 96–7; C. P. Cottis, 'Sir William de Bereford, *c.* 1250–1325', University of Oxford BLitt thesis (1959), pp. 86–9.
92. The following is based on papers given at the Thirteenth British Legal History Conference (1997) by P. Brand, J. H. Baker, J. Beckerman, P. Philbin and J. S. Arkenberg.
93. Brand, *Common Law*, pp. 57–75; P. Brand, 'The Beginnings of English Law Reporting', in C. Stebbings (ed.), *Law Reporting in Britain* (London: Hambledon Press, 1995), pp. 1–14.
94. Putnam, *Shareshull*, p. 115–18; Palmer, *English Law*, pp. 304–5.
95. Palmer, *English Law*, pp. 170–1, 217–18.
96. *RP*, vol. 2, pp. 203, 311, 368; T. F. T. Plucknett, *Statutes and their*

Interpretation in the First Half of the Fourteenth Century (Cambridge: Cambridge University Press, 1922); S. B. Chrimes, *English Constitutional Ideas in the Fifteenth Century* (Cambridge: Cambridge University Press, 1936), p. 352.

97. Putnam, *Shareshull*, p. 41; G. L. Harriss, 'The Formation of Parliament, 1272–1377', in R. G. Davies and J. H. Denton (eds), *The English Parliament in the Middle Ages* (Manchester: Manchester University Press, 1981), pp. 45–6, 48.
98. For comparison, see recent work on later chancery bills: T. S. Haskett, 'The Presentation of Cases in Medieval Chancery Bills', in W. M. Gordon and T. D. Fergus (eds), *Legal History in the Making* (London: Hambledon Press, 1991), pp. 11–25; T. S. Haskett, 'The Medieval English Court of Chancery', *Law and History Review*, 14 (1996), pp. 245–313.
99. G. L. Haskins, 'The Petitions of Representatives in the Parliaments of Edward I', *EHR*, 53 (1938), pp. 1–20; D. Rayner, 'The Forms and Machinery of the "Commune Petition" in the Fourteenth Century', *EHR*, 56 (1941), pp. 198–233, 549–70; J. R. Maddicott, 'The County Community and the Making of Public Opinion in Fourteenth-Century England', *TRHS*, 5th series, 28 (1978), pp. 27–43; J. R. Maddicott, 'Parliament and the Constituencies, 1272–1377', in Davies and Denton (eds), *English Parliament*, pp. 61–87; J. G. Edwards, *The Second Century of the English Parliament* (Oxford: Clarendon Press, 1979), pp. 44–55.
100. K. L. Wood-Legh, 'Sheriffs, Lawyers and Belted Knights in the Parliaments of Edward III', *EHR*, 46 (1931), pp. 377–80.
101. Musson, *Public Order*, pp. 133, 159; Baker, *Serjeants at Law*, pp. 504, 520; for evidence on service as parliamentary representatives, see *Return of the Names of Every Member of the Lower House of Parliament, 1213–1874*, Parliamentary Papers 1878 (London, 1878).
102. Baker, *Serjeants at Law*, p. 37 and n. 6; Wood-Legh, 'Sheriffs', pp. 378–9; Musson, *Public Order*, p. 241.
103. *RP*, vol. 2, p. 310; Edwards, *Second Century*, pp. 51–2; Wood-Legh, 'Sheriffs', p. 381.
104. J. S. Roskell, *The House of Commons, 1386–1421* (Stroud: History of Parliament Trust, 1992), vol. 1, pp. 168–71.
105. Roskell, *House of Commons*, vol. 1, p. 170; J. S. Roskell, *Parliament and Politics in Late Medieval England* (London: Hambledon Press, 1981–3), vols 2 and 3, *passim*.
106. Roskell, *House of Commons*, vol. 4, pp. 77–80.
107. Musson, *Public Order*, pp. 242–8.
108. Ormrod, *Edward III*, pp. 157–60; W. M. Ormrod, *Political Life in Medieval England, 1300–1450* (Basingstoke: Macmillan, 1995), pp. 119–24.
109. Such arguments depend heavily on re-election rates: see J. G. Edwards, 'The Personnel of the Commons in Parliament under Edward I and Edward II', in Fryde and Miller (eds), *Historical Studies*, vol. 1, pp. 150–67; Ormrod, 'Agenda', pp. 17–18, 25; N. B. Lewis, 'Re-election to Parliament in the Reign of Richard II', *EHR*, 48 (1933), pp. 364–94. See also J. G. Edwards, 'Some Common Petitions in Richard II's First Parliament', *BIHR*, 36 (1953), pp. 200–13.

110. H. G. Richardson and G. O. Sayles, *The English Parliament in the Middle Ages* (London: Hambledon Press, 1981), chapter XVII, pp. 194–205; chapter XXII, pp. 377–99; D. Higgins, 'Justices and Parliament in the Early Fourteenth Century', *Parliamentary History*, 12 (1993), pp. 3–4.
111. M. Prestwich, *Edward I* (London: Methuen, 1988), p. 292.
112. A. J. Horwood (ed.), *Year Books 33–35 Edward I*, RS 31 (London, 1879), p. 82, discussed *inter alia* by Plucknett, *Legislation of Edward I*, pp. 72–3.
113. Higgins, 'Justices and Parliament', pp. 12–14.
114. Richardson and Sayles, *English Parliament*, chapter XXI, p. 13.
115. H. Cam, *Law-finders and Law-makers in Medieval England* (London: Merlin Press, 1962), pp. 132–58; Harriss, 'Formation of Parliament', pp. 45–8.
116. For what follows, see E. L. G. Stones, 'Sir Geoffrey le Scrope (c. 1280 to 1340), Chief Justice of the King's Bench', *EHR*, 69 (1954), pp. 1–17.
117. For what follows, see Putnam, *Shareshull*; B. H. Putnam, 'Chief Justice Shareshull and the Economic and Legal Codes of 1351–1352', *University of Toronto Law Journal*, 5 (1943–4), pp. 251–81.
118. Ormrod, *Edward III*, pp. 63–8, 77–80.
119. Putnam, *Shareshull*, p. 54. The regulation of labour was on the agenda set in Shareshull's opening speech to this parliament: *RP*, vol. 2, p. 225.
120. *RP*, vol. 2, p. 228 (8).
121. *RP*, vol. 2, p. 228 (3).
122. Ormrod, *Edward III*, pp. 124–6.
123. Harriss, *Public Finance*, pp. 376–400, 410–16; W. M. Ormrod, 'Edward III and the Recovery of Royal Authority in England, 1340–60', *History*, 72 (1987), pp. 10–11.
124. *RP*, vol. 2, p. 238 (7). For what follows, see J. G. Bellamy, *The Law of Treason in England in the Later Middle Ages* (Cambridge: Cambridge University Press, 1970), pp. 59–101.
125. Harriss, 'Formation of Parliament', pp. 47–8; Putnam, *Shareshull*, p. 54.
126. Verduyn, 'Attitude', pp. 138–9.
127. Brand, *Common Law*, pp. 244, 290, 318.
128. 25 Edw III st. 1 (*SR*, vol. 1, p. 310). For the background, see also *RP*, vol. 2, pp. 139, 231.
129. J. B. Post, 'Sir Thomas West and the Statute of Rapes, 1382', *BIHR*, 53 (1980), pp. 24–30.
130. Brand, *Common Law*, pp. 287–99.

Notes to Chapter 6: Conclusion

1. For another attempt to classify similar material, see J. Coleman, *English Literature in History, 1350–1400: Medieval Readers and Writers* (London: Hutchinson, 1981), pp. 60, 65–7.
2. For what follows, see R. F. Green, *Poets and Princepleasers: Literature and the English Court in the Late Middle Ages* (Toronto: University of Toronto Press, 1980), pp. 135–67; J. Watts, *Henry VI and the Politics of Kingship* (Cambridge: Cambridge University Press, 1996), pp. 13–80; L. Coote,

'A Language of Power: Prophecy and Public Affairs in Later Medieval England', in B. Taithe and T. Thornton (eds), *Prophecy* (Stroud: Sutton Publishing, 1997), pp. 18–30; G. R. Owst, *Literature and Pulpit in Medieval England*, 2nd edn (Oxford: Basil Blackwell, 1961).

3. J. H. Fisher, *John Gower* (New York: New York University Press, 1964), pp. 154–9; J. Kail (ed.), *Twenty-Six Political and Other Poems (Digby 102)*, Early English Texts Society, Original Series, 124 (London, 1904), discussed by Coleman, *English Literature*, pp. 98–111. See also the manuals compiled for the instruction of justices of the peace in the fifteenth century: B. H. Putnam, *Early Treatises on the Practice of the Justices of the Peace in the Fifteenth and Sixteenth Centuries*, Oxford Studies in Social and Legal History 7 (Oxford, 1924), pp. 60–107.
4. R. W. Kaeuper, 'Law and Order in Fourteenth-Century England: The Evidence of Special Commissions of Oyer and Terminer', *Speculum*, 54 (1979), pp. 735–6 and n. 11.
5. A petition heard in parliament in 1354 was altered (by another hand – presumably in chancery) to include a specific accusation of treason in order to allow the resulting commission of oyer and terminer to include powers of inquiry into treasons as well as felonies and trespasses: SC 8/97/4825, resulting in *CPR 1354–8*, p. 554.
6. T. A. Green, 'Societal Concepts of Criminal Liability for Homicide in Medieval England', *Speculum*, 47 (1972), p. 672; B. A. Hanawalt, 'Violent Death in Fourteenth- and Early Fifteenth-Century England', *Comparative Studies in Society and History*, 18 (1976), pp. 298–9.
7. 13 Edw. I (Statute of Winchester) c. 1 (*SR*, vol. 1, p. 96); for comment, see J. G. Bellamy, *Crime and Public Order in England in the Later Middle Ages* (London: Routledge & Kegan Paul, 1973), pp. 4–5; Kaeuper, 'Law and Order', pp. 735–6. For a recent attempt to quantify the claims made in 1285 (so far as homicides were concerned) see H. Summerson, 'The Enforcement of the Statute of Winchester, 1285–1327', *Journal of Legal History*, 13 (1992), pp. 234–5.
8. For a notable example see 2 Ric. II st. 1 c. 6 (*SR*, vol. 2, pp. 9–10).
9. Putnam (ed.), *Proceedings*, pp. xxi, xxii.
10. J. R. Maddicott, 'The County Community and the Making of Public Opinion in Fourteenth-Century England', *TRHS*, 5th series, 28 (1978), pp. 27–43.
11. Maddicott, 'County Community', pp. 36–7.
12. For common petitions not published in *RP* that make explicit references to statutes, see SC 8/80/3951 (printed in *SCCKB*, vol. 3, p. cxvi); SC 8/80/3959 (discussed in D. Rayner, 'The Forms and Machinery of the "Commune Petition" in the Fourteenth Century', *EHR*, 56 (1941), p. 553); SC 8/100/4964.For similar petitions made in the name of county communities, see SC 8/110/5473 and SC 8/152/7592 (both cited by Maddicott, 'County community', p. 36); *RP*, vol. 2, p. 155 (43); C 81/147/3811. For a similar petition from the community of the liberty of St Edmund (Suffolk), see SC 8/266/13296.
13. See, respectively, SC 8/152/7592; SC 8/39/1937; SC 8/32/1551; *RP*, vol. 2, p. 177 (9).

14. 25 Edw. III st. 5 c. 14 (*SR*, vol. 1, p. 322); Putnam (ed.), *Proceedings*, pp. ciii–civ; E. C. Furber (ed.), *Essex Sessions of the Peace 1351, 1377–1379*, Essex Archaeological Society Occasional Publications 3 (Colchester, 1953), pp. 30–1.
15. *SCCKB*, vol. 6, no. 70; Putnam (ed.), *Proceedings*, pp. 290–2.
16. For further discussion, see M. K. McIntosh, 'Finding Language for Misconduct: Jurors in Fifteenth-Century Local Courts', in B. A. Hanawalt and D. Wallace (eds), *Bodies and Disciplines* (Minneapolis, MN: University of Minnesota Press, 1996), pp. 87–122.
17. P. R. Coss (ed.), *Thomas Wright's Political Songs* (Cambridge: Cambridge University Press, 1996); T. Wright (ed.), *Political Poems and Songs*, RS 14 (London, 1859–61); Coleman, *English Literature*, pp. 58–156; J. R. Maddicott, 'Poems of Social Protest in Early Fourteenth-Century England', in W. M. Ormrod (ed.), *England in the Fourteenth Century: Proceedings of the 1985 Harlaxton Symposium* (Woodbridge: Boydell Press, 1986), pp. 130–44; T. Turville-Petre, *England the Nation: Language, Literature and National Identity, 1290–1340* (Oxford: Clarendon Press, 1996), pp. 181–217.
18. J. Mann, *Chaucer and Medieval Estates Satire* (Cambridge: Cambridge University Press, 1973), pp. 187–202.
19. For what follows, see J. A. Yunck, *The Lineage of Lady Meed: The Development of Medieval Venality Satire* (Notre Dame, IN: University of Notre Dame Press, 1963).
20. Coss (ed.), *Political Songs*, pp. 224–30, 323–45; A. G. Rigg, *A History of Anglo-Latin Literature, 1066–1422* (Cambridge: Cambridge University Press, 1992), p. 304; Turville-Petre, *England the Nation*, p. 109.
21. T. Turville-Petre (ed.), *Alliterative Poetry of the Later Middle Ages: An Anthology* (London: Routledge, 1979), p. 49, ll. 149–55 and n. to l. 149. For dating of *Winner and Waster*, see E. Salter, *English and International: Studies in the Literature, Art and Patronage of Medieval England* (Cambridge: Cambridge University Press, 1988), pp. 180–98. For popular attitudes towards the 'green wax', see N. Brooks, 'The Organization and Achievements of the Peasants of Kent and Essex in 1381', in H. Mayr-Harting and R. I. Moore (eds), *Studies in Medieval History Presented to R. H. C. Davis* (London: Hambledon Press, 1985), p. 260.
22. L. D. Benson (ed.), *The Riverside Chaucer*, new edn (Oxford: Oxford University Press, 1987), p. 28, ll. 309–30; Mann, *Estates Satire*, pp. 86–91; S. H. Rigby, *Chaucer in Context* (Manchester: Manchester University Press, 1996), pp. 44–5.
23. For what follows, see R. B. Dobson and J. Taylor, *Rymes of Robyn Hood: An Introduction to the English Outlaw* (London: Heinemann, 1976); J. C. Holt, *Robin Hood* (London: Thames & Hudson, 1982); R. W. Kaeuper, 'An Historian's Reading of *The Tale of Gamelyn*', *Medium Aevum*, 52 (1983), pp. 51–62; J. Scattergood, '*The Tale of Gamelyn*: The Noble Robber as Provincial Hero', in C. M. Meale (ed.), *Readings in Medieval English Romance* (Cambridge: D. S. Brewer, 1994), pp. 159–94.
24. M. Keen, *The Outlaws of Medieval Legend*, rev. edn (London: Routledge and Kegan Paul, 1977), pp. 9–10; Dobson and Taylor, *Rymes*, p. 29.

25. William Langland, *The Vision of Piers Plowman: A Complete Edition of the B-Text*, ed. A. V. C. Schmidt, new edn (London: J. M. Dent & Sons, 1987), p. 243 (Passus XIX, l. 248).
26. I. S. T. Aspin (ed.), *Anglo-Norman Political Songs*, Anglo-Norman Texts 9 (Oxford, 1953), pp. 67–78; Dobson and Taylor, *Rymes*, pp. 250–4.
27. N. Saul, 'Conflict and Consensus in English Local Society', in J. Taylor and W. Childs (eds), *Politics and Crisis in Fourteenth-Century England* (Gloucester: Alan Sutton, 1990), pp. 38–54; P. C. Maddern, *Violence and Social Order: East Anglia 1422–1442* (Oxford: Clarendon Press, 1992), pp. 1–26.
28. R. H. Hilton (ed.), *Peasants, Knights and Heretics* (Cambridge: Cambridge University Press, 1967), pp. 221–72; Keen, *Outlaws*, pp. xiii–xxi.
29. C. Carpenter, 'Law, Justice and Landowners in Late Medieval England', *Law and History Review*, 1 (1983), p. 231.
30. A. P. Baldwin, *The Theme of Government in Piers Plowman* (Cambridge: Brewer, 1981); F. R. H. Du Boulay, *The England of Piers Plowman: William Langland and his Vision of the Fourteenth Century* (Woodbridge: Boydell Press, 1991); C. M. Barron, 'William Langland: A London Poet', in B. A. Hanawalt (ed.), *Chaucer's England: Literature in Historical Context* (Minneapolis, MN: University of Minnesota Press, 1992), pp. 91–109.
31. Salter, *English and International*, p. 180.
32. Langland, *Vision*, ed. Schmidt, Passus III–IV; Yunck, *Lineage of Lady Meed*, pp. 284–306.
33. D. Aers, 'Justice and Wage-Labor after the Black Death: Some Perplexities for William Langland', in A. J. Frantzen and D. Moffat (eds), *The Work of Work: Servitude, Slavery and Labor in Medieval England* (Glasgow: Cruithne Press, 1994), pp. 169–90.
34. S. Justice, *Writing and Rebellion: England in 1381* (Berkeley and Los Angeles, CA: University of California Press, 1994), pp. 67–139.
35. G. H. Martin (ed.), *Knighton's Chronicle, 1337–1396* (Oxford: Clarendon Press, 1995), pp. 221–2 (slightly modified); for an alternative rendering, see Maddicott, 'Poems of Social Protest', p. 139. The addition of the 'm' in 'Bathon' is at the suggestion of Justice, *Writing and Rebellion*, pp. 13, 133 and n. 66.
36. R. F. Green, 'John Ball's Letters: Literary History and Historical Literature', in Hanawalt (ed.), *Chaucer's England*, pp. 183–4; Justice, *Writing and Rebellion*, pp. 133–4.
37. R. B. Dobson (ed.), *The Peasants' Revolt of 1381*, 2nd edn (London: Macmillan, 1983), p. 124; Justice, *Writing and Rebellion*, pp. 133–4. Brooks, 'Organization and Achievements', pp. 250–1 discusses the relationship of Bampton with the commission. See also Chapter 4.
38. Justice, *Writing and Rebellion*, pp. 133–4.
39. Yunck, *Lineage of Lady Meed*, pp. 175, 228 and n. 58; Green, 'John Ball's Letters', pp. 183–4.
40. H. Barr (ed.), *The Piers Plowman Tradition* (London: J. M. Dent, 1993).
41. Barr (ed.), *Piers Plowman Tradition*, p. 19.
42. 'Richard the Redeless', Passus II, ll. 81–90, in Barr (ed.), *Piers Plowman Tradition*, p. 111, discussed by Yunck, *Lineage of Lady Meed*, pp. 271–2.
43. Bellamy, *Crime*, pp. 12–29; Powell, *Criminal Justice*, pp. 107–14; M. Hicks,

Bastard Feudalism (Harlow: Longman, 1995), pp. 119–24.
44. R. W. Kaeuper, *War, Justice, and Public Order: England and France in the Later Middle Ages* (Oxford: Clarendon Press, 1988), pp. 174–83, 386.
45. Putnam, 'Transformation'; G. L. Harriss, *King, Parliament and Public Finance in Medieval England to 1369* (Oxford: Clarendon Press, 1975), pp. 354–5, 516–17; Kaeuper, *War, Justice, and Public Order*, pp. 386–7.
46. Justice, *Writing and Rebellion*, p. 62.
47. R. H. Hilton, *Class Conflict and the Crisis of Feudalism*, rev. edn (London: Verso, 1990), pp. 49–65, 173–9; R. Faith, 'The "Great Rumour" of 1377 and Peasant Ideology', in R. H. Hilton and T. H. Aston (eds), *The English Rising of 1381* (Cambridge: Cambridge University Press, 1981), pp. 43–73; Palmer, *English Law*. See also S. H. Rigby, *English Society in the Later Middle Ages* (Basingstoke: Macmillan, 1995), pp. 104–44.
48. A. Harding, 'The Revolt against the Justices', in Hilton and Aston (eds), *English Rising*, pp. 165–93.
49. D. W. Sutherland (ed.), *The Eyre of Northamptonshire, 1329–1330*, SS 97–98 (London, 1983), vol. 1, pp. xxii, 5–6.
50. C 49/7/20; C 81/147/3811; SC 8/64/3156; SC 8/65/3205, printed in C. M. Fraser (ed.), *Ancient Petitions Relating to Northumberland*, Surtees Society 176 (Durham, 1966), pp. 115–16; SC 8/327/E832 (delays in assize sessions); SC 8/119/5916 (labour sessions); SC 8/73/3605 (peace sessions).
51. Maddern, *Violence and Social Order*, pp. 60–1.
52. P. Brand, *The Making of the Common Law* (London: Hambledon Press, 1992), pp. 98–101.
53. E. Clark, 'Medieval Labor Law and English Local Courts', *American Journal of Legal History*, 27 (1983), pp. 333–5.
54. Harriss, *Public Finance*, p. 517.
55. *RP*, vol. 2, pp. 2–30 (25), 241 (40), 261 (40); Verduyn, 'Attitude', pp. 133–4.
56. B. A. Hanawalt, *Crime and Conflict in English Communities, 1300–1348* (Cambridge, MA: Harvard University Press, 1979), pp. 114–83.
57. B. A. Hanawalt, 'Fur Collar Crime: The Pattern of Crime among the Fourteenth-Century English Nobility', *Journal of Social History*, 8 (1973), pp. 1–17; G. L. Harriss, 'Introduction', in K. B. McFarlane, *England in the Fifteenth Century* (London: Hambledon Press, 1981), pp. xix–xxiii.
58. 20 Edw. III (*SR*, vol. 1, pp. 303–6); J. R. Maddicott, *Law and Lordship: Royal Justices as Retainers in Thirteenth- and Fourteenth-Century England*, P&P Supplement 4 (Cambridge, 1978), pp. 40–51.
59. Justice, *Writing and Rebellion*, pp. 60–4.
60. Musson, *Public Order*, pp. 189–201; R. B. Goheen, 'Peasant Politics? Village Communities and the Crown in Fifteenth-Century England', *American Historical Review*, 96 (1991), pp. 42–62.
61. E. Powell, 'After "After McFarlane": The Poverty of Patronage and the Case for Constitutional History', in D. J. Clayton, R. G. Davies and P. McNiven (eds), *Trade, Devotion and Governance* (Stroud: Alan Sutton, 1994), pp. 11–12.
62. Maddicott, *Law and Lordship*, pp. 71–81; Powell, *Criminal Justice*, p. 114.
63. 3 Edw. I (Statute of Westminster I) c. 29; 20 Edw. III; 8 Ric. II c. 3 (*SR*, vol. 1, pp. 34, 303–6; vol. 2, p. 37).

64. For this and the next three paragraphs, see P. Brand, *The Origins of the English Legal Profession* (London: Blackwell, 1992), pp. 120–37.
65. For this and the next paragraph, see A. Harding, 'The Origins of the Crime of Conspiracy', *TRHS*, 5th series, 33 (1983), pp. 89–108, esp. pp. 98–100, 104–7; Harding, 'Revolt against the Justices', pp. 188–93.
66. Brand, *Origins*, pp. 121, 140–1.
67. *SCCKB*, vol. 2, p. cxxxv.
68. M. Bowden, *A Commentary on the General Prologue to the Canterbury Tales*, 2nd edn (New York and London: Macmillan, 1967), pp. 168–9.
69. B. R. McRee, 'Religious Gilds and the Regulation of Behavior in Late Medieval Towns', in J. Rosenthal and C. Richmond (eds), *People, Politics and Community in the Later Middle Ages* (Gloucester: Alan Sutton, 1987), pp. 108–22.
70. Faith, '"Great Rumour"', p. 44; Harding, 'Revolt against the Justices', pp. 171–2, 178–9.
71. For a recent discussion, see J. G. Bellamy, *Bastard Feudalism and the Law* (Portland, OR: Areopagitica Press, 1989), pp. 25–30.
72. Bellamy, *Crime*, pp. 121–61; R. L. Storey, *The End of the House of Lancaster*, rev. edn (Gloucester: Alan Sutton, 1986), pp. 1–28.
73. R. C. Palmer, *The Whilton Dispute, 1264–1380: A Socio-legal Study of Dispute Settlement in Medieval England* (Princeton, NJ: Princeton University Press, 1984), pp. 10–11.
74. T. A. Green, *Verdict According to Conscience* (Chicago, IL: University of Chicago Press, 1985), pp. 28–102.
75. A. Musson, 'Twelve Good Men and True? The Character of Early Fourteenth-Century Juries', *Law and History Review*, 15 (1997), pp. 132–4.
76. Green, *Verdict According to Conscience*, pp. 13–14.
77. Musson, 'Twelve Good Men and True?', pp. 134–9, 143.
78. *RP*, vol. 2, pp. 134 (67), 140 (30); 25 Edw. III st. 5 c. 3 (*SR*, vol. 1, p. 320).
79. Bellamy, *Crime*, p. 144.
80. Harriss, 'Introduction', pp. xix–xxiii; Powell, *Criminal Justice*, pp. 1–20; Powell, 'After "After McFarlane"', pp. 1–16.
81. E. Powell, 'Law and Justice', in R. Horrox (ed.), *Fifteenth-Century Attitudes: Perceptions of Society in Late Medieval England* (Cambridge: Cambridge University Press, 1994), p. 38.
82. Benson (ed.), *Riverside Chaucer*, pp. 28–9, ll. 309–60. The quotations that follow are as rendered in N. Coghill (trans.), *Chaucer: The Canterbury Tales*, rev. edn (Harmondsworth: Penguin, 1975), pp. 27–9.
83. For a summary of the arguments, see Rigby, *Chaucer in Context*, pp. 44–5.
84. Barr (ed.), *Piers Plowman Tradition*, p. 111.

SELECT BIBLIOGRAPHY

For general surveys of the judicial structure, see: J. H. Baker, *An Introduction to English Legal History*, 3rd edn (London: Buttherworths, 1990); A. L. Brown, *The Governance of Late Medieval England, 1272–1461* (London: Edward Arnold, 1989); and A. Harding, *The Law Courts of Medieval England* (London: George Allen & Unwin, 1973). G. O. Sayles (ed.), *Select Cases in the Court of King's Bench*, SS 55, 57, 58, 74, 76, 82, 88 (London, 1936–71) is a mine of information. For approaches to the history of crime, see: J. G. Bellamy, *Crime and Public Order in the Later Middle Ages* (London: Routledge & Kegan Paul, 1973); and B. A. Hanawalt, *Crime and Conflict in English Communities, 1300–1348* (Cambridge, MA: Harvard University Press, 1979). E. Powell, *Kingship, Law, and Society: Criminal Justice in the Reign of Henry V* (Oxford: Clarendon Press, 1989) provides an important conceptual approach to the study of legal history. A. Musson, *Public Order and Law Enforcement: The Local Administration of Criminal Justice, 1294–1350* (Woodbridge: Boydell Press, 1996) gives a detailed re-assessment of the period before the plague.

The model of 'transformation' outlined in Chapter 1 derives from: B. H. Putnam, 'The Transformation of the Keepers of the Peace into the Justices of the Peace, 1327–1380', *Transactions of the Royal Historical Society*, 4th series, 12 (1929), pp. 19–48; and R. C. Palmer, *English Law in the Age of the Black Death, 1348–1381: A Transformation of Governance and Law* (Chapel Hill, NC: University of North Carolina Press, 1993).

For the personnel of the courts outlined in Chapters 2 and 3, see: J. R. Maddicott, *Law and Lordship: Royal Justices as Retainers in Thirteenth- and Fourteenth-Century England*, P&P Supplement 4 (Cambridge, 1978); N. Saul, *Knights and Esquires: The Gloucestershire Gentry in the Fourteenth*

Century (Oxford: Clarendon Press, 1981); C. H. Clough (ed.), *Profession, Vocation, and Culture in Later Medieval England* (Liverpool: Liverpool University Press, 1982); M. Hicks (ed.), *Profit, Piety and the Professions in Later Medieval England* (Gloucester: Alan Sutton, 1990); and S. Walker, 'Yorkshire Justices of the Peace, 1389–1413', *EHR*, 108 (1993), pp. 281–311.

The 'law state'/'war state' opposition outlined in Chapter 4 derives from R. W. Kaeuper, *War, Justice, and Public Order: England and France in the Later Middle Ages* (Oxford: Clarendon Press, 1988). For the impact of plague on justice the classic text is B. H. Putnam, *The Enforcement of the Statute of Labourers*, Columbia University Studies in History, Economics and Public Law 32 (New York, 1908). R. B. Dobson (ed.), *The Peasants' Revolt of 1381*, 2nd edn (London: Macmillan, 1983), provides sources, commentary and bibliography on events of 1381; see also R. H. Hilton and T. H. Aston (eds), *The English Rising of 1381* (Cambridge: Cambridge University Press, 1984). The politics of justice are discussed in: J. G. Bellamy, *The Law of Treason in England in the Later Middle Ages* (Cambridge: Cambridge University Press, 1970); R. L. Storey, 'Liveries and Commissions of the Peace, 1388–90', in F. R. H. Du Boulay and C. M. Barron (eds), *The Reign of Richard II: Essays in Honour of May McKisack* (London: Athlone Press, 1971), pp. 131–52; and W. M. Ormrod, *The Reign of Edward III: Crown and Political Society in England, 1327–1377* (New Haven, CT and London: Yale University Press, 1990).

For the various case studies outlined in Chapter 5, see: R. W. Kaeuper, 'Law and Order in Fourteenth-Century England: The Evidence of Special Commissions of Oyer and Terminer', *Speculum*, 54 (1979), pp. 734–84; D. W. Sutherland, *The Assize of Novel Disseisin* (Oxford: Clarendon Press, 1973); Palmer, *English Law* (as above); E. L. G. Stones, 'Sir Geoffrey le Scrope (c. 1280 to 1340), Chief Justice of the King's Bench', *EHR*, 69 (1954), pp. 1–17; and B. H. Putnam, *The Place in Legal History of Sir William Shareshull* (Cambridge: Cambridge University Press, 1950).

For texts and discussion of the literary material discussed in Chapter 6, see: P. R. Coss (ed.), *Thomas Wright's Political Songs* (Cambridge: Cambridge University Press, 1996); T. Wright (ed.), *Political Poems and Songs*, RS 14 (London, 1859–61); H. Barr (ed.), *The Piers Plowman Tradition* (London: J. M. Dent, 1993); J. Coleman, *English Literature in History, 1350–1400: Medieval Readers and Writers* (London: Hutchinson, 1981); and J. R. Maddicott, 'Poems of Social Protest in Early

Fourteenth-Century England', in W. M. Ormrod (ed.), *England in the Fourteenth Century: Proceedings of the 1985 Harlaxton Symposium* (Woodbridge: Boydell Press, 1986), pp. 130–44. For the professionalisation and ethics of the law, see P. Brand, *The Origins of the English Legal Profession* (London: Blackwell, 1992).

INDEX

Abingdon 37, 103
  abbot of 37
Airmyn, Richard 33
Angus, Gilbert Umfraville, earl of 72
appeals
  of ancient demesne 133
  approvers' 134–8, 141, 150
  in eyre 44, 180
  of felony 17, 49
  in king's bench 17, 121, 180
  in parliament 26, 27–8, 146
  of treason 21, 28, 107–9
arbitration 132, 143
Arundel
  Richard Fitzalan, earl of (d. 1376) 71
  Richard Fitzalan, earl of (d. 1397) 108
Ashridge 194
assize
  of Clarendon (1166) 43
  grand 178
  of darrein presentment 46
  of Measures (1196) 112
  of mort d'ancestor 46, 122, 124
  of novel disseisin 46, 122–5, 132, 141
Avenal, John 210
Aylesbury 199, 200

Bakewell 194
Baldock, Robert 33
Ball, John 98, 173

Bampton, John 98, 173
Banbury 198
Bannockburn, battle of 78
Barnet 201
Basset, William 153, 155
Baynard, Robert 148
Bedford 198, 201
Bedfordshire, judicial sessions in 106
Belknap, Robert 108
Bellers, Roger 104, 135
Benstead, John 31
Bereford, William 30
Berkshire, judicial sessions in 55, 217
Berwick on Tweed 25, 194
Black Death: *see* Plague
Blyth 199
Bocking, Ralph 149
Boroughbridge, battle of 102
Boultham 194
Bradcroft 199
Bradeston, Thomas 104
Braundys, John 55
Brentwood 204
Bristol 194, 202
Bubwith, Nicholas 33
Buckinghamshire
  judicial sessions in 217
  knight of the shire for 148
Bury, Richard, bishop of Durham 33
Bury St Edmunds 98, 103, 195, 200, 201, 202, 203

Index

abbey of 142
abbot of 98

Cade's Rebellion 101
Cambridge, John 37
Cambridge 195, 199, 204
  university of 31
Cambridgeshire 132
  county court 142
Canterbury 118, 194, 195, 198, 199, 215
Carlisle 25, 71, 196
Carlisle, Andrew Harclay, earl of 78
Cattishall 194, 195
Cavendish
  John 98
  William 39
Chaucer, Geoffrey 166, 168, 191–2
  Canterbury Tales 166, 168, 191
Chelmsford 98, 200, 201, 202
Chelrey, Edmund 148
Cheltenham, William 66
Chester 195
Chester, earldom and palatinate of 9, 107
Chichester 215
Clipston 194
Colchester 199, 200, 202
Colville, Robert 66
Coterel family 80
Cumberland
  judicial sessions in 71, 134, 214
  knight of the shire for 148
  peace commissions in 66

Deptford 201, 203
Derby 197, 205
Derbyshire 80
  judicial sessions in 106
  peace commissions in 71
Despenser, Hugh, the younger 102, 120
Devon, Hugh Courtenay, earl of 71
Deyncourt, Edmund 70
Doddington 132
Domesday Book 133, 186

Doncaster, John 216
Dunstable 210
Dunwich 199
Durham
  bishopric of 36
  county palatine of 9
  judicial sessions in 45

Edward I, king of England
  judicial changes under 8, 38, 48, 60, 81, 84, 119
  judicial structure under 21, 47, 64, 125, 145–7, 189
  legislation of 151–2, 165
  parliament under 25–7
  wars of 14, 19, 78, 81, 83
Edward II, king of England 31, 33, 79, 85–6
  civil wars under 52, 102–3
  deposition of 74, 102, 135
  judicial changes under 47, 63–4, 65, 119–20, 123, 125, 142
  parliament under 25–6
Edward III, king of England 14, 31, 35, 79, 86, 112, 172
  accession and early reign of 102–6
  judicial changes under 30, 34, 47, 50, 58, 63, 84, 91, 102–6, 18, 120, 142
  judicial structure under 38, 45, 125
  legislation of 152, 153
  parliament under 25, 27–8
  wars of 81, 82, 84
Edward, Prince of Wales (the Black Prince) 149
Ely, bishopric of 36
Essex, Peasants' Revolt in 78–9, 96–7, 173
Eustace the Monk 168

Fleta 26
Folville family 80, 104, 135
  'Folvilles laws' 169, 170
France
  truces with 107, 112

wars with 3, 22, 31, 77, 78, 81, 86, 112, 113, 149
Friskney, Walter 216
Fulk Fitzwarin 168

Gascony 44, 81, 83
Gloucester 26, 194, 197, 202, 203, 204, 205
Gloucester, Thomas of Woodstock, duke of 107, 108
Gloucestershire
  judicial sessions in 215
  peace commissions in 57, 66
Gower, John 163
  Confessio amantis 163
  Vox clamantis 163
Grandpont 205
Green, Henry 38, 172
Guildford 198

Hales, John 98
Hall, John 143
Hampshire 136
Heatherslaw 194
Hengham, Ralph 30, 38–9, 151
Henry II, king of England 13
Henry III, king of England 8, 13, 25, 46
Henry IV, king of England 34, 62, 77, 107, 138, 174
  before accession 107
Henry V, king of England 19, 82, 149
Hereford 194, 197
Herefordshire 78
  judicial sessions in 217
Herle, William 33, 145, 216
Heyford, John 141
Hillary
  Henry 66
  Roger 153
Holland, Robert 64
Hood, Robin, ballads of 169–70
Hotoft, John 140, 185–6
Hungerford, Thomas 149

Inge, William 30, 31
Ingleby, Thomas 33, 148

Inns of Court 30, 140, 144
  see also London
Ipswich 200, 201
Ireland 77, 153
Ireland, Robert de Vere, duke of 107
Isabella of France, queen of Edward II 45, 102–4, 120, 152
Islip, Simon, archbishop of Canterbury 31

John, king of England 13
juries 44, 132
  corruption of 37, 49, 175, 186–8
  grand 17, 134–5, 178
  of presentment 17, 27, 130, 164, 179, 181, 187–8
  trial 15, 46, 137, 138, 179, 181, 184, 187–8

Kelshall, Richard 153
Kent
  judicial sessions in 45, 53, 64, 65, 99
  peace commissions in 64
  Peasants' Revolt in 78–9, 96, 98, 99
Kent, Edmund of Woodstock, earl of 102
Kingston on Thames 194, 201
Knighton, Henry 172
Knyvet, John 33, 34
Kyroun, John 136

Lakenheath 98
Lancashire 78, 103
  judicial sessions in 64, 104, 214
Lancaster 199
Lancaster, duchy and palatinate of 9
Lancaster
  Henry, earl of (d. 1345) 102
  Henry of Grosmont, duke of 71
  John of Gaunt, duke of 28, 71, 72, 107, 149
  Thomas, earl of 102
Langland, William 166, 171–4

Piers Plowman 166, 167, 169, 171, 172, 173, 174
Langton, Walter, bishop of Coventry and Lichfield 27, 140, 185
Latimer, William, Lord 27
Lavenham, William 148
Legett, Roger 98
Leicestershire 80, 135
  peace commissions in 71
  undersheriff of 142
Lincoln 25, 194–200, 203, 205
  judicial sessions at 119, 177
Lincolnshire 59, 70
  judicial sessions in 129, 131
  peace commissions in 66, 71, 72
Lisle, Thomas, bishop of Ely 132
Lollard Revolt 101
London 12, 14, 53, 102, 126, 171, 194–6, 229
  Peasants' Revolt in 96–7, 98
  places in:
    Chancery Lane 31
    Gray's Inn 30
    Guildhall 171
    House of Converts 31
    Lambeth 199
    Inner Temple 30
    Lincoln's Inn 30
    Mile End 97
    New Temple 30
    Smithfield 97
    Tower of London 210
  see also Westminster
Lucy, Anthony, Lord 71
Lynn 200
Lyons, Richard 27

Maidenhead 198
maintenance 37–8, 49, 51, 67, 109–10, 175, 181–2, 185, 192
  see also retaining
March
  Edmund Mortimer, earl of (d. 1381) 149
  Roger Mortimer, earl of (d. 1330) 45, 102–4, 120, 152

Mare, Peter de la 149
Mendham, Walter of 137
Middlesex 20
  bill of 20
  judicial sessions in 53
  knights of the shire for 148–9
Middleton, Gilbert 78
Molyns, John 104
Moriz, Thomas 148
Mortimer, Constantine 149
Mum and the Sothsegger 173–4
Musgrave, Thomas 67

Neville, Ralph, Lord 27
Newcastle upon Tyne 194, 196
Newenton 194
Newport 202
Nisi prius, procedure of 15–16, 58, 178
Norfolk 70, 136
  judicial sessions in 132, 137–8
  knights of the shire for 148, 149
  peace commissions in 70
Northampton 26, 103, 196, 198, 199, 203
Northamptonshire
  judicial sessions in 65, 105
  peace commissions in 66, 142
Northburgh, Michael, bishop of London 31
Norwich 102, 108, 194, 195, 197, 199, 204, 205
Nottingham 80
  sheriff of 170
Nottinghamshire 80
  judicial sessions in 59, 105, 214
  peace commissions in 65

Offord, John, archbishop of Canterbury 31–2, 33
Ogbourne, prior of 132
Old Sarum 215
Ordinances
  1305 (Conspirators) 49, 184
  1305 (Trailbaston) 48
  1311 (New Ordinances) 86, 102
  1346 (Justices) 38, 153, 180, 183
  1349 (Labourers) 3, 52, 93, 127,

153, 176, 178
1353 (Staple) 125
1372 (knights of the shire) 149
1390 (livery) 110, 165
see also Statutes
Orton Waterville 142
Otterburn, battle of 107
Outlaw's song of trailbaston 169–70

Oxford 194, 198, 205
 business school 30, 145
 university of 30, 31
Oxfordshire 217

pardons
 royal 38–9, 79–80, 86, 99, 165, 170
 general 82, 87, 99–100, 108
Paris, treaty of (1259) 77
Parliament, sessions of:
 1340 26, 92, 153
 1341 27
 1343 153
 1344 56, 153
 1346 66
 1348 56, 57, 71, 88, 132
 1351 154
 1352 57, 88, 132, 154–5
 1354 234
 1361 88, 155
 1362 88
 1363 88
 1365 88
 1368 95
 1371 43
 1375 59
 1376 (Good Parliament) 27, 28, 88, 149
 1377 133, 150, 186
 1378 150
 1379 88
 1380 96
 1381 99–100
 1382 82, 100, 150
 1383 150
 1386 (Wonderful Parliament) 28, 35, 39, 107
 1388 (Merciless Parliament) 108

 1388 (Cambridge Parliament) 101, 110
 1390 88
 1397–8 87, 108
 1399 109
Parving, Robert 34, 35, 71, 148, 153
Peasants' Revolt 10, 78–9, 89, 114, 172, 174–5, 176, 181, 186, 191
 disorder of government during 14, 39
 impact on justice 56, 96–101, 109
Penrith 194
Perrers, Alice 27, 172
Peterborough, abbot of 142
Philippa of Hainault, queen of Edward III 149
Pickering, James 149–50
Pierce the Ploughman's Crede 173
plague 3–10, 49, 63, 71, 76, 89, 93–6, 97, 112–13, 118, 158–60, 179, 186, 191
 of 1348–9 14, 52, 93, 126–7, 133, 146, 176, 178
 of 1361–2 14, 93–4
 of 1368–9 14, 93–4
 of 1371 93
 of 1375 93

Radcot Bridge, battle of 107
Reading 204, 205
retaining
 of attorneys 130, 140–4, 181–2
 by livery 174, 175
 of royal justices and sergeants 36–40, 142, 182–3
 for war 80
 see also maintenance
Rheims 81
Richard II 14, 29, 34, 35, 77, 121
 judicial changes under 118, 121
 parliament under 26, 27–8
 and Peasants' Revolt 39, 97, 99
 regime during 1390s 106–11, 174
Richard the Redeless 173–4, 192
Rochester 195

Rose, William 136
Rouceby, William 210
Roxburgh 194
Rutland 80

Sadington, Robert 34, 153
St Albans 103, 198, 199, 201
Salisbury 195, 198, 204
Sandiacre 195
Sandwich 194
Scot, William 153
Scotland
  marches of 83
  petitions to English parliament 153
  raids by 78
  truces with 112
  wars with 3, 14, 19, 22, 31, 77, 84, 86, 105, 107, 113
Scrope
  Geoffrey 31, 33, 35, 37, 59, 106, 152-3, 177, 216
  Henry 30, 35, 122, 216
  Richard, Lord 35
Shardlow, John 142
Shareshull, William 59, 145, 152, 153-5, 168, 233
Sherborne 201
Shrewsbury 14, 26, 108, 197, 205
Shropshire 78, 171
Sibthorpe, Thomas 59
Simonie, The 167, 171, 172
Skipwith, William 38, 67
Southampton 198
Spink
  Richard 132, 156
  William 132, 156
Stafford, Ralph Stafford, earl of 71
Staffordshire 59
  peace commissions in 67, 72
Stamford 195, 196, 198, 199
Stamford Bridge 199
Statutes
  1215 (Magna Carta) 9, 13, 14, 50, 92
  1275 (Westminster) 151, 182-3
  1285 (Westminster) 15, 60, 151, 214
  1285 (Winchester) 50, 51, 52, 97, 165
  1285 (Merchants) 125
  1299 (Fines) 46, 59, 64
  1300 (Articles upon the Charters) 50, 184
  1318 (York) 58
  1322 (York) 102
  1328 (Northampton) 47, 58, 59, 64, 79, 86, 152
  1330 47, 58, 59, 60, 64, 79, 86, 184
  1336 79, 86
  1340 58-9, 79, 153
  1341 27
  1344 47, 57, 61, 66, 153
  1351 154, 156
    (Labourers) 3, 53, 88, 93, 117, 127, 154, 176, 178
    (Provisors) 154
  1352 133, 154, 156, 166, 188
    (Treasons) 27, 103, 108-9, 154-5
  1354 (Staple) 125-6
  1360 121
  1361 51, 53, 57, 67, 93, 155
  1362 51, 53, 88, 94
  1363 94
  1368 94
  1377 110
  1378 93-4
  1381 124
  1382 (Rapes) 156
  1384 59, 183
  1388 (Cambridge) 56, 88, 94, 110
  1393 110
  1394 51, 67, 110
  see also Ordinances
Stonor, John 31, 38, 153, 155
Stratford 202
Stratford
  John, archbishop of Canterbury 27, 34
  Robert, bishop of Chichester 34
Stratford Langthorn 27
Stratton, Adam 98
Sudbury, Simon, archbishop of

Canterbury 98
Suffolk
　knight of the shire for 149
　peace commissions in 57, 70
　Peasants' Revolt in 98
Suffolk, Michael de la Pole, earl of 28, 35, 39, 107
Surrey, judicial sessions in 53, 64
Sussex, judicial sessions in 53

Takeley, prior of 132
Tale of Gamelyn 168–70
taxation 62, 79, 90, 94, 97–8, 153, 154, 173, 188
　and judicial change 25, 49, 86–9, 91
　poll taxes 97–8, 173
Thetford 203
Thoresby, John, archbishop of York 31–2, 33
Thorpe
　John 70
　Robert 34, 142, 147
　William 38, 39, 172
Tickhill 199
Tresilian, Robert 39, 107
Tutbury 197
Tyler, Wat 97, 173

uses (trusts) 21, 24–5, 81, 109, 143

Wales 102
　marches of 19, 78, 103–4
　petitions to English parliament 153
　wars in 14, 44, 77, 78
Walsingham, Thomas 172
Waltham, John, bishop of Salisbury 32, 33
Warwick 198, 201
Warwick, Robert 142
Warwick
　Thomas, earl of (d. 1369) 71
　Thomas, earl of (d. 1401) 108, 218
Warwickshire
　county court 142
　judicial sessions in 142

peace commissions in 72
undersheriff of 142
Wayland, Thomas 38
Wells 201
West, Thomas 156
Westminster, palace of 14, 21
　royal courts at 14, 19, 21, 25, 118, 139, 143–4, 149, 157, 192, 194–205
　great hall 14, 23
　Star Chamber 21
　see also London
Westmorland
　knight of the shire for 149–50
　peace commissions in 66, 71
Whitton, Philip 210
Wichingham, William 67
Wigan 118, 197, 199
Willoughby, Richard 39, 153
Winchester 198, 202, 205
　bishopric of 36
Winchester, Hugh Despenser the elder, earl of 102, 120
Winner and Waster 168, 171
Writs
　of assumpsit 17, 126–7, 145–6, 178
　of *capias* 15, 166
　of conspiracy 184
　of entry 123, 124
　judicial 15, 129
　de libertate probanda 132–3
　of naifty 132–2
　original 14–15, 16, 24, 46, 48, 129, 130
　pone 178
　praecipe 16
　registers of 118
　of right 123
　of *scire facias* 24
　sub pena 22, 23, 32
　of trespass 16, 118, 121, 126–7
　of trespass on the case 16–17, 126–7, 145–6, 178
Wyclif, John 172, 186
Wycombe 201, 204
Wykeham, William, bishop of Winchester 33

York 78
  mayor of 185
  parliament at 25, 195, 197–200, 202
  peace sessions at 67
  royal courts at 14, 19, 118–19, 177
Yorkshire 37, 59, 126

judicial sessions in 104
knights of the shire for 148, 150
peace commissions in 65, 71

Zouche
  family 135
  William la, Lord, of Harringworth 66